Membranes of Hope

A Guide to Attending to the Spiritual Boundaries
that Keep Lifesystems Healthy
from the Personal to the Cosmic

Theresa C. Dintino

MEMBRANES OF HOPE
A Guide to Attending to the Spiritual Boundaries that Keep
Lifesystems Healthy from the Personal to the Cosmic
Copyright © 2020 by Theresa C. Dintino

ISBN (print): 978-1-7354295-0-2
ISBN: (eBook): 978-1-7354295-1-9

Cover design by Mia Szarvas
Editing and Design: Manuscripts to Go/Book & Manuscript Services

Dedication

To the Dagara People of Burkina Faso
with Gratitude and Humility

Table of Contents

Part One

What Is a Membrane?

Part Two

Tending to the Personal Membrane

Part Three

Tending to the Family Membranes: The Importance of Ancestral Work

Part Four

Tending to the Village or Community Membrane

Part Five

The Importance of Oil as an Offering to Life and the Membranes that Contain It

Acknowledgments

Thank you to Malidoma Somé, who brought the beautiful lineage of stick divination from the Dagara people of Burkina Faso to the West. Thank you to Mark Bockley, my own mentor in this tradition who gifted it to me. Thank you to the Dagara people for their incredible generosity and to the medicine itself for its wisdom, guidance, and power.

Thank you to Domenica Colella, my great-grandmother, a holder of her own medicine and lineage which is mine too—the Italian Strega tradition. She who could see how to put it all back together again, my mentor still. The one I thank every day.

And thank you to the wedeme, my forever friends—"magical-minis" who keep me laughing and hold my hands with theirs and say, "Let's do it!"

To friends, family, clients, and all the wonderful beings I walk this Earth with who are so willing to help and work and support. Gifts, all of you.

Deepest gratitude to my daughter, Mia Szarvas, for a very careful reading of the text with thoughtful comments that made this a much better book, and for the cover design.

And last but certainly never least, thank you to my editor, Cris Wanzer. We have been working together for so many years now, we've built history and created friendship, and it is all very precious indeed.

A Few Notes About This Book...

The rituals listed in this book can apply to all of the levels and layers of membranes that are covered. Some, but not all, will be repeated in their various iterations. The reader should know that all of them can be applied to all the fractal layers—meaning those listed in the personal membrane chapter can be extrapolated to the cosmic membrane layer with a little bit of imagination.

About the shrines mentioned in this book: In the Dagara tradition, there is very defined protocol for shrine building at every level of initiation into becoming and continuing work as a diviner. The shrines listed in this book are more generalized for the reader, who is not an initiated diviner but wishes to create them for their personal medicine practice. (See "What is a Shrine?" p. 43)

The stories contained in this book are included to illustrate the feel of cultures whose membranes were intact and healthy, and will assist the reader in experiencing this reality and possibility of care.

This book has been written for people already on a medicine path, those who are just beginning, or those who simply want to be of service to their community and the Earth in some way. The reader may enter into the rituals and work offered at whatever level they wish and with whatever degree of commitment they choose. There are rituals offered for the care of the membranes at each level—personal, family, village, Earth or cosmic. (See "What is a Ritual?" p. 47) There are guided visualizations included as well. Make it your own.

Readers who decide to take up the work of caring for the membranes may feel they want to consult with the author about their work. For this I am offering 30- or 60-minute phone calls. Go to *stregatree.com* and find the sign-up page in the Apothecary under "Consultation Calls for Keepers of the Membranes."

Rituals in this Book: A Quick Glance

Shrines in this Book: A Quick Glance

The Nine Dimensions of the World Tree

Throughout this book I will be referencing the Nine Dimensions of the World Tree as articulated by Barbara Hand Clow in her book, *Alchemy of Nine Dimensions*. I understand that there are varying interpretations of the dimensional realms, many quite different than Hand Clow's. I find Hand Clow's template to be instructive and many correspondences have validated it in my own work. It has become a very important tool I use to assist in communicating complex concepts and ideas. Using this dimensional protocol does not nullify other systems of belief nor do I intend that by adhering to this one in this writing.

I offer the following overview and outline to assist the reader in following along.

About the Nine Dimensions

Through a female being from the Pleiades named Satya, Barbara Hand Clow was taught that the Earth is a realm that holds nine dimensions of consciousness that all humans can access. Now is the time for us to begin to consciously access these dimensions and become nine-dimensional humans once again. This is the Alchemy of Nine Dimensions.

According to Hand Clow, the dimensions exist along the axis of the World Tree, which is grounded in the center of the Earth. The World Tree is the cosmic creative force that creates Time[1] and all

---

[1] I capitalize Time when I am referring to it as an alive entity. I explore this concept in more depth in my book, *The Amazon Pattern*.

the dimensional realms. Belief in the World Tree is a global phenomenon found in different cultures and known by different
names. In this model, the center of the Earth is the 1st dimension
and the center of the galaxy is the 9th. (To be clear, Hand Clow is
not saying there are only nine dimensions.)

It is advantageous for us to return to relationship with the nine
dimensions. This reorients us inside the cosmology of the World
Tree. It also familiarizes us with the energies and qualities of the
unseen worlds and other dimensions in order to better interact with
and listen to them.

Being grounded in our own inner World Tree orients us in our
lives, as well as the larger stories we are embedded within. Generating the World Tree in our bodies serves as a grounding energy
for everyone around us. One way to begin to ground into our own
World Tree is to learn the nine dimensions that exist along its axis.

The Nine Dimensions

1. The 1st dimension is the iron core crystal at the center of the
Earth. The core of the Earth pulses at 7.8 times per second. This dimension corresponds to our own inner core. When we match our
inner core to the core of the Earth, we are truly centered. Being
"synched" with the center of the Earth allows us to be nourished by
the rich, dark energy held there. We must connect with the pulsing
iron center within ourselves as well as the one within the planet.

The crystal core of the Earth is in relationship with the center of
other planets and the centers of stars. We too can access these other
"centers."

2. The 2nd dimension is the space between the center of the Earth
and the surface of the Earth, also called the "telluric realm." This is
the underground Earth, which includes underground water,
mountains, and the deep magma. This is the realm of the wedeme.
These guardians and keepers of the inner Earth facilitate a relationship between Earth and humans. The 2nd dimension corresponds to

the inside of our bodies. Metals and crystals, with their power of transmission and reception, serve the same function in the Earth as in our bodies, facilitating relationship between this world and the others. It is the job of the wedeme to keep the "fires" of the inner Earth burning. They need our help with this and they, in turn, help us.

3. The 3D is our embodied 3D reality. This is the realm where humans are most focused; therefore, it is also the realm where we have the most power. We can use our power and the magic of 3D physical embodiment to affect the other dimensions. We must be firmly grounded in our 3D physical bodies to access the full power of the nine-dimensional paradigm.

If we are not properly grounded in the 1st and 2nd dimensions and our 3D physical bodies, we can misread and/or be manipulated by information from the collective consciousness of the 4D, as well as beings in other dimensions.

Being grounded in our own bodies means understanding our emotional response patterns to the feeling realm of the 4th. It means that when we are triggered by strong emotions and experiences, we are able to remain stable and be clear. We remain calm and observe ourselves in relation to these emotional events. We must feel our emotions and learn from them, but not allow ourselves to be unconsciously controlled by them.

Receiving messages and signals from the other dimensions through our 3D physical bodies is the power of the 3rd dimension. The 3D is the realm of the embodied sensual experience filtered through the Pleiadian love and light realm of the 5th.

4. The 4th dimension is a layer around the Earth. This layer collects messages from the 5th - 9th dimensions and splits them so they can be delivered to Earth. The light (information) from 5 - 9 is delivered through the lens of the 4D. The 4th dimension is also the realm of myths and archetypes, collective consciousness, and the group mind. This layer of consciousness is, in part, created by the

group mind.

The 4th dimension is the realm of feelings. If we are not firmly grounded in the 1st - 3rd dimensions, our beliefs can be easily manipulated by energies caught in or acting upon this dimension through our feelings. Collective shadows can build up in the 4th dimension and gain enough energy to take on a life of their own. I believe the energy of greed is one of these.

It is our personal responsibility to take a long hard look at our belief systems and ask where they came from, and if we are in a state of fear or paranoia, to look at why that may be. It is important to be mindful of any negative vibrations and frequencies we choose to participate with. These can easily add to or accelerate feelings and beliefs held in the 4th. We need to be consistently discerning of our own intentions.

When we are "hooked" negatively in the 4th dimension, we are run by fear or paranoia, over-identified with mythological gods and goddesses, or constantly casting blame on outside sources for our discontent. We may also be involved in emotional dramas, personal or group, that promote polarity and division.

It is up to us as fully embodied physical humans to take responsibility for what we believe and promote. We cannot receive clean information from the 5th - 9th dimensions through an unconscious, polluted lens.

Our true state of being should be one where we feel supported and nurtured by the collective realm of ancestors and the light of the dimensions of 5 - 9. If we do not feel this way, then we need to examine our relationship with the 4D and see what is out of balance. Who are your gods and villains? If you believe they have more control over your life than you do, you are mistaken. The universe is collaborative. Choose your collaborators wisely.

5. The 5th dimension is love, sensuality, and light from the Pleiades. The human heart is the channel for love in the 3rd that is mediated by the 5D. The power of love is attraction, gravitational pull,

sexuality, and sensuality: orgasm. The stars created the elements of our bodies in their burning, passionate cores. Earth is bathed in the love-orbit (gravitational pull) of the sun. What pulls you toward it? What fuels your longing? What makes you say, "yes"? Love is the opposite of and antidote to fear.

6. The 6th dimension is the realm of geometric forms and patterns. Patterns and geometric forms allow light and sound to manifest into concrete physical matter. The light from the 9th dimension and beyond comes through the 7th dimensional lens of sound, which creates geometric forms in the 6th to birth the material world we live in. It is helpful to think of the dimensions in reverse order — from 9 - 1 — to get the feel for how this works.

Forms that exist energetically in the 6th dimension are not only cubes and triangles but also "Dog," "Tree" and "Human." Indeed, the pattern of our soul is alive in the 6th dimension. By keeping a healthy relationship with the 6th dimension, we can remain united to our Source soul and the intentions we came into this physical life with from the outer dimensions.

Returning to patterns of origin is an important practice. It is worthwhile to examine any artificial imprinting that we may have adopted that is not our true pattern. Examining beliefs is not enough. Cultural conditioning and life experiences can interfere with our patterns of origin. Re-patterning is the work of the 6th dimension. Trees can help return us to our Source pattern.

Being aligned with and connected to the World Tree keeps us oriented, balanced, and grounded to true Source rather than the artificial ones we may have been re-patterned to align with.

Ritual works at the level of the 6th dimension. Rituals offer form for energy to move through. In rituals, we make offerings in a certain way, place, and Time. Group rituals at seasonal transitions were ways communities long kept themselves in synch and alignment with the greater cosmic forces they knew themselves to be embedded within. Understanding the form of the solar year and the aligning of self and community with it is a large reason for seasonal holy days and holidays.

7. The 7th dimension is the realm of vibrational resonance. The light from the 8th dimension becomes sound in the 7th dimension. Sound from the 7th creates form in the 6th. The frequencies of light and sound create all that is known to us as reality. Silence is full of sound. This is the realm of the Kontomble.

Language is related to this dimension. What we speak is a form of sound. Hearing and knowing are two different things. Do we speak what we know? Tell the truth. The frequency vibrating through your body at any given moment is your truth.

8. The 8th dimension is light. Light generated from the darkness of the 9th dimension comes into the 8th to be the "All Knowing One." This is the light and knowing of the cosmos; the crystal-clear intellect. Here is the place of diamond clarity where there is no shadow. In this dimension, we can interact with the One, or whatever you perceive the divine to be. In the 8th we can also have access to an understanding of the vastness of All Time. All Time is held here in the interfacing light patterns of All That Is. Here are the councils of great beings and what some call "the Galactic Federation."

9. The 9th Dimension is Time, the creative/generative Source of all. Here is Origin; Source. In this center of the galaxy, All Time is created. Alive Time creates all that has ever been and ever will be. In this spinning, black womb hive, tendrils of darkness flow forth and are turned into light in the 8th dimension. The light interacting with this fecund darkness gives rise to experience. Experience creates more experience and the many intersecting layers of Time. Though in the 3D, we experience these as past, present, and future. They are all part of the fecund now. Accessing the 9th dimension gives us access to all the dimensions beyond. This is the center of the vortex of All Time.

Sources: Barbara Hand Clow: *Alchemy of Nine Dimensions, The Pleiadian Agenda, Catastrophobia,* and *The Mayan Code*

Preface

She was Crafting Wombs with Wings...

This happened a long time ago and I was left with a question—well, many questions, but one main question: *What are wombs with wings?*

The journey has taken me far. I am only now beginning to understand. Certain things needed to happen first and certain skills needed to be acquired. Certain things needed to be remembered and put back in place before I could make sense of it.

Sometimes a question is enough to lead us along—the will to understand, our minds unable to let go: What? Why? How is this important?

We live in a culture of rush, quick, fast, instant. Many things need the opposite; slow nurturing and care, extended reflection, and the acquisition of skills through direct experience. Required was the slow revelation through time, stepping through the linear sway of events and layer upon layer of wisdom gained in the only way it is, through a process called "aging," "maturation." Maturation...a lost art in our time.

Now I know that to attend to the many interconnected, overlapping membranes that protect and nourish lifesystems, one must first have:

A medicine practice. A medicine practice is a defined way to work with spirits and entities to effect change in the everyday world that one has been schooled in, initiated into, and has mastered the skills of.

A medicine community. A medicine community is a group of humans that recognize and utilize those skills.

I was a single-focused writer but I had been born with a spiritual lineage. An Italian medicine lineage—the lineage of the Strega[2]. That lineage had ended formally with my great-grandmother when she immigrated to New Hampshire. My grandmother, her daughter, born here, chose not to carry it on. It did not get handed down to my father (her grandson) nor to me, her great-granddaughter. That is what I mean when I say the lineage was broken. The line was not continued, not passed on.

A lineage is just that—a continuous line of people holding a specific tradition for generations. These traditions wish to be passed on and continued. Kept alive. Lineage holders have the work of keeping lineages alive. One can be initiated into a lineage they are not born into but being a lineage holder in a certain tradition gives one special access and rank, especially in the eyes of the ancestors of that lineage.

Being a lineage holder to a spiritual tradition is important. It means one possesses a natural capacity for work that has been practiced by previous lineage holders. A lineage holder is "next in line" to take up the work. When a lineage is intact, there is a slow and steady modeling by current practitioners. There is training in tried-and-true practices passed down through the elders. Eventually, when the time is appropriate, the lineage holder is initiated. Then

---

[2] Strega (s.f.), Stregone (s.m.), Streghe (pl.)

there is additional wisdom acquired through continued practice over time.

I had the capacity to be a medicine person because I am a lineage holder and I had certain inherent abilities, but I was not taught. It was not fostered. I had not been trained. I had no skills but lots of potential and I was funneling this potential and this untrained ability into writing.

I grew up in the '70s with five siblings in the United States in the tiny state of New Hampshire. My father's family were immigrants from the Abruzzo region of Italy. My mother's family were Yankee Baptists who had been in New England since the *Mayflower*, having traveled here from Northern Europe.

When the Italian lineage was broken, my father's family became Catholics. My mother converted to Catholicism and I was brought up in the Church. In Catholicism, I had a spiritual tradition but it was not my lineage. My great-grandmother, Domenica, from Torre Dei Passeri, Italy, was from a long line of Streghe. She was what I now call a "peasant witch." My people on both sides—my mother and father—are common folk, peasants. The Strega lineage has roots in ancient paganism, pre-Roman and pre-Church, in an older version of itself called *Janarra*. It is an Earth-based tradition built on direct communication with the spirits, elements, and elemental beings. Divinatory practices and seeing, second sight, intuition, engagement, and relationship with the other nonvisible dimensions are included.

The Earth is known as an alive entity as are all the beings who live on her. My lineage is an indigenous, European tradition. In indigenous traditions, relationships are not exclusively human to human—they include rocks, trees, animals, birds, insects, the moon, and the stars. All is one web of creation that humans participate in.

The Strega fosters relationship to the spiritual dimensions and the entities located in particular dimensions, and tends to her village in this way. The ways my ancestral Streghe worked in the village my family was from is my specific lineage. Like dialects, lineages are unique to place.

My aunt (my father's sister) kept the legacy of our lineage alive the best way she could, by telling stories and reminding us of who our great-grandmother was. Eventually, I decided to try to actively find and remember my lineage. I reconnected with my great-grandmother in the ancestral realm and she began to teach me. The Dagara divination system that she led me to, and which I am initiated into, helped me acquire skills and slowly, I began to rebuild the lineage in my family and build a community in my current location. Then and only then did I begin to understand what the medicine is in its full articulation and how tending to the membranes is the main piece of work a medicine person is called to do.

Ah. But I am getting ahead of myself.

First this happened...

From her cave in the otherworld, my great-grandmother is crafting wombs with wings. The sound of water cascading from the wall of waterfalls outside is muted behind the bulk of flowering vines flourishing beneath it, creating a living door to this cave. She works, relaxed but methodical, her strong arms moving with intention and confidence. She is dressed in a chemise and bloomers, undergarments from the late 1800s, when she last lived as a Strega in Italy and America. Here in her cave, she is in her early thirties. Her long, chestnut-brown hair flows down her back. As in the physical world, so in the otherworld, she is engaged in healing.

2005

It was November and rainy outside. I was cuddled up on the couch in front of a fire reading *The Dreamer's Book of the Dead*, in which the author, Robert Moss, encourages: *Don't wait for the dead to come to you. Instead, go to them. Go find them. See where they are and what they are doing.*

This appealed to me and was different from the way I usually approached communicating with the ancestors. I usually called on them and waited for them to come to me. This day, I decided to go find Domenica, my great-grandmother, the Strega — the one who inspired the character Eva in the novel, *The Strega and the Dreamer*, whose first draft I had recently completed. I wanted to see her. I had developed a deep connection with her during the four years spent writing the book — a soul connection.

I had learned how to journey in a shamanic[3] way and had been practicing it for a few years so I knew what to do. I closed my eyes, sank into deep time, called in my guides, and went to my entry point at the base of a tree.

I didn't know where I would go. I suppose I thought I was going to some celestial sphere or otherworld place so I was pleasantly surprised when I got there to discover that she was in nature — beautiful, wonderful, Planet Earth nature.

I was in the Amazon rainforest, on a steep rise overlooking a sprawling vista of vibrant green, rolling, mist-covered hills. Around me was lush vegetation — creeping vines, colossal tropical ferns with large, pulsing photosynthetic leaves. There were awesome, cascading waterfalls — a series of them lining the half-circle of this cove-like space.

I began to walk on a path, thinking "hut" or "cottage." And that is what I began to look for. I expected to find her inside a small house. Why? I don't know. But there was no hut or cottage. I stubbornly persisted with this line of thought while the path just as stubbornly kept leading me to a place behind the waterfalls. There

---

[3] In a shamanic journey one travels through other-dimensional realms to gather information or receive a healing. They remain in their body but let their spirit travel. These journeys are often facilitated by drumming. One is trained to call in spirit guides to accompany them as they travel one of the three levels of the World Tree: lower, middle, or upper.

was a ledge of stone to walk along behind the fast and furiously moving water falling from above—a corridor with one side of falling water, the other a stone wall lined with vibrant plant life. Far below was a large lake created by the waterfalls.

I walked until I arrived at a place that spoke to me. There was a felt presence, a darkness thick with fecundity. I pulled back the ivy and vines dotted with pink and purple flowers like a curtain and there she was, in the cave behind them. Here she was in this cave behind this waterfall and these thick-with-life vines in her underwear and she was working, crafting something—but I couldn't see what it was. Though I couldn't see what she was doing, it was clear that she was doing it diligently and methodically.

I intuited that her work was somehow important to people in the physical world. I understood on a deep level that what she was doing was *keeping it going* (though I had no idea what those words meant intellectually). She continued working as she talked to me, her hands moving against the cave floor, working on something, almost like she was kneading bread or shaping clay. But it was all black to me. I could not see it. She thanked me telepathically for writing the book and said, "That was really hard for me, those operations." Then she told me, again telepathically, how painful it had been to hear about the surgeries, to know about the surgeries. The pain came with the *knowing*.

In *The Strega and the Dreamer*, Eva (the character based on Domenica), a midwife and healer—a Strega, a woman deeply engaged in the care of women, most specifically their reproductive cycles—immigrates to the U.S. at the turn of the last century. There she struggles to maintain her medicine work while simultaneously learning about the radical gynecological surgeries being performed at the time: unnecessary ovariotomies, clitoridectomies, and oophorectomies used to control women's behavior—or more specifically, women who were considered outspoken, unruly or "oversexed."

But here, in this place in the cave, I could see that she was far removed from all of that, from the anger of it. The knowing of it was still there yet held in a different way. A bigger picture kind of way. My writing of the book had *eased the pain she had experienced in that time over that issue,* she told me, commenting almost casually, detached emotionally, on what had been difficult about that lifetime. She was beautiful—her thick, straight hair falling down her back. Nurturing yet firm. She showed me around. We left the cave and walked up to the rise. There was the initial view I had encountered coming into this place—the rolling, mist-covered hills stretching for what seemed like forever. I felt my spirit soar like a bird out over the vista.

This was the first visit. I was left wondering desperately what she had been crafting, yet found myself unable to let the information in, unable to see. I was entirely blocked from receiving this information. I understand that when one cannot see in the otherworld it does not mean there is nothing there; rather, it is an indication that the seer herself has an impediment. The dark spaces live in the visitor, not the place visited.

Perhaps I intuited on some level the life-changing ramifications seeing would bring. Perhaps I resisted this change. Nevertheless, I returned and returned, trying unsuccessfully to see, until one day, along the path of my daily walk, I tried once again…and this time, I saw.

My walks are a daily ritual practice. I allow myself to be in a trance state as I walk. It is my time to interact with the trees, my inner self, and other guides. It might be that the movement of my body helped to release fear or that, in the time that had passed, my subconscious had readied itself for change. Perhaps it was merely my persistence but on this day, I was able to see and what I saw astounded and shocked me, and continues to reverberate within.

I saw that in her cave in the otherworld, my great-grandmother is crafting wombs with wings. I shudder to even write the words yet I know I must.

Wombs with Wings
Wombs with Wings

Red and porous, with healthy veins and wings of joy, pulsing with the rhythm of life.

When I finally saw what she was doing, I felt my own womb jump. It began to pulse. Now, fifteen years later, I am finally beginning to understand what this image means, what she is doing, why it is important, and that she wants me to do this as well. The wombs are the membranes and the membranes are in need of healing. The wings are for ascension — an overused but essential word. Ascension — meaning literally "going up," moving to the next level. It can even simply mean to evolve rather than devolve, strengthen rather than dissipate or fall apart, flourish rather than self-destruct, and thrive rather than merely survive. And it can only happen when the membranes are strong.

Introduction

A Universe of Nested Membranes

2020

I am now a diviner[4]. After I met Domenica, my great-grand-mother, in the cave, she began to teach me the ways of the Strega and led me to a stick divination where I was "claimed." I write about my journey toward becoming a diviner more fully in my book, *The Amazon Pattern*. It is important that you understand who I mean when I speak of the wedeme and their particular form of divination — stick divination.

According to the West African form of divination I am initiated into, the wedeme are the elemental beings[5] of the wild. In this tradition, to be a stick diviner, one must merge consciousness with one or more of these sweet and lovely beings. This "merge" is carried

---

[4] A diviner can see into the spiritual dimensions to inform, assist, and heal; a seer.

[5] The elemental beings are the wee folk: fairies, elves, gnomes, and trolls in European lore, known by various names in other cultures. You can learn more about them in chapter 17 of this book, my Tree Medicine Trilogy and at stregatree.com

out in an initiation ritual. The initiation ritual takes place after receiving multiple stick divinations and doing the work that comes through, or is prescribed, in those sessions. This can take anywhere from one-and-a-half to five years. There are many other forms of divination in this tradition but the medicine one acquires when they are merged with the wedeme is stick divination. One literally sits on a stool and holds a stick from a tree. The client sits on a stool across from them and holds the stick as well.

When one comes to a divination for personal reasons, they are told what they most need to know about the beings who are with them in the other dimensions (ancestors, guides, animal allies, elemental beings) and their life purpose. The wedeme look at who they are on a soul level and what is happening in their life currently, and communicate to the diviner how to bring those two back into alignment. Ancestral work is a large part of this system of divination, which is based on the belief that we are a culmination of those who came before us. We need their help and they need ours. Rituals are prescribed for healing and restitution. My great-grandmother led me to this form of divination probably because of its strong connection to the ancestral realms and its intimate relationship with the wedeme. Through Dagara stick divination, I was able to restore my own lineage to myself and my family. And now I help others do the same.

When I am divining, I am listening to the wedeme and translating what they are saying. They are mediators between me and other spirits. They are connectors and weavers. They understand the "warp and weft" of the cosmos and can see where there is fraying. They have an interest in weaving it all back together. They love us humans and wish to help us. And they love the Earth. She is their home and their mother. They see that humans are the ones who can effect change for and on the Earth at this time, so they are pushing for us to reconnect with them and our own lineages at a rapid pace.

After working for a while as a diviner and having a community begin to form around the work, a new style of divination emerged which we call *Group Theme Divinations*. In Group Theme Divinations, a group comes together and listens to what the wedeme have to say about certain subjects we wish to learn more about. One person divines (a different one every time) while other diviners actively participate.

For two years, in Group Theme Divinations the wedeme taught us about the importance of tending to the many layers of "membranes" that enclose and protect lifesystems. Feeding and caring for these membranes is crucial and urgent work for medicine people at this time on the planet. This book will explain what is meant by the use of the word "membrane" and more fully explain this concept.

These membranes span the microscopic and extend out into the galaxy, enclosing other galaxies, other dimensions, other realities, and times.

The Holographic Principle—which emerged, surprisingly, from the equations of string theory—points to the unseen presence of layers or "skins" in the universe. The skin itself is intelligent and contains holographic codes and patterns that create what is alive within it. This is a fundamental cosmic reality. These skins act as a sort of barrier, called an "event horizon," beyond which current scientific instruments cannot penetrate. These are also membranes.

Those of us working in the fields of other kinds of perception (including divination, channeling, psychic reading, ritual, meditation, midwifery, death work, and shamanism) can "see" and perceive these other realities. In fact, it is interesting to think of other ways of seeing as the ability to penetrate the dimensional membranes. Between and beyond the membranes and event horizons are entities that are alive and can be interacted and collaborated with.

The membranes and their health are what this book is concerned with. We can participate in keeping healthy and strong the barriers, skins, and holographic walls that are essential for life to exist.

The membrane is a fractal reality. Fractals are infinitely complex patterns that are self-similar across different scales.

The membrane, as a container and protective barrier holding within it a precious and separate interior, is a self-similar occurrence across all scales of physical and non-physical reality.

Membranes exist at the spiritual, energetic, and physical levels. There are membranes within membranes within membranes. Consider a human body or an ecosystem and all the layers and overlapping membranes held within them. The strength and health of each membrane affect the strength and health of the whole. We need the membranes at each level and scale to be healthy and strong to keep lifesystems healthy. Membranes hold all in integrity and wholeness.

Membranes nurture, feed, and inform what is within them as the within feeds and supports the membranes.

We want to keep the membranes elastic and supple and not allow them to become frayed or hardened, as that compromises all that is within them. At this time on the planet, as medicine people, this is our work—becoming aware of these membranes and working toward nurturing and repair. We must learn once again how to keep them healthy and strong to protect the lifesystems within them. The largest part of a medicine person's work is tending to the membranes, the containers of life, the wombs with wings.

Part One

What Is a Membrane?

Chapter 1

Countless Containers of Safety

The first act of life is to create a boundary, a membrane that is the cell's identity. It defines an inside and an outside, what it is, what it is not.[6]

A membrane is a "selective barrier" that allows or denies access to that which it is protecting. There are synthetic membranes (those created through chemical synthesis), biological membranes, and energetic membranes. Biological membranes "consist largely of a lipid bilayer… Lipids give cell membranes a fluid character, with a consistency approaching that of a light oil."[7]

In this book, I am addressing biological membranes and extending this concept out to what we might call "etheric," "energetic," or "spiritual" membranes. Since it is often difficult to separate these from each other, a better term may be "bio-energetic" membranes.

The creation of the biological membrane on Earth occurred

---

[6] Margaret J. Wheatley. *Who Do We Choose to Be?* 63.
[7] "Membrane." *Encyclopædia Britannica*, 25 Sept. 2019, https://www.britannica.com/science/membrane-biology.

about 3.8 billion years ago with the creation of the first cell in the early sea. Cosmologist Brian Swimme cites the emergence of the cell membrane as one of the most crucial developments for the presence of life on Earth. He describes the early Earth system and the existence of molecules in the early sea. For a long time in this early Earth system, complexity is created, then washed away by the ongoing forces of nature. But there is a "moment where a **molecular web** folds around a complex chemical interaction and that molecular web protects what has been developed."[8] This is the birth of the cell. All other life forms emerged as a result of this moment of creativity.

The cell could not be created until it had a membrane, a system whereby the cell could close itself off from external influence. It is important to draw the reader's attention to the use of the word "web" in the above quote. We can think of membranes as webs as well: netting — woven and braided light energy.

The membrane acts as a filter, screening carefully and intelligently what it allows in while preserving the integrity of the center.

Until a cell had a distinct boundary between outside and inside, it could not become an integral whole. Its energies were constantly dispersed into the environment that surrounded it.[9] The invention of the membrane out of fatty liposomes found in the early sea allowed the cell to maintain itself while interacting with the outside world.

Membranes also possess the power of discernment, deciding what to allow in and what to keep out for the overall integrity of

---

[8] Personal notes from a retreat, *Powers of the Cosmos*, Santa Sabina Center, San Rafael, CA, October 2002.
[9] Brian Swimme and Thomas Berry, *The Universe Story*. 87.

the cell. "The membrane protects complexity and creative power."[10]

It is important to remember that what is being held in integrity is that which is inside the membrane. The membrane, by acting as an active, alive, intelligent boundary for its contents, holds the space so that what has been created may grow and change according to its own internal experience. The membrane has what we might call a kind of intelligence.

Similarly, the Earth's atmosphere offers a protective shield or boundary to the planet, allowing it to bring forth a wide variety of life forms while acting as a screening device for UV radiation and other harmful cosmic substances. Without the protective, circular embrace of the atmosphere, the planet would not be able to sustain life. "The atmosphere contains a complex system of gases and suspended particles that behave in many ways like fluids. Many of its constituents are derived from the Earth by way of chemical and biochemical reactions."[11]

The atmosphere can be seen as another form of bio-energetic membrane. The magnetospheres of the Earth and the sun can also be seen as layers of protective membranes that enclose and protect. The membrane is the container for a separate, individuated interior.

The membrane protects and preserves the creativity within to assure that this unique creation will not only stay alive, but thrive.

---

[10] Video clip, Workshop on Race and Cosmology, Sophia Institute, Holy Names College, Oakland CA, June 2005. http://www.caroline-webb.com/Video.htm
[11] Atmosphere - Biology Forums Dictionary, http://biology-forums.com/definitions/index.php/Atmosphere.

The membranes that contain life forms are not to be confused with the synthetic wrappers covering the products we throw in the trash. Rather, they are alive. The interior and external forces surrounding this protected center inform the alive membranes. The membrane adjusts to both of these in order to keep the interior healthy and strong, while remaining mutable and malleable to outside forces.

The membrane is a fractal reality of the container—contained space. When everything is in balance and healthy, we are held within countless containers of safety. We are held within layer upon layer of membranes that are permeable, yet protective.

The membranes can also be seen as the "Archetype of the Womb," which is carefully held, contained space. Carefully held, contained space creates more carefully held, contained space. The cosmos is a series of nested womb-like structures containing all within itself. The membranes containing these precious interiors need to be healthy at all levels.[12]

These are Domenica's wombs, the wombs with wings. This is the work of the medicine people.

The Importance of Holding and Containment

Holding space and creating safe containers within which beings and life forms can thrive and become the best realization of themselves is a familiar concept to most of us. For a baby, a young one, the parents hold the space, which is not only accomplished through nurturing and tending but protecting, listening, and responding to the needs of the child in relation to the world outside of them. We can understand this easily when we consider the very young and

---

[12] I have written more extensively on the *Archetype of the Womb* in the book, *Notes from a Diviner in the Postmodern World: A Handbook for Spirit Workers*.

4

vulnerable, or from a psychological perspective of "holding space" for a person as they process deep issues or unweave emotional entanglements that are unhealthy for them. But holding and containment have more applications than that. It is also something that is present and necessary in every form of life in every fractal layer of the cosmos. Membranes are the containers for what is inside them and these membranes must be strong as well as porous. It is a delicate balancing act. At each layer or level, there are ways to care for the membranes, which this book will discuss.

Lifesystems Create Their Own Membranes From Within

Membranes arise from that which is held within them. They are organic to life. Life must have a membrane, all phases and stages. The membrane is determined by what lies within it and the health of the membrane reveals the health of that which is inside it. This dual reality is how life works and we can participate in this consciously if we only begin to understand and value it.

The wedeme inform us that the many layers of nested membranes that protect life and help it thrive have been compromised and are in need of attention and repair. We are being asked to begin the work toward repair and recovery of our many membranes, be they biological, energetic or spiritual. The membrane needs to be fed and tended to, kept supple and permeable. This is the work of the medicine people. Just as there are those who care for the physical condition of humans, animals, water, and villages, as there are those who govern, there are those who care for the spiritual or unseen dimensions of humans, animals, villages, Earth, and beyond. These are what I call the "medicine people." They come in different forms and traditions with various titles. "Medicine person" is the general term I use to be inclusive and broad but medicine people arise from their local ecosystems, know their communities intimately, and tend to them.

One medicine person cannot attend to everything yet many can attend to their local space and together, tend to the all. It takes more than a village—it takes multiple villages, multiple lineages, and multiple medicine traditions. All of these are called upon for this work in whatever level of depth one wishes to enter into it. This is work for all of us. We will learn more as we all get on board.

Part Two

Tending to the Personal Membrane

Chapter 2

The Origin of the Personal Soup

Choosing to come to Earth to experience a lifetime embodied within Earth's reality is a deliberate act. We choose to do this in order to experience biological life in 3D through the consciousness of the Earth. There are most likely many other opportunities for embodiment in the universe; however, in this book, I am speaking only about choosing to come to Earth.

Earth is an alive consciousness, sometimes called Gaia[13], who agreed to be a place where light energy can coalesce into solid form. Earth agreed to host biological life[14]. There are myriad forms of biological life on Earth, all interrelated and in communion. Being a human being is just one of these forms. Though Earth is most probably not the only planet that agreed to host it, biological life is still a rarity in the cosmos.

---

[13] This name for our planet was popularized by James Lovelock's *Gaia Hypothesis,* that Earth is an alive entity with consciousness and self-regulation. He chose the Greek name for the Earth Goddess, Gaia, to convey this.

[14] A statement made by the wedeme in divination.

Complex lifesystems require this nested membrane design to exist and continue to exist, passing down their learned and successful accomplishments to the next generation. Early cellular life captured a foreign mechanism within itself, added more, and eventually created complex life forms. Cells contain mitochondria and photosensitive components that can eat the sun through photosynthesis. A human is a complex life form that contains other life forms within it, each with its own membrane. The Earth too created systems within herself, all with unique identities and membranes.

The Interiority Of a Thing Is What We Call Soul

A soul is a consciousness contained within and separated from its surroundings in a way that allows it to have its own integrity while living within a community of other integrated wholes. The collective of these separated consciousnesses creates another kind of consciousness—a collective consciousness activated and enhanced through many forms of communication and the sharing of information through physical, biochemical, electric, and verbal signaling.

One of the reasons we choose to come to Earth as humans is to process light through a physical body that is able to feel and sense. The sensuous experience of life on this planet must not be underestimated. It is a great gift. *Sensuous* does not mean only sexual, though that is certainly a part of it. The sensuous experience of life on Earth is one that includes all the ways we experience life here: through smell, taste, touch, sound, and sight. The vision we experience through our physical eyes — seeing color — is part of the sensuous experience embodied life on this planet offers.

Human eyes take in light in such a way that enables us to see green grass, blue skies, each other, a rainbow, clouds, and a sunset. This kind of vision took billions of years to evolve on Earth and it is a form of creativity unique to the experience of life on Earth. If you ever wonder why you are here or what the point is, ponder for a moment the ability to see. If you cannot see, then ponder the ability to hear.

If you are currently embodied on Earth, it took a lot of planning and effort on your part to get here. What is shared in this chapter is but a small peek into the vast mystery of how that happens. These are important components that have come through divination; however, it is acknowledged that they are but pieces.

We Are All Source

We all come from Source, whatever you perceive Source to be: Goddess, God, The All. Source is Origin and is an ongoing reality. Though we place it at a start time far, far away, that is not the truth of Source. Source is an ongoing, evolving reality that we all participate in. Even Time is a manifestation of Source, which enables Source to experience itself uniquely at differing vibratory levels. This helps create what we call different dimensions.

There are layers of energy within and around each other that form a rich tapestry of what we experience as "reality," though we see and sense very little of it through our primary human senses. Through the five senses—touch, smell, sight, sound, and taste—we experience physical life. There are also ways to experience non-physical reality while embodied, many of which we have forgotten or have not encouraged. But Original Source is one of the layers of energy that exists and is accessible always, right here and right now.

Before we come to Earth, we are wholly with Source, a non-differentiated aspect of The All. Source is not a person or one being. Source is All. We all comprise Source. When we choose to incarnate, we are choosing the experience of differentiating ourselves in a lens through which Source can experience itself differently. This is when the kernel for our souls is born, at this point of differentiation when we begin to have an "identity" separated from Source, held within it, creating a membrane with a within and a without.

Source holds many energetic manifestations within itself. These manifestations take different forms such as trees, planets, and stars but they are never separate or disconnected from Source. Becoming human is but one manifestation of Source. Source is not above, below or outside of us. Rather, we are it.

Feeling separate from Source is another way that Source can choose to experience itself. We may have chosen to experience that through our human embodiment.

The Stars and Star Beings Help Us Plan Our Incarnation

Through divination, I have been told that the stars are involved in helping to create the intentions and plans for our individual journeys here on Earth. We not only come from Source but we are all, in fact, Source brought to Earth from and by the stars.

When we move into the intention of incarnating as a human on Earth, we move into a time of working with the stars, star beings, and others, to plan our incarnation. This is not a set and rigid "destiny" but rather a framework for us to work within while we are here. This is a framework that can be edited and altered while we are on Earth according to decisions and choices made both consciously and unconsciously. We always have free will.

When we are working with the stars and the star beings (and others) to create our journey on Earth, we already have a more solid aspect to our being. Already there is a particular energetic pattern within a circle (or membrane). The wedeme call this our "soul origin pattern." I am shown this literally as a circle or sphere containing a pattern of lines within it; a design or even geometric form. This soul origin pattern has an interior, which differentiates it from the exterior. This interior is then held in integrity by the etheric membrane surrounding it. Though we are not separated from

12

Source, we are differentiated by this unique interior pattern for the duration of our embodied lifetime. This soul origin pattern can be thought of as "potentiality."

Potentialities are not realities until they are consciously or unconsciously activated. This potentiality already has individual consciousness. It has intent. Once we become embodied, this soul origin pattern is held for us in the 6th dimension (see Part Seven) and in our star of origin as well. It is a template and resource we can refer back to throughout our lives. It is our "library." The information is all there but only when we open one of the books can we access it. We can visit the library of our soul origin pattern, read the "instruction manual," and make changes to it or "edit" it.

I often see soul origin patterns when a woman of childbearing age comes in for a divination. The soul origin pattern will appear on her ovary and light up on a star simultaneously. It looks like a three-dimensional pattern held within a circle. It took me some time to understand that the pattern blinking on the ovary and the pattern blinking on the star were connected. In these cases, the soul origin patterns feel akin to what we would label "consciousness" and it is asking to be born through this woman's body into its physical embodiment.

Sometimes there are two—twins. The woman has a choice to say yes or no. If no, the consciousness will look for another way to embody. It seems that it doesn't always have to be a human embodiment. Sometimes the woman is unable to physically bring forth the consciousness in embodied form and the being wants to stay by her as an angel or spirit guide. As I said, I do not fully understand the mechanism here but I see these kernels of consciousness with intention and a soul origin pattern. I also stress emphatically that the woman has a choice and is never told that she must bring this being through.

Nurturing Our Connection to Source

Though we are never truly separate from Source, nurturing and keeping the connection strong is a good practice. If it becomes frayed, our physical lives can be in danger. In the Dagara tradition, this connection entity is called the *siura*.[15]

The siura guards and protects the connection to Source throughout our embodied lives. It also connects us to others at a deep soul level. In other traditions, this is often portrayed as a guardian angel or a luminous white cord. In the context of this book and as we journey through its pages, we can begin to think of the siura as the membrane as well. We can see that this is not unique to our personal soul. All things that are alive are ensouled. All things that are ensouled have a membrane and all those membranes connect to Source. This includes family systems, groups, places, planets, and galaxies.

If the soul is the interiority of a thing, the membrane is that which creates, allows for, informs, and protects that interiority.

This is fractal reality that extends out and in—multiple layers of membranes, multiple layers of interiors, precious interiors, holies of holies, and the life-giving wombs that support them.

The within nurtures the without and the without informs, protects, and contains the within. Lifesystems are held in balance in this way.

---

[15] You may read more about the *siura* in my book, *Notes from a Diviner in the Postmodern World,* Chapter 9.

The "Codes for Ascension"

We each carry, in our unique souls, individual "codes for ascension." Codes for ascension are pre-programmed opportunities to grow, learn, and actualize our soul's intended trajectory. To ascend is to fly. You will recall that Domenica's wombs were winged and that was necessary for ascension.

We all have the potential to ascend when we come into physical embodiment. The codes for ascension are held in the original pattern. They appear as little bubbles of potentiality embedded within it. There are many of them, which present themselves as opportunities as we move through linear time. If we miss one, another will come along. It is our choice, through our actions, whether or not we activate them. The available ascensions are also those we chose as potentialities before we came in.

Ascension does not happen to us. We choose to ascend or not.

Chapter 3

Our Personal Membranes

Since the wedeme suggest we work *from the inside out,* one of the first membranes to attend to is the membrane around our soul—our personal membrane. Within this membrane is our physical body, which also has many membranes within it. Each organ has a membrane. Our consciousness has a membrane. Our cells have membranes. Our personal membrane includes all of these membranes within it while simultaneously existing within other membranes: family membranes, community and village membranes, and Earth membranes. Our individual soul within our personal membrane is a precious inner space—the holy of holies within us.

The within nurtures the without and the without informs, protects, and contains the within. The quality of our precious interior space determines the quality of our personal membrane. Personal membranes help hold us in integrity within a sea of other personal membranes around us.

Poet John O'Donohue refers to this space as our "interiority." He remarks on how in the Western world, this space is no longer talked about or left room for. We are not schooled in how to attend to this interior space. Instead, we are encouraged to be outward focused. O'Donohue feels there is "an evacuation of interiority going on in our time."[16]

What we call our soul is connected to the Source soul and soul origin pattern. It is our interiority, our inner darkness. It is uniquely ours. What we have gathered through lifetimes of experience, what we brought with us from the stars, the memories of all our lifetimes, the precious jewels we have polished in the fires of transformation, are all there. Did you know that you could be in such intimate relationship with it? That *this* relationship is the most important one you will ever have? That you can interact with this and even change agreements made that you no longer wish to agree to, from this place? Our lives are ever-evolving works of art, controlled and designed by us. Actively engaging with our own libraries and interiority helps us sculpt what we feel is delicious to us. The soul is not something *outside* of us. We carry it within and it is ours to interact with and shape and dance with.

We must nurture and attend to our interior — what I like to call the "Library of the Soul" — and its contents, which are uniquely ours.

Knowing the Library of the Soul

The library of the soul is the place within us that belongs uniquely to us. And to know this place inside is absolutely essential to retaining our power. Sometimes, for me, this place or space simply feels like a pocket of thick and fecund darkness, a presence of depth and potency within. I have my own ways of finding it and

---

[16] "John O'Donohue - The Inner Landscape of Beauty." The On Being Project, 31 Aug. 2017, https://onbeing.org/programs/john-odonohue-the-inner-landscape-of-beauty-aug2017/.

feeding it: long, silent walks; writing and reading; pondering and questioning; ruminating. There is information there (another reason I call it a library) akin to what we call "intuition" or knowing. It is our personal database. This is the place from which arises what are often called "other ways of knowing." Dreams live here.

We have our own symbols in this place that have special meaning to us and help us make meaning of our lives and experiences. Through our experiences, impressions, and memories we create what could be called our own vocabulary of symbols and words. Associations. Only we can follow the trails of these breadcrumbs to the nuggets of information trying to be revealed to us through all we have stored and accumulated in our library. Some symbols have profound meaning to us that would mean nothing to another. It is important for us to understand our own vocabulary.

Exploring the library of the soul often and being in intimate relationship with it can help us understand the meaning we make of things based on our past experiences, intuition, and relationships with all the dimensional realms. We can access memories and dreams from this place to better understand information trying to come through to us. But it is also a place where we can go for quiet retreat and reflection when we feel depleted and exhausted, weary or worried.

As we continue to go there, the library becomes a portal to other times and places and we may experience deep insights. It is a place where we can make connections between seemingly random occurrences—a place of deeper understanding. In this space, we are no longer separate. In this space that is uniquely ours, we experience the connectedness of all.

If this spark within us is not appreciated, explored, and nurtured, we may experience what is often referred to as "losing ourselves." We may not have a strong "sense of self" and so look to others to provide that for us. We may look to jobs to do that for us or seek external approval. We may attempt to build ourselves up from the outside which, in the end, is ineffective because it leaves a hollow core. Everyone has a library of the soul. To go there is only a matter of acknowledging it, visiting it, experiencing it, and becoming intimate with it. It is important to form a deep relationship with it.

Knowing the Library of the Soul Helps Us Retain Our Power

This interior space is the well from which arises our will. It is what causes us to act and make decisions in the world. It is the core of what we are as a person. Being in touch with and retaining access to this place makes our actions, thoughts, and experiences authentic to who we are at our deepest core. When we are in alignment with and acting from who we are at our deepest core, we are in our power. When we are in our power, we are not only in touch with, but are true to our core essence — that which we call the soul. Being in our power is being grounded in our uniqueness, our passions and beliefs, our convictions and desires, our longings and aspirations, and our purpose and impetus. To use a cliché, being in our power is being true to our innermost selves — being able to speak from and for that place unapologetically with integrity.

If we know what this is and can return to it often, and let it evolve and grow with us, we will not be knocked off our center by the daily events of life or huge trials along the way. That is what I mean by "retaining our power." Fighting for this place means giving it priority and importance. It means giving ourselves access to this room of our own and tending to it. It means allowing ourselves to cherish ourselves. So, no matter what is happening in the outside world, events, or day-to-day living, we have this solid, weighted, and grounded core. This, in turn, keeps our membrane strong.

Journey To the Library of Your Soul

The following is a guided meditation or journey to find and become familiar with the library of your soul. To listen to this, go to *stregatree.com* and find the free download under the "Guided Meditation Journeys" tab or you can read the text below.

✳ ✳ ✳

Preparation: Give yourself at least 30 minutes to do this guided meditation. Find a comfortable position, sitting or reclining, with a light covering in case your temperature drops. Have a journal and pen available in case you wish to sketch or write after the recording.

The journey: It's time to journey to the library of your soul. You enter this place through the heart. First, become quiet and peaceful, taking a few deep breaths in and out. Become calm. Release cares, stress, and worries. Breathe in and exhale slowly. Breathe in again and exhale slowly. Breathe in, exhale slowly. Life is busy. But this place is not. This place is nurturing and secluded and yours alone.

Allow your consciousness to settle into the space in your chest where you feel your heart. Again, take deep breaths to feel what is there. There may be some unexpressed feelings that need your attention. Happiness, love, grief, pain, sadness, joy. Take a moment to listen to them. Then imagine a white light in the shape of a spiral over your heart. Let this spiral begin to spin in a counter-clockwise direction. Allow the feelings to latch onto this spiral and dissipate with its swirling movements. Let the spiral continue to spin.

Behind it is the door to the library of your soul.

Take some time to project that spiral into the space in front of your body. Allow the spiral to become larger until it is large enough to completely fill the space in front of you, as large as your body if not larger. You may need to breathe some more to allow this form to enlarge. Take some time to do that.

Now the light turns into a misty substance and you begin to see the door to the library of your soul in front of you.

What does it look like? Take some time to notice. Is it wooden? Or stone? Does it have a pattern or design on it? Does it have a door handle? What does the handle look like? Is there a sound, a feeling, or perhaps light coming through this door?

Begin to feel the presence of this space. Is it familiar? Does it have something to say to you? Stay in front of this door as long as you need to. When you are ready, open the door and walk inside.

Now that you are inside, what do you see, feel, perceive? You may not see objects but rather perceive a feeling, a word, a pressure, or an energy. Take notice. Go with what is happening. There is no right or wrong way to do this.

Are there walls? Is it a cave? Is it soft? Are there bookshelves? Is there a table with a nice armchair and tea? Perhaps it is a garden? Notice what is there. Are there any animals? Is something you do not want there? Kindly ask it to leave. Is there anything you would like to be there? Take some time to bring it in. Sit or recline inside this room. Welcome to the library of your soul. Begin to get to know it.

Stay here for ten minutes.

It is time to begin to come back. When you are ready, thank the space and tell it you will return. Come out of the library of your soul and close the door. Put the room back in your heart. You can move your hands to do this if you like. See the spiral of light again in front of your heartspace. Spin it the other way, this time in a clockwise direction.

Return to normal consciousness: Now come back into your body inside the room you are reclining in, inside your home, inside your town. When you are ready, take some time to write about the journey or draw.

Chapter 4

Tending to the Membrane of the Library of Your Soul

Personal Boundaries

Caring for and tending to the interior is one way to care for the membrane. A healthy and supported interiority keeps the membrane strong and supple. This is true for all the membranes we will speak of. Another way to tend to it is through what many people call "personal boundaries." Boundary work is very important. But it is important to not think of it as a defense mechanism—rather, it is a nurturing, caring container that keeps what is inside safe and healthy. This boundary is created by and emerges from the interiority itself. This is an important concept we will revisit throughout this book.

The interior of a thing creates its membrane and the membrane supports, guards, and protects the healthy interior. For the membrane to be strong, the interior must be kept healthy and strong.

The membranes allow in new information, new ideas, new people, and new physical material, which the interior accepts or rejects.

I see my personal membrane as a golden egg-like form around my-self, which begins from within the heart and extends out in concen-tric circles. It has an oily substance swirling within it, kind of like that bubble stuff we used to blow through a small, round wand to create fabulous bubbles when we were young. The glycerin, which is a kind of oil, created the membrane that would swirl, catch the light, and create color. The magical substance resulting from treas-uring my interiority, my soul, my tender holy of holies, my caring of myself, creates the golden hue that swirls within my orb. And it is this which is the boundary. Not a hard concrete wall but some-thing created by my own opinion of myself, my self love, and care.

My personal membrane is created by my own concern for my pre-ciousness, my own understanding of my holy of holies within. My own "golden membrane," spun from my union with divine Source and its multiple iterations of being through that which I call me. It is created from the inside out and not built-up from the outside in.

Building boundaries from the outside in is defense and keeping out, which is the opposite of what we are after. Experiences like abuse can fracture, tear, and infect this membrane. Suddenly, we have been dirtied or soiled. Suddenly, there is pain and soreness in this interior space, which if left, can fester and create resentment and the desire to hurt others. We must watch for situations that feel toxic and say no to them. We must limit our time with other hu-mans who do not respect us and do not treat us with respect.

Overdoing, overworking, and overexposing ourselves to media and outside influences can also threaten this membrane. They can push up against it and cause it to constrict and become smaller. Eventually, there is no space or time for ourselves, for our interior to breathe, for our own precious library. We must allow enough time for ourselves to be alone, to be free, to wander, and to listen to what it is we need. Silent time by water and walks in the forest can nurture this membrane. Reading poetry, dreaming, resting, visioning, silence, and entering into the darkness can help. With enough space, our wings can open, flutter, and we can fly.

All things that are alive have a soul. And many things that we often do not consider to be alive are, in fact, alive. Rocks are alive, ancestors are alive, the medicine is alive, lineages are alive, relationships are alive, communities are alive. All souls are protected by their membrane and are kept in touch with Source in this way.

In this book, we will explore the many layers of ensoulment and their membranes. To each of these soul entities and membranes there is a shrine that a medicine person watches over, feeds, and protects. We will explore this as well.

Tending to Our Personal Membranes by Reducing Overexposure

Divination Time

I wanted to know about the nature of the sun as a spiritual being, so I did a Group Theme Divination on the sun. In the divinatory space, I was shown the image of a person in a spotlight, on a stage, in front of a lot of people and getting a lot of attention.

"Do not stand in the bright lights for too long," the sun warned. "You should be reflecting me. Do not overexpose yourselves."

When the sun said this, it was clear that the word *overexposed* had two meanings. One was to not be overexposed to the literal sun. Retreat, find darkness, go inside, seek shelter. But also, don't overexpose yourselves to others and activity. Do not overdo. We must take care of this ourselves. If we stand in the bright lights for too long, constantly seeking, needing and/or getting attention, we will indeed burn out.

"The spotlight cannot reflect."

We should be emulating the sun, beaming light back to it and to each other. We should not be taking it all in for ourselves. We are indeed not the sun.

Most of us currently live our lives in a state of overexposure to everything. We take in too much and we put ourselves out there too much. There must be times where we have absolutely nothing to do, where we can be idle, wander, and where we can dream. Time out in nature with no agenda. Sitting by water or walking in the forest. Times where we can play. And wonder. This feeds our interiority. This nurtures our soul and creates strength in the membrane.

The sun itself said, "Don't overexpose yourself to me, retreat to the darkness to nourish and restore yourselves, otherwise, you become toxic and dangerous."

Protecting Others from Ourselves

We must protect others from ourselves.

It is necessary to look at the ways that we ourselves can be too large and find ways to protect others from overexposure to us. If we are not centered and our membrane feels frayed or burnt around the edges, we must take ourselves away to center, to ground. We must take ourselves out of exposure for a time, to and from others, information, and experience. Protecting ourselves protects others. Do not expose other people to your unprotected (and possibly toxic) light caused by your frayed and burnt membrane.

"Even When You Can Choose Not To Be, Please Be Noble"

At the close of the divination, the sun left us with two requests.

"Please shine your light back to me and upon each other. And please be noble behind your shields of reflection, deflection, and protection."

Unlike the sun, we can hide. But the sun petitioned us to:

"Please be noble, even when no one sees it. Even when you can hide, even when you can choose not to be, please be noble."

At times of overexposure, when you are worn out, the soul-washing ritual listed in the rituals section is a good thing to do.

Chapter 5

The Importance of Dreaming, Dreams, and The Dreamers

One way our personal membranes, as well as those of Earth and village, are held and sustained is through a process that we call dreaming. At one time, humans built special chambers in deep, underground caverns in which to do this. They built temples where dreaming was sought after, held, and facilitated by priests and priestesses of this realm.

Knowing the Landscapes of Our Dreams

In most ancient and indigenous cultures, dreams are considered a shared experience with which to gather information for the community. It was sometimes a collective act. This is often the case but sometimes they are deeply personal and sometimes they are both. We will delve more deeply into community dreaming in Part 6. Here, we will attend to personal dreaming and developing our own vocabulary around our dreams.

Dreaming is very healthy for us. It is a time to interact with the library of our soul and be fed by it, to explore the subconscious parts of ourselves, and be held and nurtured by the dark goddess of the inner Earth: *The One Who Brings the Dreams*. Scientific research is currently discovering the importance of dreaming to our overall health and well-being.

There are many dictionaries and systems for dream interpretation; however, I encourage everyone to develop their own vocabulary around their dreams. They are the landscapes of our soul and other lifetimes, images and layered impressions of personal experiences we are transforming or coming to understand. In fact, dreamtime is the chance to integrate and more deeply understand all of these.

I posit that we are integrating more than this lifetime and dimension alone. I believe dreaming is a transdimensional affair. Our souls span all the dimensions and dreaming is a chance for them to gather all their many aspects and continue to evolve. Since no one else knows the landscape of our soul, we are the best interpreters of our own dreamscapes. Having said that, it is an art to begin to decode them and see this vocabulary for what it is: a language for one to come into intimate relationship with. It is not difficult to understand. Simply begin by paying attention.

There is a lot going on in dreams. Sometimes they are important and sometimes not. It is crucial to categorize one's dreams so we know which ones to investigate. Some are simply day-processing dreams. We can recognize these by the circumstances of the dream and whether they seem to be derived specifically from events that transpired that day. Some are anxiety dreams—missing an appointment, being late when we have an important meeting or early flight to get to the following morning. Others are messages or warnings from our subconscious, some are downloads of valuable information, some are ancestral, and if one is a medicine person, some are medicine dreams. Sometimes dreams are for and about others but we cannot know if we have not explored well and studied our own terrain.

Since I became a diviner, I have discovered a whole new level of dreaming: dreaming landscapes, ancestral dreams, medicine dreams, integrity dreams, and prophetic dreams. Each type has its own signature feel that I identify and recognize as I am dreaming or upon awakening. Often, I divine into these dreams or ask another diviner to look into those I cannot understand. Yes, dreams can be divined into. For this, I recommend a six-shell roll, which some of the diviners on the Strega Tree (stregatree.com) site offer. You can inquire more about this on our *Meet our Diviners* page.

To follow is a list that is useful to start to understand more fully the different landscapes that can present themselves in dreams.

Ancestral Dreams[17]

Ancestral Landscapes

If we dream frequently, we begin to notice the feel of certain dreams. Some have more depth and texture than others. We begin to notice that there are certain "landscapes" we revisit over and over. The landscape may not look the same but in the dream, we know we are at a certain place or it is referred to in the dream, or there is a feel to the "landscape" that is the same.

For me, an ancestral dream is usually at my parents' home, the house I grew up in, in New Hampshire. Sometimes it is in a different location but I know it is an ancestral dream by the number of people there—a lot— and that we are mostly related. There is wine and feasting. It feels like a holiday or party on that side of my family, my father's Italian side. In these dreams, people are always kissing and hugging me. That was the experience of my childhood with these ancestors. This is my personal ancestral dream landscape. That does not mean the ancestors in my dream are limited to my

---

[17] Read more about ancestors and the ancestral realm in Part 3 of this book.

father's side, just that this is the landscape of an ancestral dream for me. It can be ancestors from both sides. This recurring landscape is simply the way I am to understand that this is an ancestral dream. My own notes to myself. My own soul's language to me.

When I have these kinds of dreams, I understand that the ancestors have something to say or convey to me. These dreams are recurring and they all have this same quality.

Your ancestral dreams will be different and have their own unique qualities, which you will begin to recognize. Yours may not even seem to be relatives but a crowd. Most often, a defining factor in an ancestral dream is the crowd or group quality — the feeling of a function or an event.

Decoding the Dream

What happens in the dream is indicative of what is going on in the ancestral realm. Often I have these dreams when there is a big event happening or upcoming on the Earth plane, our 3D reality, that the ancestors are happy about and celebrating just like we are on Earth.

Possibly there is an initiation ceremony on the calendar, a wedding in the family, or a party for the medicine. The dream may be telling me the ancestors want to be included and fed. They may perhaps even show me in the dream what they want, or that they want to be included, remembered, or invited. I may have lost my manners and forgotten to invite the ancestors — literally going to the ancestor shrine, telling them about the event, asking for their blessing and encouraging them to attend, and letting them know that they are welcome. The dream may be reminding me to do this and that the ancestors are involved.

Once we establish the ancestral dream landscape, we can look at the specific contents and feel of the dream for what the ancestors are trying to say to us, or possibly something that they need from us or want to help us with.

Ancestral Nightmares

Conversely, sometimes these dreams are turned inside out for me and I realize all is not well in the ancestral world. The dream is not a crowd of hugging people at all, rather, I am on the streets of a city alone or with a few others and the "bad guys" are after us. I am marked and being chased and I cannot get away. There is a sinking feeling in my stomach throughout the dream. There is usually a family member in the dream with me, maybe one or two, and we are in danger. It is dark — literally, nighttime. These dreams are dark in the other meaning of the word too: a dark, heavy, frightening feel. There is violence, literal or threatened. I wake up shaking from these dreams.

Now I know, through a teaching from my mentor in the Dagara tradition and repeated experience, that these dreams often indicate stress in the ancestral realm. They are trying to protect me in my work and keep my family safe but they are worn thin and in need of more support in the form of material offerings from me. When I awake, I make many offerings to the ancestors to give them extra fuel for their support and protection and all the work they are doing for me. (See Strega Tree Apothecary's YouTube video, *How to Make Physical Offerings to Spiritual Entities,* for instruction on this, and the *Top 5 Physical Offerings to Make to Spiritual Beings* listed in Chapter 11 of this book.)

I then try to define the situation I have gotten myself into that may be stressing them. This could be a client with a lot of ancestral debt, possible sorcery, or ill will aimed at me from other medicine people who do not have my best interests in mind. Or perhaps I am engaged in an Earthly relationship or behavior that is really not good for me. I need to tighten up my boundaries and fix the places where I have become sloppy. I need to analyze these factors and make changes to keep my family, community, the ancestors, and myself healthy and safe. Usually, after I make my offerings and ascertain what is stressing the ancestors, the nightmares cease.

Medicine Dreams

Some dreams are medicine dreams. Examples of these are:

* ❀ Being visited by a spirit animal or another entity you work with, or a new one that is presenting itself to you. Often animal totems or new entities (a Goddess, angel, or guide) will appear in a dream as a message or just to make themselves known to you. If this happens, it is always good to make an offering the next day as an acknowledgment of this. *I see you and thank you. Here you go.* Simply make the offering onto the Earth or leave it on your kitchen counter for a few hours.
* ❀ Working with an element (fire, water, Earth, mountain/mineral, nature/wild) in a new and magical way.
* ❀ Receiving information about medicine work or being taught in the dream by an elder in the medicine.
* ❀ Given work by being shown a ritual, an issue that needs looking into, or where to look for information. Many people see inside books or are given words.
* ❀ Being shown things the spirits want us to make or acquire. I have seen rings and other jewelry in my dreams that the wedeme want me to acquire, new tools to make or acquire and how to use them, even concoctions or remedies to make.
* ❀ Seeing oneself as a medicine person working in a past life and one's guides from that lifetime.
* ❀ Dreaming of my medicine tools. Perhaps they need an offering or are simply wanting to interact with me in this space and come into better relationship with me.

I often deliberately ask for these dreams or they are prescribed in divination. "Put a quarter under your pillow and ask for a dream," people are often told in divination. When I want to understand something better, I whisper it into a shell or seed and put it under my pillow as I sleep. Tree medicine came to me through meeting a tree being in two separate dreams. Dreamtime is an important, interactive space for any medicine person.

Integrity Dreams

I was so happy to understand that there is a cap on what we are allowed access to through what I call *universal integrity tests*. By this I mean exactly what I say: the universe sends us tests and we either fail or pass. These tests are checking up on our integrity in life and with the work. If we pass, we are given greater access. If we fail, we have less access. Access to what? Information, teachings, and the work in general.

In a liminal space between sleep and waking, I was shown a literal ceiling we will meet if we fail to stay in integrity. We will be stopped if we do not handle the medicine correctly. We will lose access. That does not mean we cannot make mistakes and correct ourselves. It is not said to create or imply punishment. It is just another cause-and-effect action of the universe. If you are not in integrity with the medicine, you can still do medicine and some magic but you will stay at a certain level and will not advance.

Who is conducting these tests? Our guides. It seems to be something we have all agreed to because they appear to be pretty standardized.

It is also not for us to judge the integrity of another and make assumptions about their level of access. Humans could never be trusted with that. What we need to be concerned with is ourselves and our own relationship to the medicine, not anyone else's.

We all deal with integrity tests regularly in our daily lives. These are moments where we have a choice to make concerning our own behavior as well as how we handle situations that may be triggering, challenging, or emotionally charged for us.

But the dreams come too. It's nice to get the dreams because they give us a chance to try things out and see where we may be vulnerable to acting with less integrity. I remember one dream where I was tempted to betray a friend. In the dream, I was extremely close to doing it and it was very seductive. When I awoke, I realized it was an integrity dream and that I had been truly tempted by the seductions laid before me. If I had indeed betrayed her, I would have been in better graces with the person in power who was encouraging the betrayal. I had to do a lot of soul searching around the temptations that were seducing me in this dream and why they had appealed to me.

Other things that can be common integrity tests are situations where we choose to be greedy rather than generous, where we allow our jealousy to get the best of us and deliberately try to denounce or destabilize someone else, or where we are encouraged to cross the line with our medicine work over into sorcery.

Sometimes, I am not sure whether I have "passed" but then receive some kind of new information later that makes me aware that I have increased access. I suspect that I may not be aware of the tests I do not pass and lower my access. I think part of being out of integrity is not even knowing when we transgress. That is why it is good to do a scan on ourselves from time to time—to take time to be alone and check in with ourselves, and do the sweeps and soul washings described later in this book with regularity to make sure we are dealing with our shadow.

Especially in this culture, where projections of grandeur are cast onto spiritual workers and leaders, we must be mindful to hold our boundaries and be in proper alignment with our power. We must be careful not to indulge our egos and buy into those projections of adoration and holiness that can make us believe that we do not have to abide by common rules of conduct.

Prophetic Dreams

Prophetic dreams are when we are shown an event that may come to pass in the future, or we are given a warning about a person or possibility that could arise out of our current life trajectory. They can also simply be showing us our own futures. They can be confusing as we might feel uncertain about what it is we are being told or shown. These dreams can be divined into to determine exactly what the message is and if there are actions that can be taken to offset the possibility or mitigate the damage of these events if they are catastrophic in nature. We can begin to work with these dreams by recording them and seeing if what we are told indeed comes to pass. Then we can begin to categorize them to better understand their meaning and levels of priority. Sometimes dreaming of catastrophic events can be speaking to our emotional lives rather than an event that is going to take place literally on the Earth. Working with dreams consciously helps us to begin to discern these differences.

Visitations and Visions

Some dreams are not really dreams at all but are visitations or visions that have a dreamlike quality. Often at night, I am awakened by what I call a *visitation.* I am awake, not asleep, but they mostly happen in the middle of the night. Is this because the liminal state between waking and sleeping allows me to be more open to the visitation? Or is it because I am quiet and they are sure they can get my attention and force me to listen? Is it because I am a captive audience? I am unsure but in these cases, actual entities, ancestors, places, energies, and stars come into the room and speak to me.

They float above my bed as a sort of light-form or visual picture. Usually, with a visitation comes an order, a request, or a plea. I don't tend to ignore them.

Visions are spontaneous shifts to another reality when we are suddenly able to see through another dimensional lens. They can come with a meditative state, while deeply pondering something, sitting by water, or even when we are speaking to someone. They often carry information about what we are considering at the time but they can also be completely random and spontaneous. These too are worth recording and categorizing to better understand and derive their meaning.

Your dream list will look different than mine. Just know that you and your dream landscape are worthy of studying and exploring as much as anything else. It is a language worth learning.

Chapter 6

Dying Before We Die

Part of the work of taking care of our personal membrane includes coming to terms with death and our own mortality. We will die. Others will die. But when we die we will not, in fact, be dead. Not in the way we currently think of it, anyway.

The wedeme and ancestors get upset at me whenever I call them dead. "That cup is dead," they say, pointing to the ever-present teacup in my hand. *"We* are alive. We are not dead. You can talk to us, right? How then can we be dead? We continue to grow and change, right? Then how can we be dead?"

Yes, they indeed have a point. Some of the most alive interactions I have are with those we consider to be "dead." Simply put, they are no longer in physical form but they are not dead. They are alive in another dimensional realm and time space. They no longer have physical embodied form, which is what we often call dead, but they still have an energetic presence, which is how we can interact with them.

2005

After I met Domenica in the cave, there was a second exercise from Robert Moss's book that I wanted to try. In *The Dreamer's Book of the Dead*, Moss talks about creating a space for yourself in the otherworld that you will go to when you die. He says to create it now and visit it often, have it feel very much like a second home so that when you die, for the first few days when you might be disoriented, you will have this familiar place to go to. I thought this was a valuable teaching since so many of us these days have no firm belief or expectation of the afterworld, and very little interaction with the otherworld. I understood that my soul might be confused upon death and that I wanted to create a place for *then*, but I also wanted a place in the otherworld that was mine alone for *now*. I essentially hungered for it. I had been working on seeing the afterworld as the otherworld, meaning seeing it less as a linear place that happens after death and more a place that exists perpetually and is here with us now, held within another membrane.

It felt more accurate to me that the otherworld is the afterworld and that it is here now, and that interacting with it here and now would facilitate my transition to the death state as well as greatly enhance my present life in the physical realm.

In the Western world, we have come to believe in a hereafter (for those who believe in that) as something or somewhere that happens and we go to after death. But this is a limited way to view reality. What we call the "otherworld" is a separate reality interconnected and interacting with the physical world that we moderns are more accustomed to experiencing.

To create my own place in the otherworld, I built a strong fire in the fireplace, lit candles, and chanted before getting into a comfortable position for a journey. Then I went. I went back to Domenica's cave.

I found Domenica right where I had left her, in her cave behind the waterfall working dutifully on her wombs with wings. I asked her if I could come there after I died. She said yes, I could, but I needed to create my own room. I built a room within her cave and brought things into it that felt like home, then I sat out in the main cave to chat with her.

She said, "You mustn't interfere with my work."

I said, "Yes, I understand."

But she repeated it, this time in a more forceful manner. "You can be here but you cannot interfere with my work."

I felt slightly wounded, though she had not said it with any harshness or anger. It was simply a very firm boundary that revealed to me that what I wanted from her, to hang out and get her approval, wasn't what she was about and wasn't what I should be about either. There it was, perfectly laid out before me. *Ouch.*

My intentions for sharing space with Domenica were not clean. They arose from a needy place. I realized I needed to find a different place and not ask her to attend to those needy parts of myself.

I returned to my start point of the journey and this time found myself inside a tree. I stood inside her empty husk, waiting. The tree turned into a boat and fell gently into a running current of water with me lying inside it. It was a canoe-type boat, which took me across the water. The boat swayed with the soft waves. I lay there completely enclosed by its edges, looking at the daytime sky above me and feeling the rhythmic rocking. There were voices, like a choir, and many beings escorted me. It was as if I had died and was being led to the otherworld by these wonderful guides and this magnificent music. I understood that what I was experiencing this time, in this try, was a true practice of dying.

While we can journey and interact with other dimensions, places, and times while we are still embodied, the experience of "death" is different in that we withdraw from our physical embodiment and all that accumulated around that creation, leaving it behind.

Whereas before I had experienced an otherworld journey, now I was, in fact, rehearsing my own death. It took me a little time to realize that I had died and that I was actually leaving. I felt emotional and sad about leaving my life while simultaneously letting go in layered succession. The entire time a part of me was aware of what was happening and observing with interest. I expected to feel desperate over dying...but I didn't.

Finally, my boat landed on a beach in a cove of fresh water. As I landed, the boat disappeared and it was only me sitting on the edge of the water. The sand was soft brown and there were gentle waves, just a soft pulsing rhythm of water meeting the Earth. Many animals came to me as I sat there on the shore. They sat around me: orca, bear, weasel, owl, dog and cat, hummingbird and parrot, koala and snake. There was a lot of color here — bright green, energetic reds, bright blues, and stark white in contrast. The colors were of a brightness and intensity not found in the physical reality. I kept saying internally, *Well, that was that...* meaning the life that had just passed, *well that's over with,* in a very detached way similar to how Domenica had spoken of her previous life.

I remember noticing consciously that this must be what it is like, a rather detached observation of the lifetime experience one had only just left. And to me, that offered great relief. I thought if I could be a little bit more like that in my daily life, it would truly be easier. However, while I had that thought, I simultaneously understood that there is a certain amount of enmeshment that comes with incarnating as a human that makes it inherently difficult to acquire this kind of distance. From my place in the cove, it appeared that the enmeshment may be limited to the human realm. Therefore, it must be part of the learning. If this is the case, shouldn't it be something that is ultimately embraced? Perhaps that is what ancient cultures had in mind by celebrating sacred sexuality and Dionysian rites — to celebrate and wholeheartedly embrace this experience of utter and total enmeshment that comes with physical embodiment — not only with each other but with the Earth herself, the plants and the other beings, and the air that we need to breathe.

I sat for a while in this cove, noticing how I no longer had the tendrils of attachment. The animals were very tender with me and loving, remaining cluttered about me like children wanting to hear a story. I felt an amazing amount of protection and gratitude from them.

Suddenly, I became aware of Domenica and that is when I realized that she was working in her cave in the mountaintop above me. I was in the cove below her — with her but not with her. I realized happily that I could create my own space down here, near her but not bothering her. It was clear from here that her work was imperative, was somehow *holding the world together*, though, again, intellectually I had no idea what that meant. Here in this place, I was so thankful for her work and definitely did not want to interfere with it in any way.

I sat on the edge of the beach and thought, *It was hard for me to be alive when I thought the Earth was dying.* It felt similar to the way Domenica had mentioned the operations the first time I had found her — how, in the lifetime I had just finished, this had been the thing, the knowing that had been difficult for me to hold, difficult to not be overwhelmed by, difficult to have a big-picture view of. But as I sat there, the Earth said, "I am all right. I am fine."

I was surprised, envisioning the destruction I had seen to her habitat in my lifetime. She said, "Look around you, am I not okay?" And in this place of natural beauty, it was true, I could see no sign that she was not okay. Then the Earth that I was on, the "spirit Earth," this otherworld Earth, moved like a translucent shadow over and onto the physical Earth and wrapped around it, becoming one with it, and I understood. They were one, not separate at all, and I felt a healing and an inner knowing that she was well. "I am taking care of myself," she said. I understood that she is doing this partially by bringing forth healing consciousness from this, this otherworld.

The cave in this cove, beneath Domenica's, is my cave. It is my special place in the otherworld. I began to slowly fill it with things of mine. Owl, my faithful guardian and companion, was there with me. Though I was afraid it would, it didn't feel cold at all. It was more of a porous and blanket-like presence. Here I would do my own work and not disturb Domenica but I could visit her as often as I liked.

Chapter 7

What is a Shrine?

A shrine is a place or object that represents, holds, and makes a space for a certain entity, component, idea, or belief. At the shrine, offerings are made or prayers are said to and for what is held there.

The practice of building shrines has many functions, some of which are psychological in that they allow us to *externalize* certain ineffable concepts and ideas like the soul, or a relationship to a powerful but unseen being. Externalizing means giving form to something that we only feel, perceive, and understand as untouchable, within, or numinous. The practice of externalizing helps us to actively work with them, and consider and care for them in a way that is different from when they are internalized only. With the shrine, we can take that relationship, being, or concept, place it in a concrete form outside of ourselves, look at it, and interact with it in a real-time, three-dimensional way.

Though many may think of shrine building as primitive or an old-fashioned superstition, this is simply not true. This practice arose out of a common-sense need to give expression to something intangible and create form for something that is formless. Shrines have served and continue to serve a useful purpose throughout human history. It is potent and effective, even from a strictly intellectual point of view, to consider a thing from a different perspective. Externalizing a concept or entity like the soul or a god, and building an image of them in our understanding of them, helps humans interact with this part of themselves or the universe. It offers a feeling of agency over our lives as well as interaction and participation with these unseen entities.

Shrines Make the Invisible Visible

Shrines help humans to remember to engage in an ongoing, reciprocal relationship with things we cannot see or touch.

Many of us are familiar with altar-type shrines—a bench or a shelf upon which we place items that are precious or sacred and interact with them in that way. For this book, I will differentiate the word "shrine" from the word "altar" in that when I speak of a shrine, I am speaking of the item that is crafted for the purpose of worship or interaction itself.

In the Dagara tradition I am initiated into, shrines are built out of clay from the Earth in a special ritual. They are crafted for a specific element, entity, or concept to give it embodiment; a place to live inside our homes. Onto these clay figurines, offerings are poured. The more one interacts with the shrine, the more powerful it and the relationship become. The shrines begin to hold space of their own and anchor the diviner and their medicine in a concrete and active way. They become potent portals for healing.

Chapter 8

Creating and Tending to a Personal Soul Shrine

For this shrine you will need:

❈ A gourd or small basket

In many indigenous cultures, when one is born, a personal soul shrine is built for them. A personal soul shrine is a shrine that is created at or before birth to represent the soul of the individual who has come or is coming into embodiment. It is a place to honor the unseen part of them, to tend to it and feed it, and care for it in a very intimate and loving way. Parents tend to this shrine until the child reaches the age where it is appropriate for them to care for it themselves.

For many of us, this did not happen or maybe it happened within the context of a religion we no longer feel aligned to. If this is the case, we can build ourselves a personal soul shrine if we wish to.

Everything that is alive has an interior. We may call it a self or a soul or whatever we wish but it is this that the shrine attends to. It is the space within from which the inner voice arises, the one who thinks and feels and imagines, the one who intuits and the one who dreams.

The personal soul shrine is small and round, like a womb or container or membrane. One idea for the creation of this shrine is a small gourd that has been cut in half or has some of its shell cut off for an opening; a small woven basket, perhaps lined with feathers like a bird's nest; or to knit or felt a small, rounded container. Glass and pottery are breakable so are not the best material for this particular shrine. The interior of this basket or gourd is left empty. But it is not really empty — it is full of our interior, our library, our soul. You may put things inside this to represent certain aspects of yourself, your soul, your interior, or your preciousness but they are not the all of it. The all of it is eternal and cannot ever die or be broken, so material objects simply cannot be it.

This shrine is tended to by us. We tend to our soul and personal membrane through interaction with this small, round shrine. It should be kept somewhere out of public view yet also in a place where it is nourished and cared for. From time to time, take this shrine out and polish it, sit with it, feel with it, take care of it, and sleep with it beside you. Work with this shrine, make offerings to it, and talk to it as a way of interacting with your own precious interior in an intentional way.

Chapter 9

What is Ritual and Why is it Important?

Ritual is a time out of ordinary time. There are varying degrees of rituals—large, group rituals; long, intense rituals; and then there are the small, everyday offerings that are also rituals, and these are the most common in this work. When I offer milk on my shrine for the grandmothers, I consider that a ritual. When I walk to the water and make an offering for a person in need, that is a ritual. When I pour water asking for conflict to be cleared and communication to be eased, that is a ritual.

Ritual is so common to human experience that most of us don't notice how many we participate in within the span of a day. Do you call your children or your parents often and regularly? This too could be seen as a ritual: special time set aside just for them. Do you pray or say affirmations? Engage in gratitude thinking? These too are rituals. Do you visit a place regularly to commune with nature? This too could be seen as a ritual.

Rituals are offerings and intentional physical acts we carry out to have an effect in and with the nonvisible world. We may sing a song to the trees, asking for help with a certain issue. We may bury an egg, asking for certain energies to be metabolized by it. We may offer hibiscus to the Earth to repay the debts of our ancestors. All of these are rituals in that we are acting them out to effect change through the dimensional layers of existence. We are carrying out these acts in a ceremonial way that separates it from ordinary, daily acts.

For me, an important component of any ritual is clarity and focus of intent. Ritual allows us to take sections of the quotidian to focus clearly and with intent on something sacred or meaningful. The ritual space has power because it allows us to interact with other dimensions, and in that space, leave ordinary time and have access to All Time. Carving out room in our busy days to focus and make offerings, send healing energy, and offer gratitude creates vortices of intention that concentrate our energy in intentional ways that have power. The more we do it, especially with intention, the more we become aware of this. Ritual allows our energy to be focused and like a laser, which is a more coherent form of light, create a more coherent form of energy.

Rituals interacting with specific beings in the spiritual dimensions, when done intentionally, pack an extra-potent punch. Because we are entering into and growing this relationship with each ritual, our lives expand beyond the usual parameters and we feel ourselves becoming part of a much larger, more expansive reality. Our souls expand and we feel supported in ways possibly not felt before. And the best thing about ritual is that often there is a powerful response. They are meant to be interactions and communications and those are meant to garner a response. The response deepens and we begin to experience the reciprocity of the world and the universe we live in.

Rituals do not have to be complex. They can be simple and subtle. But getting quiet and focusing is required, and that in and of itself is healing and a gift, given the times we live in.

Rituals create a membrane around time and space, separating them from the routine and day-to-day elements of our lives. Ritual space and time is its own interiority, offering access to our power and the power of the universe.

Chapter 10

The Importance of Invocation

One of the main ways we keep personal membranes and the membranes around our rituals strong and supple is through the practice of invocation. Invocations are the words spoken before a ritual that state our intentions and call in the allies we need to do the ritual. The invocation creates and seals the space (creates a membrane) for that ritual and separates it from our day-to-day lives.

Invocations are an important part of any medicine work. We must speak our prayers loudly and with strong intent so that they are well heard. When we do medicine work, we must call in our allies and state our purpose so that we, as well as others, are clear about what we are doing. And by "others," I mean those present in the flesh as well as those in the other dimensions. Invocations are different from incantations in that they are not words to speak a spell; rather, they are imploring or beseeching, asking with humility for aid and assistance in our work.

When we take time before a ritual to invoke, this allows us to tap into our interiority. We become grounded when we invoke and speaking our intentions helps us listen to both the interiority of the other dimensions we are calling upon and to the sacred space of the ritual. If we are carrying out the ritual with a group of people, it helps to cohere the energy of the group and ground everyone in the same intention. In invocation, we express our humility, we express our awe, we are reminded to ground and focus our intention, and we make our deepest prayers for healing.

I am calling on the spirits of the water to help carry out this healing for _____, whose heart is broken and in need of healing...

Words are important. They open doors. Our voices possess the power of sound and the words we choose fine-tune that power. Invocation is intentional speech directed toward a specific outcome. Choose your words well. Often in divination, when the wedeme prescribe a ritual, they will deliver to the client specific words to use. They understand that certain words carry certain energies and the wedeme are sometimes tireless in their insistence that we say the right word at the right time.

I call upon the spirits of this grove, the grandmothers and all the women who have walked this path, the ancient ones, sisters through time, mothers and daughters, witches and midwives, tree priestesses, to help us open this portal and find the way back to the ancient grove locked away in time...

The invocation opens the portal to other dimensions. The vibratory resonance of our voice in the invocation we speak sets the tone, literally, for what is about to happen in the ritual following the invocation. The invocation is the time to state our purpose, our intention, what we want and need, and what we hope to accomplish through the following ritual along with who we are asking to come and help us with it. It's a statement of intention. And it includes humility. Humility is the master key to all the doors in this work.

I call upon the wedeme. We are so thankful to you for all you have given us and taught us, for your commitment and dedication to the Earth. We are so grateful and so I call upon you today to come and help us listen to this place, to hear what it needs for healing and how we, at this time and in this place, can be of service...

It is important that invocations are not set or rehearsed and that they come from our hearts in the moment for the present moment. They ground us firmly into the moment and solidify the purpose of what we are doing. Speaking that aloud, with conviction and strength, helps us gain clarity and presence, therefore invocations must come from us explicitly.

Many people are shy about invoking aloud in front of others but I encourage people to do this so that they can get used to it. Listening to another's invocation is a great gift and is often inspiring. By example, we learn. Invocations can be loud and forceful or soft and gentle, but make sure the soft and gentle is authentic and not out of shyness. If you are doing medicine work, you need to be in your power and use your voice, and you need to feel comfortable doing that.

You have your own medicine, borne of all the unique qualities and components you came in with and those you have cultivated during your time here. Allow that to permeate your work in the world. Allow your prayers to move spontaneously through your body, which is the container of all you are. That is how it becomes rarefied and precious and therefore, effective.

I am calling upon my grandmother to come and teach me and show me the wise ways...

There are many ways to invoke. Some invocations may be voice only. If other humans are present and also invoking, take turns speaking aloud your prayers. With the voice, we can add in a tapping onto the Earth. If you are in a group, others tap onto the Earth along with you as you invoke as a gesture to affirm your invocation. This is a powerful thing to do when we invoke outside but even inside, one can tap on the floor or table as another invokes. We can also invoke with rattles and bells. In a typical Dagara divination, bells and rattles are used along with voice. We can invoke with drums. We can invoke with song.

Some people see beings arrive before they call them in, and

include greetings and welcoming them as part of the invocation.

Some say, *I greet and welcome…*
Some say, *I call upon…*
Some address them directly, *Old ones…*

We all have our own style.

When we invoke, if it is not a formal divination in which there is a clear protocol, we invoke the entities we need to join us in the specific ritual, we invoke the ancestors, the elemental beings, the spirits of the place where we are. We let the spirits know what we are doing and why, and what we may need from them by way of help or support.

It is important to remember that invocations are calling in the spirits. We are invoking to call them in. We need them to help us, so call them in well. And know that if you call them, they will come.

This is another piece of invocation. Mean it. Say what you mean and mean what you say. If self-doubt comes knocking at your door—which for those of us who live in the paradigm of the Western world, it surely will, you can count on it—just send it packing. That's all. Just pay it no mind. You will always have to deal with self-doubt. It's part of the split nature of the mechanistic mind we in the West have all inherited—the one that says only that which we can experience with our physical senses is real. We are all educated into it. It is part of our terrain and constantly in the field. So, don't feed it. Just push past it. Truly, do just that. Good-bye and thank you.

Most times after invoking, you can feel a change in energy. The presence of those we have called in is palpable.

Invocations are not to be minimized. They are one of the most important parts of the work. Speak your prayers well.

Chapter 11

The Top Five Physical Offerings to Make to Spiritual Beings

If you feel yourself to be a medicine person but have not found your path or lineage and don't know what to do, begin by doing the rituals and suggestions in this book. Trust that you will eventually be led to a path that teaches you skills and leads to an initiation of some sort through which you will develop your unique style of medicine work. If you only want to do a few of the things in this book and do not wish to seek further training, that is fine too. You do not need to be initiated to do the work set forth in this book.

One thing many people just beginning to do this kind of spirit work ask me is, "What are the most common offerings made to the spiritual dimensions?" Here is a list of the top five from the divination system of the Dagara people from Burkina Faso.

Ash: Meaning ash from a wood fire. Any kind of fire—it does not have to be a special or ceremonial fire. Ash from your wood stove or fireplace is good enough. It is often nice to sift the ash so it is easier to work with. If you don't have a wood stove or fireplace, find someone who does. I am sure they would be willing to share. Ash is offered only and always with the left hand. It is used frequently to create a barrier or boundary of protection, to seal off a ritual space, or seal off an offering meant only for an intended recipient. But it is also a major offering in and of itself. It has high potency in the otherworld and is a precious gift.

Water: Water is a frequent offering to the spirits. You can have many kinds of water available to offer if you wish. Rainwater is seen as the cleanest and best. You can easily gather this by leaving containers out to catch the rain. You can make moon water by leaving water out under a full moon, star water by leaving water out under the stars, and all kinds of flower and herbal waters. Collect water from important water sources close to you—lakes, ponds, the ocean, rivers, and streams. But you can use tap water too. I leave my tap water out in the sun for one full day to clear it. Water is an offering in and of itself, as well as an element that is used most frequently to "clear the way." If there are obstacles or blockages, or you want to open communication or increase the flow of energy, you can pour water onto the Earth and ask for the way to be cleared, and state what it is you are wishing for clearing around. You are asking the water to clear the way. The water is doing the work. Water is also good for clearing conflict and discord, purifying and cleaning negative energy, and bringing freshness and opening to any situation.

 Milk: Any kind of milk—soy, rice, coconut, hemp—will do but the spirits do prefer cow's milk. Milk is white and is a symbol of purity and innocence. It is used to clear experiences of violation and upset but it is also the most common offering to the female ancestors and entities. It is called upon for nurturing, healing, soothing, caring, and sustenance. One of the most common offerings to the star beings is milk poured into any natural body of water.

Hibiscus juice: The teaching I received when I was training to become a diviner was to use hibiscus flowers steeped in boiling water as a substitute for a blood offering. I do not make blood offerings (meaning blood from an animal I have sacrificed) nor do I train people to do so. The reason for me to continue with this substitute I was taught, is because I do not feel myself to be in appropriate relationship to the animals I would be asked to sacrifice in order to carry that out. This is not a judgment call on others who do blood sacrifice. People need to make their own decisions based on what feels right to them. To create the hibiscus juice, steep 2 tablespoons of dry hibiscus flowers in 8 ounces of water. This equals one portion. Sometimes we are asked to offer two or three portions or more. This is considered a very big offering and you should understand that. If hibiscus is called for, it is a signal to you that this is a big offering and that a possible debt of some kind is asking to be filled, or that the ritual you are carrying out is of significant importance. If you feel you need to make a big offering for an ancestral debt or you are asking for a big favor from the spirits, then hibiscus juice is a good offering.

Spirits: Meaning alcohol of any kind but the clear kind is often preferred: gin or vodka. The spirits love spirits. This is a very high-energy fuel for them. They can extract a lot of sustenance from fermented beverages. If you have a problem with keeping alcohol around or simply do not want to engage in that, you might consider kombucha or other fermented beverages as an alternative.

Many other foods are asked for but the above are the staples and the most requested. You will develop your own particular offering bag based on the spirits you work with. Mine always has anise powder in it as a nod to my Italian ancestors. My great-grandmother's other favorite herbs are often asked for as well as colloidal gold. But this is particular to me personally. Offering some of your meal is a good practice too. This is commonly called the *spirit plate*: a small portion of a meal is set aside on a special plate and left for the spirits.

On the Strega Tree Apothecary YouTube channel, you will find instructions on how to make these offerings if you wish to learn.

Chapter 12

Rituals to Care for the Personal Membrane and the Space Within

Here are some simple rituals to help keep the personal membrane clean, refreshed, supple, and golden, and to nourish and feed our deep and unique interior.

1. A Basic Cleansing "Sweep" for Energetic or Spiritual "Dirt"

For this ritual you will need:
* Water—fresh-running or tap water—in a large mixing bowl
* Ferns or branches of rosemary or trees to create a small broom
* Optional: essential oils or healing charcoal[18]
* Wood ash

---

[18] Healing charcoal is a powerful medicine made by merged diviners in special ritual.

❊ This ritual requires two people

The basic sweep or *"dompla"* in the Dagara tradition is a common ritual prescribed often in divination when one needs "dirt" cleaned off of them. "Dirt" is a term the Dagara use for any personal body fluids of another, negative energies one has been exposed to through unpleasant experiences, and circumstances that have stuck or malintent "sent" by someone else through ill will, jealousy, or gossip. This "dirt" can collect for any number of reasons. We often do not need to know why. It is common to need a sweep. Alarm need not be present in this ritual.

The basic sweep attends to the skin and the membrane or *siura*. Cleanings for the interior or soul come later in this chapter.

If one feels "icky," psychically burdened, emotionally weighted down, the victim of "bad luck" or if one is physically ill, a sweep may very well be needed. It always feels remarkably good to receive a sweep and is equally potent to be the one doing the sweeping.

Fern is the plant most often used for this ritual. In the Italian tradition, the fern, *le felce*, is called the "herb of accord and discord."[19] It is viewed as possessing the shape of a hand with fingers that can be separated or reconnected.

Le felce or the fern, together with the power of water, can be used to heal great disconnection and fragmentation in a person, possibly even removing curses. If there is no fern available, one can also use branches from a tree or herbs such as rosemary.[20]

---

[19] Estella Canziani. *Through the Apennines and the Lands of the Abruzzi*.
[20] Always ask permission to take branches from a tree, or cut fern or herbs. Explain to the plant why you need them and if they are willing to be used in that way. Listen for a response. If you receive a "no," be respectful and go find another option.

The *dompla* is traditionally performed by an outdoor body of water—a creek, stream, river, or ocean—but it can also be successfully achieved with a bowl of water outside in the backyard.

The *dompla* can be carried out by anyone. One does not need to be a merged diviner to carry out this ritual.

The element for healing in this ritual is the water. Be aware that this is a water ritual. Now and then, something is added to the water—essential oils or healing charcoal, for example—but that is rare.

If one chooses, they may invoke before, though it is not necessary.[21] Often I invoke the Earth, tapping upon it with a stick and calling my and the recipient's ancestors, the wedeme, and kontomble.[22] If by a stream or river, I call in that place and the common name of its water, its helpful allies, and the spirit of the plant I am using, to help carry out this healing and cleaning. It is good to invoke to help settle everyone's nervous systems and to be clear on our intention. Sometimes the recipient is also instructed to invoke but again, this is not necessary and very rare. Use your judgment and instincts here.

Performing the Sweep

❋ Once the invocation is complete, create a circle out of wood ash for the person to stand in.[23] Encourage the recipient to

---

[21] See Chapter 10 for instructions on invocation.

[22] In the Dagara tradition the wedeme are the elemental beings of the wild and kontomble are the elemental beings of the water.

[23] Wood ash creates the container of safe space within which the ritual and healing can take place. This means the ash left from a wood fire. Any wood fire, it does not have to be special fire or special ash. All ash is special. If no ash is available, create the boundary with water. Your intention as you create this circle is for only helpful energies to be allowed inside and for a container of safety to be created for the ritual to be performed.

remove any eyewear and close their eyes, if they are comfortable with that. They should know this is an intimate ritual with physical contact. Make sure they are comfortable with this. If not, perform the sweep at the outer edges of their energetic field as you perceive it so that no actual physical contact is made. I typically ask the person I am sweeping to be barefoot if that is comfortable for them. I try to always be barefoot as well.[24]

❋ Form the gathered branches into a sort of broom shape in your hand. Dip the branches into the water and shake them off, away from the person. Starting from the top of the head, in the front of the body, begin to brush and sweep the dirt off of them in downward, out, and away movements. Literally sweep the dirt off of them from the top down. Branches may be re-dipped in the water if it feels necessary. As you sweep, you may begin to feel "stickiness" in the energetic field around the person as you do this. This can be perceived as a thickness or twisting energies, knots or negativity. You may sense emotional material like pain, grief, or anger. If so, extend the sweeping out beyond the limits of the physical body and clear the energetic field as well.

❋ I tend to carry out the sweep on the four sides or directions of the body, using as many strokes as I feel necessary on each "side" — front, left, back, right; north, east, south, west — moving around them in a circle, re-dipping in each direction, starting at the top of the head in each direction. I lift arms and do underarms; I open hands that may be closed to sweep palms as well. I make sure to sweep between legs (using discretion, of course) and under feet.

❋ Everyone has his or her own style and the sweep is largely

---

[24] As a general rule it is always best to be barefoot when doing ritual.

determined by how it feels once you begin. Go with the flow of it. You will be led. Once completed, I gently touch the recipient's heart with the branches to let them know we are finished. Then I allow them time to integrate.

❋ Once all is finished, if in the wild, the branches are offered to the water by gently placing them within it as a gift. If at home, place them on a shrine or at the base of a tree as a gift or offering, or compost them if there is no other option. If using a bowl, the water can be returned to the Earth at the base of a tree.

In the Dagara belief system, we need to be swept often as we walk through much dirt or negativity in our daily lives and are exposed to the unhealthy vibrations of others on a regular basis. It is a practice I consider to be in the category of general hygiene. This tends to our primary personal membrane, our skin, and so, just as the floors need to be swept often, so do we. It keeps the filters clear in our membranes and helps them work more effectively.

2. Egg Rituals for Deeper Clearing, Cleaning of and Extraction from Our Interior Space

For this ritual you will need:
❋ 1 raw egg
❋ Healing charcoal (optional)
❋ A place alone in the wild
❋ This ritual can be done alone or with another.

Why an Egg?

Whole, raw eggs represent wholeness and completeness, health, and coherence. We are asking for wholeness to be restored in these rituals. Wholeness is health. We are asking the egg to restore the wholeness while extracting and taking into itself the dirt that has become embedded. Being "restored to wholeness" is a phrase that means that all the connections are working and flow is restored so the system is operating at full potential. It does not mean you are broken by asking to be returned to wholeness, just that your system is able to function as one coherent whole again without any broken parts or blocked passages.

The wedeme are very concerned with places where connections are broken or detached. They see all as a web of interconnection and see disconnection as an unhealthy thing. Blockages and obstructions block connection.

Eggs for Extraction

Sometimes the dirt has become more deeply embedded, meaning it is more than "skin" deep and requires intervention stronger than a basic sweep. We must tend to this form of dirt as this can quickly turn into physical illness. Conventional wisdom states that illness first exists on the energetic or etheric planes. It is easy to clean them off at this skin-deep level but once they begin to settle more deeply into our energetic fields and even physical bodies, they can quickly turn into physical illness. This usually occurs over time with repeated insult or injury or with issues that are left unattended and allowed to sink more deeply into our fields.

The wedeme inform us that there are membranes around each organ and system in our bodies. We must tend to these as well. The membranes protect what is inside. If the membrane is compromised, the interiority is at risk and the wholeness of the system is in danger.

Often in divination, I see a spot or shadow on someone's heart, womb, liver, or throat chakra. In these cases, an egg ritual is prescribed. Egg rituals are to collect and clear deeper dirt. Rather than a sweep, these rituals are the removal of stuck, problematic energies that have settled into the physical body. Egg rituals are extractions.

When we look at a body in a divination, we want to see a clean flow of energy moving through it. Anywhere we perceive energy to be stuck, clumping, hardened or thick could indicate an issue that might become a problem. There may be emotional material like anger or grief that have not been expressed, there may be memories of violation or abuse or actual physical injury, and there may be ancestral issues made evident by these blockages or shadows. We want a healthy flow, always. Obstruction can lead to physical illness and could be causing emotional or psychological issues. We want to look for healthy flow of energy in our clients.

If a diviner perceives shadows or unhealthy energy in your body, or if you feel there is illness in a place or certain organ or system of your body, it is often necessary to ask an egg to help with this clearing.

Many people are told to do this on their neck and thyroid area, their womb spaces, their hearts, places where surgeries have been performed, or where injuries from accidents have happened and bones or tissue have still not recovered from the trauma.

These egg rituals are also often used to address issues of what we might label "karma." I see karma as embedded dirt that has been carried for one or more lifetimes and is sitting at the soul level. This dirt is heavily embedded and is often a stain from events, relationships, past agreements, and activities that have not been dealt with, consciously transformed, or properly metabolized. By "metabolized" I mean digested and cleared, worked through so that they are no longer bothersome. Troublesome events and experiences must be fully processed and cleared, otherwise, they create what we call karma. We can clean our karma even if it involves another person by cleaning up what we are carrying from it in our own body and psyche. For karmic "smut" or embedded "soul stains," an assisting material may be needed to help process the even deeper-down dirt. Often, healing charcoal is spread on the outer shell of the egg or upon the body area indicated, or sprinkled upon the egg once the extraction has been performed. Healing charcoal can help move and process these things.

If one is unable to acquire healing charcoal from a diviner, they may use water in its place. Wash the area with water after, or pour water over the egg after the extraction. Water is very cleansing and purifying. It helps things move and can encourage flow. Ask the water to help carry out this healing. Again, trust your instincts.

The Ritual

* In this ritual, it is the egg that is doing the work. First, take the raw egg into your hands and ask it to carry out this healing for you. Thank it for being willing. Then tell it specifically what you are asking it to do.
* Rub the egg directly on the area of concern, asking for this healing, allowing it to suck up the leftover anger, the embedded hurt and pain, the grief, the upset. Often these rituals are done out in the wild so the egg can be left there to freely metabolize the materials it has extracted, allowing the wild creatures and the forces of nature to organically compost it.
* Once the ritual is complete, the egg is put into the water, left by a tree, or even thrown and allowed to break. Other times, the egg is buried.
* If you are not a diviner and have not consulted one, but wish to carry this out, trust your instincts with how to offer the egg once the extraction is complete. If you are unable to

do this in the wild, try to leave the egg somewhere outside in your yard or under a tree in a local park. It is fine if an animal eats it and fine if one does not. Let the process go once you are done with it and trust what happens to the egg is what is meant to happen. Don't worry about the egg once you are done.

❊ In rituals like these, pay attention to what comes up when you do them. Information often comes to the surface in the form of feelings, sensations, images, or even sounds. Know that this is the emotional or psychic material you are loosening and moving—which is the whole point of healing. Once movement happens, memories, feelings, sensations, etc. are loosened and can rise to the surface of your consciousness. This means you are successful in your work.

❊ Close the ritual by thanking the egg, the place where you are working, and the other elements you have called in for this clearing.

3. Clearing The Inner Lens to Help the Membrane with Discernment

For this ritual you will need:
❊ Water: The water needs to be rainwater or water that has sat in the sun for a full day.
❊ A clear quartz crystal
❊ A transparent glass jar with a lid
❊ Dry white sage to burn
❊ 8oz hibiscus tea[25]

---

[25] Make this hibiscus tea offering by acquiring dry hibiscus flowers and steeping 2 tbsp. in 8oz of hot water, or you can use a tea bag in 8oz of hot water. This is a substitute for a blood offering. See Chapter 11 for more information.

❀ A journal or notebook
❀ A local place where you honor water

The 6th chakra is often called the third eye—the place above and between your physical eyes. It is what helps us access the other dimensions, other ways of seeing, and perceptions beyond the ordinary 3D. If it is foggy, our perceptions can be skewed on all levels. Often the third eye can become cloudy and needs clearing. This will affect the personal membrane as well as our interior space. If one feels they are muddled and unclear in receiving information, the following ritual helps to clean this lens.

The Ritual

❀ Hold the clear crystal to your third eye. Allow it to sync up, meaning the energies will eventually match. Ask for the lens to be cleansed and purified. Ask for clarity of vision and the cleaning of intent.
❀ Take the crystal away from your third eye as if you are removing the lens from your forehead.
❀ Put the crystal into a jar of water. This is a "stand-in" for the lens of your third eye and as it is cleaned, so too will be the lens of your third eye.
❀ Burn sage and use the smoke to cleanse around the jar containing the crystal and water.
❀ Leave the crystal in the water overnight.
❀ Let the jar of water with the crystal sit in contact with the Earth while you sleep. Pay attention to dreams overnight. These may indicate what is foggy and in need of clearing,

or what you are being prohibited from seeing.

* In the morning, make note of any dreams or information you received overnight.
* Retrieve the crystal from the jar with the water. Put the lens back into your third eye by holding it near your third eye and asking it to return, cleansed and renewed.
* Later, in the following week or two, offer this crystal to the ocean with one portion (8oz) of hibiscus tea. If you do not live near the ocean, offer it to a place where you honor water.
* The water that held and cleared your lens overnight is now medicinal. The alchemy that happens overnight is the medicine. You may be called to use it as an offering or for healing.
* This ritual can be carried out as often as needed.

4. Soul Washing to Attend to the Contents of Your Personal, Interior Space

For this ritual you will need:

* A fire in a fireplace, wood stove or outdoor fire pit. If you do not have access to these, a candle will do.
* Milk (any kind you prefer)
* Healing charcoal (optional)
* Hyssop essential oil (optional)
* One raw egg
* A bowl large enough to hold the egg covered with milk

In this ritual, we are washing our interior space. This is different from the basic *dompla* or sweep because the sweep cleans the outside — the skin, the membrane. Here, we are reaching for our internal, private, vulnerable soul space — what lies within the membrane, the place only we have access to and that only we know completely, or *can* know completely.

The Ritual

❋ Come to a place of quiet and calm. Light the candle or build the fire.

❋ First, we are going to go deep within ourselves and do a scan to see what is there. As we go in to clean this private interior, we must first address any shadow material that is lurking around it, on it, or present within—any "sins," blemishes, negative energies or thought patterns. It is time to look at each of these, one at a time, and begin the work of transforming them. Close your eyes and allow yourself to observe your interior. What are you holding on to that is no longer serving you? Are there hurts, wounds, or places where you are stuck? Is there anger, judgment, reactivity? This is between you and you. No one else. It is time to clean house—your interior house.

❋ As you identify each one, ask it what it would like to be transmuted into. After you have done this, offer it to the fire, asking the fire to do the work of transforming it, transmuting it to what it would like to become. For example, in a soul washing I did recently, my impatience wanted to be turned into friendliness. My sarcasm into tenderness. You can do this by making a list on paper, then offering each to the fire, one at a time, literally allowing the fire to burn the paper. Or you may do one at a time with your mind instead of writing it down, just energetically offering them to the fire. Go at your own pace, continuing to scan until you feel you have fully addressed the shadow part of your soul material. You may be surprised by what they ask to be transmuted into. Once you feel you have addressed the shadow material on your soul, it is time to begin the interior washing.

❋ The egg is now standing in for your soul. Take it into your hands, hold it, and *connect with it* deeply as your soul. This is now your soul externalized that you are holding in your hands. Hold it up to your chest, to your heart. Offer it love, feel into it, connect with it. You are about to wash this egg, your soul, clean of any impurities. Offer it nurturing and refreshment so you can continue with your life renewed, re-freshed, and washed clean.

❋ Once you feel ready, set the egg in the bowl and cover it with milk. It is up to you if you feel you need to add a bit of healing charcoal into the milk to deepen the cleaning, or hyssop essential oil, an herb that helps consecrate and pu-rify. Once you have all your ingredients in the bowl, begin to wash the egg, your soul, with the milk. Milk is used to cleanse, nourish, and purify. It also connects us back to the Source soul. Source itself. The numinous. Take your time, be gentle, and feel into it. Let it speak to you as you bathe it. Offer it what it needs. Know you are offering this to your-self, to your own secret interior.

❋ Once complete, offer the whole egg to the Earth somewhere for it to be metabolized by the forces of nature and offer the milk at the base of a tree.

5. The Milk Bath to Heal Violation and Transgression to Your Body and Soul

For this ritual you will need:
❋ 4 cups of milk (any milk you choose is fine)

❀ A bathtub
❀ Candles
❀ One raw egg
❀ Wood ash or salt

The milk bath is commonly prescribed for women[26] for healing issues of violation, rape, incest, assault, and transgressions against their bodies and being. This healing may be extended to an entire female lineage, biological or otherwise, or to one ancestress in particular who would benefit from it. Offering healing through our physical embodiment for one who no longer has a body is a common prescription. Men who are transgressed against in this way may also use this ritual as a way to heal and cleanse these violations.

The Ritual

❀ Before the bath, take a raw egg and roll it over your heart, asking it to take all the pain into it to be metabolized and healed. When complete, leave the egg outside in the wild for the forces of nature to eat it or transform it.
❀ If you have wood ash, place a thin line of it across the threshold of the bathroom door to seal the space and create a safe container. If no ash, you may use sea salt or another material that feels right to you. You are stating your boundary as you set this down: *Only energies with my best interests*

---

[26] Women are indicated most here as they are the victims of these kinds of assaults more than 90% of the time through no fault of their own.

in mind may enter this place.

❊ Draw the bath and pour the milk into it. If it feels right, you may light a candle or two for protection or any other intention you wish to set.

❊ Before entering the water, ask for healing, ask the water to clear you and the milk to clean you and nourish you.

❊ Once submerged, tell yourself this should not have happened to you. It was wrong. Tell your body you understand how it feels, how it suffered. At this point, you may state that you are extending out the healing to all the women in your lineage or a particular one. Sit quietly in the water, feeling. Allow the milk and the water to penetrate all the levels of your being. Offer yourself healing. Offer your grief to the water. Offer yourself compassion and care—love.

6. Crossroads Rituals to Strengthen Our Inner Experiences and Create Personal Membranes Around Change

For this ritual you will need:

❊ *A Crossroads*

Choose your crossroads wisely. They can be automobile intersections—not too busy as you need to be able to go to the center and drop the quarter safely, yet have sufficient traffic to constitute a true crossroads. The crossroads used can be a bicycle or walking trail as well—anywhere where at least three paths intersect with traffic of some kind crossing over them daily.

❊ *A quarter or another coin of that weight if you do not live in the U.S.*

I advise that you take some time with your quarter before going out and doing this ritual, perhaps sleeping with it under your pillow, meditating with it, getting comfortable with your request, and fully comprehending the crossroads you are at and what it means to you.

Crossroads rituals are often prescribed in divination.[27] Classically, it is when a person is approaching or anticipating a change in their life, or holding a question about making a change. This ritual can have many variations.

For the membrane of our personal interiority, this crossroads ritual is important because it acknowledges a change, however subtle, in our personal life and configuration, different than a larger, more obvious life change event held by the community like coming of age, marriage, or the death of a loved one.

These more subtle, personal changes are often held close to our chests. Often we don't even know we are going through them. Acknowledging them for and to ourselves is important for the health of our interiority. We are telling ourselves we care about ourselves.

Transitional thresholds should not be minimized. A new job, moving homes, relational crossroads — all are potent times to be respected and often good times to ask for spiritual guidance from whomever you feel can lead you through safely.

Agonizing over a decision is another useful time to go to the crossroads with your quarter. It then becomes, in part, a ritual of surrender — allowing your intuitive mind to open to listening, receiving, and feeling, thereby ceasing the intellectual "spin" created in your head by thinking about something over and over.

Change is predominant and constant in our lives yet it is not always easy. Transitions need to be honored and it is good to ask for help at these times.

---

[27] I learned about Crossroads Rituals from my original mentor in the Dagara tradition.

Why Crossroads?

Some interesting Italian traditions around crossroads are found in *Italian-American Folktales,* collected by Catherine Harris Ainsworth. One tale reveals how the shepherd "would station his flock in the middle of the crossroads" for protection from the "perils of hungry wolves, thieves or severe weather." Another tells of the mother of a sick newborn child burning pieces of the baby's clothing at the crossroads at midnight to help the baby gain weight. In Italy, crossroads are often associated with the Goddess Diana or offerings are left more generally to the *Lares Compitales* (Spirits of the Crossroads).[28]

In Ancient Greece, the Goddess Hecate was the Goddess of the crossroads and indeed, in many of the crossroads rituals prescribed in my divinations, the petitioner is told to make their prayers and offerings to the Goddess Hecate. Hecate, also identified as a moon goddess, is often portrayed as having three faces, probably due to her tripartite nature: maiden, mother, and crone.

Hecate, like many powerful goddesses, has been demonized and made into a "wrathful hag." But that is not the truth of who she is. She is indeed wise and embodies the crone as part of her trinity but that is not the reason we invoke her at the crossroads. The reason we invoke Hecate at the crossroads is because she can see far and so can guide us safely to where she can see we need to be. It is Hecate's vision we are asking for when we invoke her at the crossroads for she is a seer. We are asking her to guide us because she can see things that we cannot, though they might be right in front of our faces.

Just as the crossroads have long been viewed as powerful locations on the Earth, the crossroads of our lives are equally powerful points in our trajectories. Though transition can be difficult, it also

---

[28] Catherine Harris Ainsworth. *Italian-American Folktales,* p. 45.

74

has the potential to lead us somewhere we have been trying to go but have not been able to. We need help and guidance to get there.

Asking for help is important. It is always there for us but it is indeed incumbent upon us to ask for it.

The Ritual

❀ At dawn or dusk, go to a crossroads with the quarter.
❀ If you feel inclined to make more of an offering to the Spirit of the Crossroads than the quarter (food, tobacco, spirits, surrounded by a circle of wood ash if you have it), this can be made in another location near the crossroads or at your home.
❀ Deposit your quarter with intention at the center of the crossroads, uttering the phrase, "Spirit of the Crossroads (Hecate, Diana, entity of your choice), guide me safely through these crossroads."
❀ Walk away. Do not look back. You are moving forward now.

7. Becoming Oriented in the Place Where We Live and the Times We Inhabit to Protect, Extend, and Deepen Our Connection to Our Personal Membrane

For this ritual you will need:
❀ A compass

The Importance of Orienting Ourselves

Another important way to care for the personal membrane, which the wedeme iterate over and over again, is to be oriented in space and time no matter where you are. On this planet, there are four cardinal directions (north, east, south, and west) that orient us in our place and location. Where do you live and how do the directions line up when you place yourself at the center? This is where you are located. This is your place.

What season is it? Are you interacting with the past, present, or future? This is what Time it is.

Orienting Ourselves in Space

Orienting ourselves in space, the place where we live, work, and love, does just that. It orients us, meaning we are centered, know our center, and know where things are in relation to us. We know our place and where we belong. We are oriented rather than disoriented. If we are oriented, we can plant our intentions, ourselves, and our lives in ways that keep us rooted and grounded. We know what we are doing and why. That is what being oriented means. Orienting ourselves in space also creates a larger and stronger membrane around us as it pulls in larger energies for us to work with for support and grounding. The mountains, big bodies of water, wild places, forests, and the directions themselves are large and powerful energies. We can and should interact and form relationships with these.

We are stronger when our sense of place extends beyond our *selves*, homes, and places of work. It's good to root further out into and through the local ecosystem, and eventually into the outlying areas of where we reside. We begin with ourselves, our soul, our interiority. What is inside us? What is our inner compass, our True North? Stay lined up with that. Then, where do we live? We start small, from where we live, extending to farther reaches, understanding more and more the layer upon layer of belonging we are held within and how the membranes hold these in place.

Where are we located? Our family, our community, our extended community? These communities include all the beings in the ecosystem. Held within these membranes are all forms of life in all dimensions. If we could feel the complexity of our existence and feel ourselves firmly and fully rooted and committed within that, what a different life experience we would have.

Who are the people and beings we are tending to, including mountains, waterways, trees, animals, plants, and what we call the land; the geographic circumference of our lives? Our lives and identities want to be firmly embedded within these concentric circles of membranes to have the fullest effect and to be experienced for the fullness that they are. Indeed, no human is an island. We are richly included in the many tapestries and layers of our relationships with all beings. Why would we ever believe otherwise? In our strange forgetting of this, we feel untethered and unrooted. We lack a feeling of belonging. This is not a natural state of mind. The place to begin is in orienting ourselves first in the place where we are.

The Ritual

* **The first thing to do** is orient yourself by finding out where the cardinal directions are in the place where you live, work, and do medicine—north, east, south, and west. If home, work, and where you practice medicine are three different locations, do this for each place. You can discover this easily by using a compass. Most of us have those on our phones.

❋ **Creating a Simple Medicine Wheel.** There are many ways to do this, depending on how simple or how complex you wish to get. You can make a small circle or "medicine wheel"[29] on the ground in your yard or garden, notating the directions you discover with small lines, a stone, or a crystal. The simplest medicine wheel we can make is a circle with a cross drawn in it creating four distinct ends, one for each of the cardinal directions. It can be that simple.

Or, you may choose to go to the edges or boundaries of your property and establish a marker there for its corresponding point on the horizon. Ideas for markers are a stone, a birdbath, a tree, a bush, a shrine—whatever you want to place there to mark each direction. Some of these markers may be natural features that are already there. For example, if there is a pine tree in the north, that can be your marker for north.

As time goes by, after you have set up your medicine wheel, you will begin to understand these directions as alive energies. You will perceive characteristics and traits for each one and will feel each one as a unique presence. You will begin to distinguish them from each other and they will begin to feel like friends. You may wish to interact with them by making offerings to and at them, observing them throughout the day, season, and year, and seeing what you notice. You may receive a response.

Some of you may wish to do only this part and that is enough.

❋ **Placing an Element in Each Direction**

Some traditions place a certain element (see Part 4 for more on the elements) in each direction—fire in the south and water in the west, for example. Many people I divine for have been

---

[29] *Medicine Wheel* is a Native American term.

told to notice the major natural landmark in the direction where they live and place the corresponding element there. For example, I have a large local mountain to the east, so I place the element mountain in the east. The ocean is to my west, so I place water there. That is just the way it has worked out for me.[30]

Either find a template for what element you wish to place in which direction or you can choose to listen in for your own. "Listening in" means interacting with the directions for a while and noticing if anything arises in your consciousness, almost intuitively or instinctively. You suddenly "know" what belongs in each direction. Listening in is taking the time to ask and hear the answer in your own way.

If you choose to go with the local landmark template, make it a point to eventually go to each landmark with their directional orientation in mind and commune with them in that way. If ocean is in the west, go to the ocean and interact with it as your far west and begin to feel the qualities of that western space with regard to where you live and work.

You may also listen for who is present in each direction. Is there an entity there? Certain guardians in each direction? This kind of information and knowing will increase as you deepen your practice. Perhaps there is a color associated with each direction for you.

❀ Honoring the Center

In the center of your medicine wheel can be a marker as well. If you wish to designate Center, then know that out of that comes Above and Below, Earth and Sky, and then you begin to be in harmony with Time.

---

[30] In the Dagara cosmology, mountain is one of the five elements: Fire, water, Earth, mountain/mineral and nature/wildness.

❋ Orienting Ourselves in Time

The sun and moon create our reality of Time on this planet. We have the 24-hour circadian rhythm — the day and night cycle created by the spin of the Earth. The seasons are created by the axis of the Earth and its relationship to the sun. Monthly moon cycles are created by the relationship of the Earth, sun, and the moon. This creates Time. Cyclic Time. Though most of us do not live in deep relationship with this anymore because of our mechanical clocks and phones, our primal and ancient selves still observe these deeper, more organic rhythms. Aligning ourselves to them is orienting for us as well.

To deepen your practice, you can begin to notice the seasons and observe the quarter and cross-quarter days. This is a wheel with sections of eight.

❋ Quarter and Cross-Quarter Days — The Wheel of the Year

This division of the Earth year is observed by humans globally. There are varying names for these days but the basic idea is the demarcation and ritual honoring of solstices and equinoxes and the halfway points between.

Dates listed are where they roughly fall every year. The Southern Hemisphere is reversed for seasons.

- Winter Solstice: Dec 21/22
- Imbolc/Candlemas/Groundhog Day: February 2
- Spring Equinox: March 20/21
- Beltane/May Day: May 1
- Summer Solstice: June 20/21
- Lammas/Lughnasad: August 2
- Autumnal Equinox: September 21/22
- Samhain/Hallowmas: October 31
- Start All Over Again (Different cultures viewed the beginning of the year at different seasons. Some celebrated it at the spring equinox, others at the autumnal equinox.)

Once you understand the different phases of the quarter and cross-quarter days, you can begin to observe how they interact with the directions of your medicine wheel by noticing where and when the sun rises and sets at these times, the color and quality of the light and how it changes with each season, and the shadows and how they shift. You can root even more deeply by paying attention to the moon phases in relation to your particular medicine wheel. If you want to go even deeper into your own orientation, begin to watch the stars and galaxies, constellations, and cosmic events.

Orienting ourselves and carrying out the rituals listed above reveals to us the many membranes of Time and space we are embedded within. Understanding, noticing, and interacting with them strengthens the membranes and what is held within them. Strengthening the membranes of our lives and further protecting and holding that which is within them brings a deeper understanding of why our ancestors and predecessors put so much Time and effort into honoring these cycles of time and space.

Concurrently, we can begin to understand the seasons as the seasons of our lives. Which one are we in? What are the qualities of these seasons of time? There are membranes around each decade of our life. Each decade is a membrane around our life and experience. This may help us age more gracefully and understand the time of life we are in more fully.

In many pagan rituals, people "call in" the four cardinal directions and those who are held there as an invocation before a ritual, greeting and asking each of them to come and hold the ritual container or membrane around the ritual being performed. This practice may emerge for you out of your medicine wheel practice.

Chapter 13

Story

The following story is included to help you to feel more deeply into the ways humans attended to the personal membrane in ancient times. Encourage your soul self to relax here...imagine here...remember here. Rest in the feeling this story evokes in you. Notice what arises within you as you read it.

Notes on the Setting

The story is set by the blue-green waters of the Mediterranean Sea on the islands of Malta and Gozo, where the remains of no less than 43 Neolithic Temples dated to 4000 BCE have been found. The limestone slabs used to build them are so enormous (some weighing up to three tons), we cannot begin to speculate how they were created.

Many of the temples on Malta have a cloverleaf design which, when viewed from an aerial position, conveys the image of a huge, rounded female. Rounded females predominate on Malta, where many sculptures of robust women wearing flounced skirts and with exposed breasts were recovered. The entryways to many of the temples were tunnels. The petitioner entered the large, round woman by crawling through a narrow passageway — a literal return to the Source, the mother, the Earth, the womb of the Goddess.

Because the temples are so overwhelmingly present and so specific in function, some scholars speculate that the islands may have served as a Neolithic retreat or healing center.

One of the most intriguing discoveries on Malta is the underground chamber or "hypogeum," a labyrinthine maze of rounded rooms carved into the limestone that descends deeper and deeper into the Earth as one travels within it.

Many of the rooms have façades of lintel design carved into the stone mirroring the design of the temples above. Within the hypogeum is a large, oval-shaped hall surrounded by many smaller rooms. In one of these rooms, the "oracle room," is a small hole less than halfway up the wall which, when spoken into, resonated sounds throughout the hall and surrounding rooms. I believe that early people understood the properties of stones, sound, and darkness and the absolute power of the combination of the three.

In the hypogeum were found small sculptures of full-bodied women reclining upon small boat-like beds, sleeping, dreaming...perhaps a little bit of both.

Pilgrimage to the Goddess

Malta 2600 BCE

We have been traveling a long time on this boat, over many waters. Waters blue and green, green-brown, blue blues and at night, endless black. The waters slap a slow rhythm against the boat's edges. *Slap...slap...slap.* We will be on this boat forever. I sleep within its wooden roundness, listening. *Slap...slap...slap.* We rock together upon the waves. My mother guards me from the everywhere-sun's light with a covering of cool cloth.

Awake, I wonder over the other pilgrims. Why do they travel? What do they seek? We are on our way to the sacred islands of Malta — islands of visions and voices — to Her temples of healing.

A time ago, my mother woke with a face full of knowing. On the next event of the rounded moon, she consulted with the council of elders. I know not what words were spoken there. I only know that after her visit with them, she entered the temple each day and prayed for long periods of time. She brought with her many offerings, even my festival robe. Still, she told me nothing. I wondered until the question became me and I became the question. Then the wondering left me.

It was heated moon time. The community spent most of the strong sun in the brown waters of the wide part of the river our village sits beside. We sat and told each other stories at the place where the trees bend their long branches over it, offering coolness.

In the cove of the singing rocks, I sang my song, which the tall rocks sang back to me. I sent them more songs and they sent more back until it sounded as if a whole village was singing. It was here that my mother found me the day she told me we were to leave for Malta.

"Malta?" I exclaimed. I was in true surprise. "Now?"

"Yes. Now," she answered.

I splashed out of the water and up the hill toward her, barely bidding my friends farewell. For three days we walked, taking turns carrying the clay vessel we were bringing as a gift, before we reached the boat that would carry us to Her.

The journey has been long.

My mother wakes me to the sight of Her islands rising in curving shadows of hills from the waters that everywhere surround them. Enormous stone temples stand tall upon the crest of one of them, their rounded walls leaning out toward us, beckoning us near.

These temples are the largest ever built. It is said they were built by the Goddess Herself, in one evening, a child at her breast.

On the shore, priestesses greet us bearing fresh water and ripe fruit. They are all dressed the same — proud breasts curving freely over bell-shaped skirts that sway below their knees. Each wears a necklace of stones hung between tiny, delicate shells. These necklaces seem to identify them to one another. Each wears a different one bordering gently around the base of her neck.

One of them approaches me and my mother. She is a woman at the late stage of maidenhood, older than me. Her black skin highlights the white cowrie shell of her necklace. Her long, thick, curly hair hangs over her shoulders. Her eyes are large and contain kindness. She introduces herself as Martiki. My mother treats her in the manner of a friend. I know that we have never met this woman. Martiki considers me with great interest. She takes me by the hand and leads me up the hill.

There are a lot of people on this island. It is clear from the variety of clothing that they have come from many different places. Martiki leads us to a flowing stream of fresh water. We bathe ourselves in its sparkling coolness. After bathing, we are led to a small hut that sits on a hill overlooking the calm waters of the afternoon sea. Martiki instructs us to rest.

"Tomorrow, when you are better yourselves," she says, "I shall take you to Her."

I lie in the hut looking up at the place where the sun's fingers push through the straw roofing, creating patterns of square weaving within the room and upon my mother sleeping within it. Her silence overwhelms me.

Martiki meets my mother and me as the morning mists are rising off the waters. She escorts us to a grove in the valley below the temples. Grapes, quince, sheep cheese, and breads overflow in piles upon a large table for all to consume. This will be our last meal until tomorrow morning. We will sleep in the underground chambers tonight.

"The Goddess wants you empty," Martiki says. "Clean."

Pilgrims are scattered about, eating beneath cypress trees, sitting alone in silent thought, visiting in small groups. Above us hover the imposing temples of stone; their flat roofs stretching toward the sea. Young girls wearing red robes, which flow around their ankles as they walk, tend to the food supply.

Martiki notices me watching them. "Those are priestesses in training," she tells me. "They have all been called to this island to serve the Goddess, handpicked by Her from many different places. They serve in this way until initiation, at which time they shall assume the specific function the Goddess has chosen for them."

Below my navel, something softens and turns over to melting. It moves painfully through my chest, then to my throat and neck, tightening around it. When it reaches my head, the spot above and right between my eyes, I push it aside.

Martiki is looking at me. She is waiting.

I look at her and say nothing.

When we have finished eating, she leads us to the temples. In the entryway is a large stone engraved with the circling spirals of life. Martiki crawls up on it and, on her hands and knees, enters the temple. I follow behind her, barely getting up onto the large rock by myself. When I have crossed the stone threshold, I try to stand up but the ceiling is low above me. I must crawl further upon my hands and knees through a narrow passageway that bears no light. I am relieved when the tight crawlspace opens itself into a large, circular room of stone.

There are a few lamps lit high on the walls. Otherwise, the room is dark and cave-like. The walls seem to be pushing in toward us from something behind them. The stones emit vibrations as though, if one listened carefully, one would hear them whispering. We sit in a circle of three. I observe the other pilgrims sitting about. Martiki and my mother pray.

We crawl through another passageway, which leads to three adjoining circular rooms. Within this rounded, cloverleaf of shrines there are altars, ritual cleansing bowls, and small, square walls with holes in them for oracular consultation. In these temples, there are many priestesses. I understand only now that many of the pilgrims in the other room await individual consultation.

My mother calls my attention to a long, low bench altar to our right that has many offerings upon and around it. Together, we present the Goddess with the gift we have brought Her.

Later, when darkness covers the land, Martiki leads us to the underground chambers. It is here that the Goddess speaks to those who have visited Her temples above in the light of day. We descend a long row of stairs down into the deep depths of her warm, encircling caves. The only light is the one that Martiki carries in front of us, leading the way through long, narrow tunnels. Inside a small room carved into the stone, she points to two boat-shaped beds.

"You shall sleep here tonight," she says, taking her light with her as she leaves.

I lie awake, my eyes open, waiting for them to adjust to the thick darkness. My mother's breathing deepens slowly into sleep.

I wake to the voice of a woman chanting, rising from the ground below me, surrounding and enveloping me. I have never experienced anything like this sound — it is all-consuming in its beauty and strength. Whole, pure, and clean, it vibrates within me as I lie upon my bed in the deep blackness. My skin pulses, tingling outward. I float upon its current; swaying, rocking, weightless.

In the morning, outside the temple, I ask my mother if she has heard the singing.

"Yes," she says, holding my hands within hers. "I have never heard anything so wonderful."

Tears fill her eyes. She has not yet received her vision. We shall return to the caves tonight. No one leaves Malta without receiving their vision. The Goddess speaks to all who journey here. One must patiently await their turn.

I cannot stop thinking about the chanting. When Martiki meets us at the morning meal, I observe her with renewed interest. My eye keeps returning to the place where her necklace lies, almost possessing the smooth skin that covers her collarbones.

I tell her about the chanting.

"You are very lucky," she says. "The Goddess does not sing every night. She has looked favorably upon you."

"Why does she not sing every night?"

"Many nights She is silent. We know not why. We are always there, ready for Her, waiting."

All day I try to remember the melody I have heard. I practice singing it into a rock by the sea. I go to the temple alone. I thank the Goddess for Her song. I ask Her to please sing to me again tonight. I have never wanted anything so completely. My body aches with memories of floating.

In the small boat of a bed, I welcome the darkness. I pray for sleep.

While sleeping, I am sound, passing through a circular hole in the wall, growing within the underground chambers, dancing up out of the Earth, bouncing off walls, repeating myself back to myself, flowing down hallways and dark tunnels, and spreading myself through large, dug-out caverns.

A woman kneels, swaying over something, chanting. Her white, creamy voice enters a hole in the wall near the floor above which she sways. She turns her head, revealing to me my own face. The song enters me from the Earth below me, passing through my body like a strong, fiery breath. It billows up through my open throat, out of my receptive mouth, vibrating lastly off my red, tingling lips. I am stunned by its power.

In the morning, I say nothing. I leave the underground chambers alone. I walk to the sea. I let the warm waves lap at my legs, immersing myself in Her watery depths. I sit cross-legged in the temple with my eyes closed, swaying, asking for guidance.

At night, Martiki leads us again across the waters to Her temple of darkness. Again we descend Her steep staircase and follow the narrow passageways. This time, we pass the small room we have been sleeping in and journey deeper into Her until we reach a large belly of a room whose rounded red walls curve gently into a domed ceiling above us. Many pilgrims are spread about, waiting for sleep.

My mother and I lie beside each other, shoulders touching. Sleep takes me quickly, almost landing upon me.

I am awakened by whispering in my ears. The whispering grows louder and louder, tripping around the great hall, making itself into more whispers, swelling into voices. When I open my eyes, I see small, white flowerets of light rising out of each of the pilgrims who are lying in this room with me. From within their open chests they emerge, climbing slowly, then releasing themselves swiftly into the roundness. I watch these lights bounce off the walls, ceilings, and each other, dancing above me within this darkness.

I observe my mother bathed in this light. It shines, glowing down upon her broad forehead, exposing her eyebrows, thick and almost meeting; her sharp, angled cheeks; her strong, nurturing body. I thank her for all she has given me. I stand up. "I am ready now," I say.

I walk among and between the pilgrims. They see me not. All that exists for them is this sound; this most sacred healing voice that I follow. It leads me up a few steps into a small room directly off the great hall.

Inside, Martiki kneels, swaying over a hole in the wall near the floor. The Goddess is singing through her.

My mother's boat moves slowly away from the island. My eyes will remain upon it until it disappears, rolling over the crest of the horizon. The warm wind from the sea blows the soft fabric of my red robe against and between my legs. She can come to visit me as often as she wishes. I await her return.

Part Three

Tending to the Family Membranes: The Importance of Ancestral Work

Chapter 14

Family Systems

"Life is social. It exists in communities and collectives."[31]

Parents or other important adults in a family system tend to the membrane of their family, keeping the boundaries permeable yet firm. The adults set the tone of the family system, agree on what is allowed in and what is kept out, and who or what is allowed into its innermost space, its soul. Those who tend to the membrane help manage conflicts, watch for illness or dysfunction, and work to maintain health and balance within the system. The condition of the group or family's interiority is mirrored by the health of the membrane.

Concurrently, the grandparents or elders may be the ones to hold the container of care and tend to the membrane of the extended family system. By paying attention to and caring more indirectly for all who are held within, they attend to the tone and tenor of the system, thereby nurturing the membrane.

---

[31] James Lovelock. *The Ages of Gaia: A Biography of Our Living Earth.* 18.

Once again, the health of the membrane emerges from what is within it.

All of the rituals prescribed in the personal membrane chapter can be applied to a family system. Especially in times of stress, the soul-washing ritual can be carried out for the soul of the family. Although we would hope that the elders would be the ones to do the tending, we also recognize that this is not always the case. Others may perform these rituals when they feel things are out of balance. One might sweep a tree that is important to the family as a stand-in for the family membrane when things have happened to "dirty" that family membrane. This can be extended to all the levels and layers of the family. Treating the family system as such, an alive system with a soul that needs care, is effective membrane work.

Ancestors and the Membranes

Another way a family keeps its membrane healthy is by attending to the ancestors. If things are not well in the ancestral realm, our family systems, and even community and village systems, will not thrive. Attending to the ancestors keeps the membranes happy and healthy. And developing a healthy relationship with the ancestors allows them to help hold the family membrane as well.

In a family, unresolved issues in the ancestral realm can cause problems for the individuals and all subsequent descendants. Ancestor work gives depth and complexity to our lives and adds texture to who we are. It is nurturing for both our ancestors and us. Working with the spiritual or energetic dimensions is always a reciprocal relationship.

Knowing where we came from helps us know and feel that we belong, and to whom we belong. It helps us live our lives more consciously knowing that one day, we too will be ancestors. How do we want to be remembered? What do we want to be remembered for?

Some helpful information to try to find out about ancestors is: Where did they come from? Where did they spend most of their lives? Is there a quality about them that remains and wants to be remembered and passed on? Where are they buried? Is it possible to visit their graves?

Some ancestors were not great people in their human, embodied lifetimes and we may not want to have them around. We are allowed to set our own terms and boundaries around our ancestral interactions. Keep in mind, however, that souls continue to evolve, grow, change, and learn after death. If there were troubles and hardships, we can acknowledge them, consider how they live on inside us, and make offerings for their healing. If the issues are extreme, contact a diviner.

Letting our children know where they came from and to whom they belong is important. (If one is adopted, they belong to both the adoptive family and the birth family.) It allows them to feel embedded inside a community of other humans before and after them. They have stories within which to locate themselves. It is also essential that our children understand that relationships do not end with death, and this will help them navigate these passages when they get to them. Depending on our personal biographies, telling the stories of our ancestors to our children can be an important practice. It grounds them in their lives and opens a place for the oral tradition inside them. The stories they hear about their ancestors and where they came from help them consciously shape their own stories.

Further Nuances in the Word "Ancestor"

The word *ancestor* has many layers, the complexities of which are not often discussed in this culture. There are the just recently dead, the long dead, the unhappy dead (ghosts), the still-working dead, the restless dead, and then there are the ancestors. In our general use of the term, the word *ancestors* encompasses all of those previously named. But the reality is, the ancestral realm is a place and a dimension, and everyone who is dead is not there. There are also the longer-dead ancestors who have become even more potent, radiant, and thinly transparent. They are closer to the fire of origin, *gossamer, diaphanous: the Nyamping — the old, old ones.* In any healthy village, all of these must be attended to. This ensures the continued health of the system.

It is important for us to know that we must honor those who have come before us: we must honor their lives. And we must help the dead. *All* the dead — those who lived wonderful lives, those who were not so terrific, and especially those who died in traumatic ways. Their lives gave us life and we give life to all who come after us. If they were not good people, it is upon us, the medicine people and descendants, to help them heal after death. If they left things undone it is also necessary to help those things become completed. This is one of the reasons for *Finding Divination* at death. Family members go on behalf of a loved one who has passed, intending to attend to unfinished business on the spiritual planes and to assist the recently deceased in finding their way to the ancestral realm. We want to help our ancestors move on as easily as they can. It all affects us and our lives and the lives of our descendants.

Those beloved dead who have made it to the ancestral realm are very powerful and can help us enormously in our lives. It is essential for the medicine people to have a working relationship with them, especially in the realm of conflict, community crisis, and family disputes. The ancestors help the recently dead and also help us with difficult beings, entities, and no-longer-embodied humans who may have made seriously bad choices during their lifetime. Ancestors are also called upon for energies such as "possession" and what we may call "evil."

Some of My Ancestral Stories

My Paternal Ancestors

My father's family emigrated from the Abruzzo region of Italy at the turn of the last century to Keene, New Hampshire, and formed a small Italian-American community there. When I was growing up, I heard many stories about my paternal ancestors that made me believe our deaths are events we can choose and design. Some were stories of relatives who, when they reached a certain age or state of declining health, went to bed one night with the deliberate intention to never awake. They were successful at this. Others were described as "dying of a broken heart." I was told that my great-grandmother willed herself to die due to despair over a tragic event that happened to a neighbor's daughter. It took a couple of days but she too was successful.

When my grandfather died, I was told his heart had given out. "He was done," my father said. "Just done. There was no pain." His funeral was a weeklong celebration.

From these stories, I came to believe that when it was time to be done with life, a person found a way to be done. They had this option and ability. Many of my great-uncles walked into the local river, the Ashuelot, after their wives died. They didn't want to live without them. "They were very dependent on their wives," my mother explained.

"Found Pete's hat today downstream," came my dad's hushed voice from the kitchen one day as I sat coloring in the dining room. "Only a matter of time till they find his body." A few days later, the conversation changed to where they found him and where they guessed he had walked in.

Then funeral plans would be discussed. Though it was obviously suicide, the Church, who was supposed to reject those who took their own lives, buried these men like all the other congregants. "He slipped," the funeral attendees rationalized, shaking their heads. "Got too close, of course. Don't know what he was doing out there like that."

The mile-long walk to my local Catholic grammar school traversed the Ashuelot River twice. I had an odd fascination with those waters. As I stared over the green steel bridge's railing into the river's brown, murky depths, I often scared myself with the thought of suddenly seeing one of my great-uncles looking up at me. I imagined they would be bloated and dead, like fish lying on their sides amid the old, rusted tire rims, shopping carts, and tall river weeds. When the river reached low points at certain times of the year, I never allowed myself to look down at it.

I wondered what it felt like to walk into cold river water with all your clothes on and continue walking as the water filled your lungs. I thought about how they walked in even after they could no longer breathe. It seemed very brave to me that they did not turn around and run away as I was so sure I would have done.

Reflecting on these stories makes me wonder now, is it indeed possible to choose when we are done and will it to be so? In this age of "medicalized death," I wonder, did my ancestors understand something important about the end of life that we have forgotten?

On the other hand, this pattern of despair in my family needed tending to so that it would not continue with future descendants. Contacting these ancestors and asking what they need to heal is a beneficial practice. Recognizing and making general offerings for their pain can be helpful too. Often energies that are unhealed or need metabolizing simply need to be acknowledged and offered food for healing and remuneration. Then they settle down.

My Paternal Great-Grandmother, Domenica (Colella) Ciandella (1856-1943)

The Village Strega

Domenica, my great-grandmother, was a Strega. Strega is the word for a wisewoman, healer, witch, or shaman in Italy. I have recently come to learn of the word *Janarra*, which predates the word Strega in Italy as a shaman or female healer.[32] I call these women "medicine women" to encompass the broad scope of the role across cultures. Domenica held the ancestral lineage and called me back to it. Ten years in, I am still only beginning.

When I wrote the novel *The Strega and the Dreamer*, I was shocked to see the extent of the jobs these Streghe held in their communities and what the loss of them has meant. I didn't understand until I was writing *The Strega and the Dreamer* that the loss of them has ultimately meant the loss of those who tend to the membranes. It was this that Domenica was showing me when I first met her in the cave — that life exists in layers of encased and enclosed interiority, space within space held within more withins, a built-up series of nested interiors with tender wombs surrounding and protecting each layer; that these womb vessels, or membranes, are essential for life to exist and thrive, and that medicine work is about protecting, caring for, and tending to this layered interiority and the membranes on all levels of being.

In the cave, Domenica was showing me the medicine work in its fullness, its highest articulation, knowing that even in the lifetime of hers I had just written about, it was diminished.

---

[32] Personal communication from scholar and goat man Massimiliamo Palmesano.

There is no use caring for and building up interiorities if the membranes are too frayed and weak to support them, and there is no use tending to the membranes when the interiorities have become radically toxic.

My great-grandmother wished to teach me about this. She was asking me to take up the work. This is another way to work with the ancestors — to receive teachings from them for our current lifetime.

Every culture has its own style of medicine people. They have different names and presentations but they are all generally holding the same role. In times past, the medicine women were also the midwives, tending to all things female-health related. But "midwife" is also a perfect term for one who tends to the membranes — midwifing life on all levels to come forth and flourish in the full expression of itself, its soul.

In Italy, there were male Stregone. The plural word for the medicine people in Italy was Streghe. The word "Strega" literally translates to "screech owl" and "witch" in Italian. However, my great-grandmother would have been very unhappy with the term "witch." By the nineteenth century, that word had been so demonized and negativized that she would not have called herself that. The general belief then was that witches were those who dabbled in sorcery or black magic. This is not the true meaning of the word "witch" and many of us are endeavoring to reclaim it from this misnomer, but in Domenica's time, that was not possible. Recently, I learned from Massimiliamo Palmesano that the word "Strega" was applied to the *Janarra* lineage during the Inquisition. My great-grandmother was called and called herself a Strega, so I will continue with that but it is fascinating and illuminating to find the deeper layer of the tradition, pre-Inquisition.

My great-grandmother was dead by the time I was born. My grandmother, her daughter, broke the lineage, which means she did not carry it on or pass it on to her children. This too needed healing in my family and has become my life's work. Spiritual lineages are traditions held in a family or group that are carefully passed to the younger generation so that they can continue.

My great-grandmother knew how to midwife babies, she knew herbalism and doctoring, and she knew how to attend to the community's spiritual needs. None of this was passed to me as a girl, which is the ordinary order of events when a lineage is intact. When I speak of lineage being broken, this is what I mean. I would have been trained in the craft from a young age by one of my family members. Especially in the Italian lineages, family lines hold them and this is very important to the lineage itself, that it continues to be passed on through the family line. Not all lineages are like this. They are not all necessarily family lines. When members of a lineage cease to pass on the teachings of their medicine, the lineage is broken.

In my Tree Medicine Trilogy series of books (*The Amazon Pattern, Notes from a Diviner in the Postmodern World,* and *Teachings from the Trees*) I speak of the journey I went through to recover the spiritual lineage of the Strega to my family. But I am not a midwife or an herbalist. Those parts I do not have. Those parts others in my community and medicine group will handle. Holding the spiritual component of tending to and interacting with the energies and non-physical aspects of the work, tending to shrines, and carrying out divination has come to me but handling physical illness with herbs and midwifing babies probably never will. The full articulation of the lineage may never return as it was held in my great-grandmother's time and as is illustrated in *The Strega and the Dreamer,* for she was integrated into a very small village and could hold many roles: diviner, shrine-tender, midwifing birth and death, herbalism, and tending to all aspects of village life. But even by the time of my great-grandmother, the role was radically reduced. The full articulation was when the women were fully in their power and not fearful of persecution or being ostracized. Then they could hold the full depth and breadth of the work and the community held them in their roles as well. The Catholic Inquisition radically reduced the role of the village Strega by torturing and murdering the wise-women and calling them witches in a derogatory way.

The Persecution of the Witches of Europe— A Tear in the Membrane

The "witches" of Europe were women and men from villages all across Europe who were involved with their indigenous spiritual traditions. Each small village in Europe had its own rich customs about the natural world and the unseen realms. These traditions arose organically from the ecosystem itself. The place, the trees, the mountains, the water, and the important landscape features made the witch's craft unique to each area. Though customs differed, they always involved the same work: tending to the ancestors and Earth spirits and keeping open the gates of communication between dimensions. It was not important how this was done but very important that it *was* done. Tending to the energetic balance of places and communities is very important work. The Streghe are part of this tradition.

From 1486 until the early 1800s, these women and men were murdered en masse. The lowest total estimate of those burned at the stake for the crime of witchcraft is 300,000. Others estimate the count to be millions murdered during this time. Eighty-two percent of those murdered were women. There only needed to be one person to accuse a witch. She was not allowed to defend herself. Witches were burned publicly in the village square. Before they were burned alive, they were also publicly tortured. This is a painful part of the history of the Earth.

If you are of European descent—whether your ancestors were the witches, the children who witnessed this torture and murder, the accusers, or the perpetrators—all the people in this story are your ancestors. And all of it is asking to be healed.

Reclaiming these lost lineages is an important part of healing this collective trauma.

My Paternal Grandmother's Devotion

My paternal grandmother, Annie (Ciandella) Dintino (1899-1995), was very devoted to her own form of Catholicism. Since she was a first-generation Italian-American, it was laced with pagan overtones. In the village of my ancestors, the Catholic Church had taken over but underneath that layer is a very ancient (pagan) tradition that yet flourishes: shrines on the side of the road where people make offerings, prayers, and appeals to the spirits for specific healings. Also, lavish feasts for the ancestors and processions for the saints who were once the gods and goddesses of Rome and before, singing and dancing of the *tarantella*, evil-eye beliefs and evil-eye rituals, and garlic hanging to ward off vampires. Traditions that are now called witchcraft prevail. All over my grandmother's home were shrines to the saints and pictures of ancestors with candles burning feverishly day and night.

Every morning she walked to the 8 o'clock Mass at her church in the small town of Keene, New Hampshire. She was a member of this congregation for most of her life. She lived to be 95. Her spiritual largesse flowed out of her and into her daily life. Everyone wanted to be around her. She had an energy that was uplifting and buoyant. Despite many difficulties in her life, there was something that got her through them and let her come out the other side optimistic and loving.

She never pushed her peasant village form of Catholicism on anyone or preached about it. It was simply hers, what she chose to pray to and devote herself to. Through this daily practice, she was centered and strengthened. Every day after Mass, she stayed for a couple of hours and cleaned the candles, tending lovingly the community prayers and petitions. She did it without complaining. It was her way to give back.

She was a very powerful prayer leader. She spoke her prayers from the heart, pounding her foot on the ground to accentuate each beat. She did not read them. She knew them intimately and she sang them with exuberance and joy. Hearing her say the rosary at a Catholic wake, escorting the dead on their journey, was powerful and transformative.

Now, if I enter a church anywhere in the world and light a candle, I think of Gram. As I do so, I pray wholeheartedly to her saints, invoke her infectiously joyous presence, and send her my heartfelt love. Though I have not followed the path of Catholicism, I believe that witnessing her dedication helped me enter more strongly into my own chosen path, and continues to do so every day. Despite her difficulties and challenges in life, I have her modeling of persistent devotion, which grounds and enriches my life.

It does not necessarily matter what the path is. If we are devoted to our own chosen practices and regular engagement in the places inside us that need nurturing, steadily following the path is valuable modeling for others. And it keeps the membrane strong. It creates a container in which people, family members, and others feel held within, nurtured, and cared for. My grandmother's inner devotion fed the membrane container of my youth. I knew she was tending to things that were important so I could relax in that knowing. Elders should provide this for the youth.

My Paternal Grandfather

In his very large garden in Keene, New Hampshire, my grandfather, Fiore Dintino (1892-1972) grew the most beautiful food. I grew up eating fava beans fresh off the growing plants. They were so delicious. I could not get enough of them. After taking the fat

pod off the stem, I popped it open, fresh and hairy, and let the suc-
culent peas enter my mouth. The taste was more than sustenance;
it was a sweet, etheric, and physical sensation all at once. I felt the
whole world, my whole ancestry, entering me as I ingested these
pods of love. Most kids beg for candy but we, my five siblings and
I, begged to go out to the garden to imbibe truth.

Did he enjoy seeing us do that? Did anyone know what it felt
like to us? I have no idea. The sun was in those green droplets. The
love was in those droplets. He, my grandfather, his hard-working
hands and thoughtful tending of the soil, was in those seeds.

On the way to the fava beans were the rows and rows of bleeding hearts bending their delicious heart blossoms toward our tender child calves. Directional arrows of pink and red hearts led us
forth to the juicy *faavs,* as they were called in my family — the most
eloquent jewels one could eat in the early spring.

Growing food for our families is so much more than we think.
When you grow your own food, you put yourself, your love, and
your wisdom into it. Literally, the family gets fed from you. It is so
much more than growing food simply to satisfy hunger. When I ate
the fava beans and all the rest of the food my grandfather grew —
the tomatoes, fresh and canned, in the pasta sauce every Sunday;
the greens and the chard — I was receiving a transmission. These
teachings live in my body, my blood still. He fed me and I grew
from his soul food.

Now older, I know what it takes to maintain that kind of garden, the care and planning that goes into bringing a seed to fruition
that your grandchildren eat. Then, to have the generosity to allow
child energy to enter the neat and weedless rows of your deep hoe
work to pick their own food...all of that I now understand as a very
great gift.

My grandfather came to this country as a young man. He was a
highly intelligent man. He taught himself English and Chinese
through reading the dictionary. He worked as a janitor in a factory

where his employers never knew his name. They called him John. He was a proud man and worked hard to attain the house and land that he cared for so lovingly.

The Italian-American neighborhood was very close to the college in town, which was growing and expanding. Eventually, the whole neighborhood was overtaken by the college. Through the law of eminent domain, the college took one house at a time and turned it into more buildings for the students. Now, where my grandfather's house and garden were, are dormitories. Some of the trees remain. I walk to them when I am home. Many of my nieces have graduated from that college and my sister worked there for 25 years. Life goes on.

On the day they were to tear down my grandfather's house and do the rebuilding for the college, the person in charge of the demolition told his employees to go and take the topsoil. He knew it was the best topsoil in the city of Keene and he did not want it to go to waste. My grandfather's topsoil was taken and spread into the city's flowerbeds and gardens and many other places around the city we will never know about. The understanding of topsoil is so different now. We understand it as a very precious, finite resource. Somehow this was intuitively understood and so my grandfather's topsoil was harvested and spread around the city of Keene, where it continues to offer sustenance and wisdom to gardens to this day.

My Maternal Ancestors

My mom's ancestors can be traced back to the *Mayflower*. They came from France and England, I was told, but further research reveals German descent as well. There is not a lot known about their lives in Europe before they came but we know from history that the ones who left at that time were in search of better lives and freedom from religious persecution. They came and found a small patch of land in New Hampshire called Sullivan. When I visited the graveyard there, I could see that most of my ancestors had inter-married. My grandmother on my mom's side married the hired help on her father's farm. She was sixteen at the time but apparently, my grandfather was irresistible.

These people were hard-working, New England stock and they were Baptists. My mother's marriage to my father, a child of Italian immigrants, was a radical act as well. She was marrying into the odd, foreigner side of town. Of these radical women was I born. While neither of them would ever look to my particular style of radicalness and call it their own, it is.

My Maternal Grandmother

Dorothy (Wright) Ball (1918-2016), "Dot," was a compellingly strong woman who didn't mince words and held her family strong and firm. In her earlier life, she didn't talk much about her child-hood and her ancestors but in her older years, she couldn't stop. She spoke often of how her father was the love of her life. She thought he was the most fabulous man that ever existed. His disap-proval was gut-wrenching to her. She did not receive it much but at age 90, she was yet stung and worried about the few times she had. She never wanted to do anything to make him unhappy or have him think ill of her.

Dorothy was a young mother, birthing her first child at 16. As many mothers of young children are wont to do, she fell asleep ac-cidentally in the afternoon and her two eldest daughters wandered across the street to her parents' home. When she awoke and found them, her father threatened to take her children away if it ever hap-pened again. That was one of those times.

Dorothy worked hard. For a very long time, she lived without electricity in a cabin in the forest with six kids. Her husband was away all week with his job, so she was left to do all the work alone. She carried water to the house from the stream down the hill, washed the clothes by hand in a tub, cut and carried wood in the colder weather, and raised the six children. They were raised with good Yankee values. There was no waste and no frivolity. They were taught to help out and do good.

Eventually, her farmhand husband came into money. He started his own road construction business and Dorothy did not need to work so hard any longer. She moved into a big, beautiful house built just for her, complete with luxury items like a washing machine and a dishwasher. She never looked back. There was no nostalgia for the old days in this woman.

Dorothy was a woman who scared me when I was a child. She was strict and seemed stern but as I grew older, I became accustomed to her nature and began to feel incredible warmth behind it. Appreciation. She appreciated people. She liked to joke and poke and she loved a political argument—and you can bet we were not on the same side of the aisle.

After her husband died, we experienced a radical change in Dorothy. She became lighter and freer. It seems that she was loyal to her husband and so tolerated and remained silent to his points of view, many of them racist. When he died, she changed her life, became a community leader at the senior center, opened a ceramic studio, and even had an affair with an Italian man! It was beautiful to witness and even better to experience.

Another experience she spoke of a lot when she was older was one of her elder relatives whom she was sure was a witch. They were told to not interact with her. She would ride fast around town on her big, black horse and always carried broken crackers that she offered to Dorothy and her sister as treats when she came upon them playing. They loved them and took them guiltily because they knew she was a witch and they were not supposed to.

After I wrote my tree book, while my mother was visiting her, my grandmother asked her what I was up to. My mother rather sarcastically said I was "talking to trees." My grandmother shocked my mother by saying, "Well, of course she is. Don't you? Everyone talks to trees. I do all the time. All you have to do is sit down and listen. You don't talk to trees? What's wrong with you?" My mother was completely flabbergasted but I wasn't. I agree. This woman grew up in the forest with no electricity or TV. Of course she talked to the trees.

Dorothy lived to be 98, and the greatest pleasure in her 90s was great big bear hugs from her sons-in-law and grandsons-in-law. And she was not afraid to ask for them. She missed being hugged.

My Maternal Grandfather

My mother's father, Clifton Ball (1917-1980) was a farmhand from New England who had been abandoned by his mother when he was just a child. The story is really upsetting. His mother had three young children and had an affair with a man in town. When it was found out, she left the town and abandoned her children. A few years later, she came back but never acknowledged them as her children. They grew up in the same town as her. People pointed her out to them and said, "That's your mother." It was excruciating for them.

Lucky for my grandfather, my great-grandfather remarried to a wonderful woman who took over mothering the children. They considered her their mother. She was a very powerful, strong woman named Ella Swet. I claim her as my great-grandmother. She never once treated them as anything other than her own children and my grandfather loved her dearly.

My grandfather made a success of his life and lifted himself up through several classes of income. He was a hard worker. I did not know him well. He seemed quiet to me but that is only the impression from a child's point of view. I remember him feeding squirrels from his hand. He had many squirrel friends. As a child, I felt envious of this.

I have to say here that he was terribly afraid of black people, which showed itself as racism. When my sister was dating a black man, he told my grandmother he was terrified that he would come over to our house one day and that young man would be there, and he wouldn't know if he could shake his hand or not. He actually lived in fear of this possible moment. How sad. On his deathbed, he was attended to by a black nurse who he came to know and love. Through that experience, he was able to release all the years of racism he had carried and become unafraid. It was a beautiful gift. Some said that he had never met a black person before and that contributed to him being a racist.

Creating and Tending to a Family Ancestor Shrine

For this shrine you will need:
* A designated space indoors or outdoors where you go and interact with the ancestors.
* Optional: pictures of ancestors, mementos from ancestors, jewelry from ancestors, rocks, crystals, or candles

One way for anyone to honor the ancestors in the broad sense of the word is to create a family ancestor shrine. In fact, everyone can benefit from carrying out this practice. If we have children, young or old, this is a great gift to them as well. It can be as simple or elaborate as we choose.

An ancestor shrine or altar is a place to honor and remember those who came before us and gave us life. It is because of them that we are here and, in part, they have made us who we are.

Honoring our ancestral legacy keeps us connected to the cycles of life and brings those who came before us into the present. In some ways, it actually keeps them alive. We may honor specific ancestors—a grandmother, a great-uncle, great-great-grandmother. Or we might choose to honor the homeland of our ancestors—Italy, Spain, Burkina Faso, Mali, Peru—and the traditions and culture associated with the ancestry. It is up to you and how you choose to do it.

Remember: Shrines make the invisible visible. They offer embodiment to those who are no longer embodied.

At the shrine, we make offerings of spirits (wine, beer, vodka in a glass), small plates of favorite or shared food, flowers, rocks, crystals, mementos, seeds, and more. The offerings are gifts but also food (fuel) for their journey and the work the ancestors are doing on the other side. We clean these offerings away periodically when the energetic essence has left them, and replace them with fresh ones.

My paternal grandmother's home was full of shrines. There were pictures of loved ones who had passed, statues of saints, and lit candles in many corners of the rooms of her home. For me, as a child, it indicated the presence of others I could not necessarily see with my eyes. Often, after hearing stories of the ancestors told around the Sunday dinner table, I went looking for them in one of those shrines. If I located their picture, I would speak to them there, at the shrine.

My grandmother kept her ancestors alive so that I felt I could freely interact with them, though they were long "dead." This gave my life depth and the understanding that life continues, relationships continue beyond death, and that they who came before us or left us early are still important members of the family.

How to Create the Shrine

Ancestral shrines can have many forms. Use one that fits perfectly into your space and lifestyle and is not burdensome, but rather a joyful experience.

* The shrine can be a shelf, table, or any surface where, on top of a nice cloth, you place pictures, mementos, statues, or candles, leaving space for offerings to be added. A shrine is an interactive space.
* You can also keep it simple and have one picture and one candleholder in which you continually replace tea light candles.
* Or you can build your shrine outside under a tree, with rocks in a circle on the ground, or up against a fence. You can incorporate plants and bushes, outdoor statues, and prayer flags. It is however you wish to create it. With children, it is fun to create and maintain it together. Visit it on holidays or important family times, inviting the ancestors to the celebration and feeding them. You can leave notes to the ancestors, tell stories, or read poetry together there.
* Trees are great shrines because you can hang things in their branches. One can sit under a tree and listen or meditate. Trees, with their deep, unseen roots supporting them (ancestors), strong trunks grounding and centering them (parents and adults), and their branches with young shoots growing toward the sun (children), represent a family system just by being who they are.
* However you choose to create it, let the shrine be a place that you go to periodically with the intention of interacting with your ancestors. Eventually, they will come to inhabit it. The relationship will come alive and you will feel supported and cared for, as will they.

Part Four

Tending to the Village or Community Membrane

"Living organisms are open systems in the sense that they take and excrete energy and matter. In theory, they are open as far as the bounds of the universe; but they are also enclosed within a hierarchy of internal boundaries. As we move in towards the Earth from space, first we see the atmospheric boundary that encloses Gaia; then the borders of an ecosystem such as the forests; then the skin or bark of living animals and plants; further in are the cell membranes; and finally the nucleus of the cell and its DNA. If life is defined as a self-organizing system characterized by an actively sustained low entropy, then, viewed from outside each of these boundaries, what lies within is alive."[33]

---

[33] James Lovelock. *The Ages of Gaia: A Biography of Our Living Earth.* 27.

Chapter 15

Systems Theory and Autopoiesis: Membranes as Self-Organizing Systems

The networks and layers of community that we exist within are numerous, and each layer's membrane must be tended to and nourished. While public works takes care of the water, energy, and organization a village needs to operate, the medicine person tends to the soul of the village and its corresponding bio-energetic membrane. Keeping it strong keeps the village protected.

The community membrane exists at what we call the "village" level — those both human and other, which live together in a certain location. Within this overarching village membrane are nested layers of smaller, interconnecting systems, each held within their own membrane. All the varying systems are interconnected in a network or interwoven web. Here we reassert the thesis mentioned earlier: The health of the smaller systems' membranes affects the health of the village membrane. Likewise, the health of the village membrane affects the health of the family and other membranes held within it.

Within the overarching village membrane are groups of people brought together by a common interest, which may include

115

ethnicity, religious beliefs, hobbies, or work; family systems, from the nuclear family to the extended; and networks of friends and extended friends and families. Being held within a membrane, personal or group, is often experienced as identity.

"Living things such as trees and horses and even bacteria can easily be perceived and recognized because they are bounded by walls, membranes, skin or waxy coverings. Using energy directly from the sun and indirectly from food, living systems incessantly act to maintain their identity, their integrity."[34]

For humans within a village, each of these groups or collectives is constantly maintaining and upholding their identity through the persistent rearticulation of their membrane. This is one of the functions of the bio-energetic membranes at the cultural level of humans in an ecosystem. If we extend this out further beyond the village we may experience tribalism and nationalism. These identities help humans orient themselves within a sea of other humans. The way the boundaries are held and tended to is revealed by how we experience those identities as well as their membranes.

"Living systems create themselves. They (we) are all self-authoring. We always and only organize around an identity, a membrane or boundary that distinguishes us from everything else. Without identity, there would be no means to differentiate one thing from another. There would be no possibility to organize into greater complexity and order. Without identity, it would be a never-ending mess of primordial soup devoid of form and possibility"[35]

---

[34] Ibid.,17.
[35] Margaret J. Wheatley. *Who Do We Choose to Be?* 64.

Membranes provide differentiation. With differentiation, each can grow its own identity within a sea of other multileveled and multilayered identities. Each membrane, no matter how large or small, contains a living system. Systems Theory helps us understand the complexity of living systems and teaches us that within a system, everything is interconnected and in constant communication with everything else. Living systems are autopoietic, meaning they are self-authoring and self-organizing and emerge organically from the interactions of the components, species, or life forms within them. The system organizes itself into a coherent whole and sets its own terms and conditions by learning what best maintains the whole. Sensitivity is the way a component or part understands what it needs to do to best fit with the system and keep itself healthy while helping to maintain the balance and health of the whole.

"Each organism maintains a clear sense of its individual identity *within* a larger network of relationships that helps shape its identity. Each being is noticeable as a separate entity, yet it is simultaneously part of a whole system. While we humans observe and count separate selves, and pay a great deal of attention to the differences that seem to divide us, in fact we survive only as we learn how to participate in a web of relationships. Autopoiesis describes a very different universe, one in which all organisms are capable of creating a 'self' through their intimate engagement with all others in their system. This is not a fragile, fragmented world that needs us to hold it together. This is a world rich in processes that support growth and coherence through paradoxes that we need to contemplate."[36]

---

[36] Margaret J. Wheatley. *Leadership and the New Science*. 20.

The "identities" from the above quote equate to what we have been calling "soul" throughout this book. From a "membrane" perspective, this would mean that each individual membrane holds within it a self-organizing system (identity, soul) that cares for itself while also caring for the membrane of the village. In lifesystems, each part is independently working to thrive while also remaining sensitive to the health of the whole. Developing human capacities back to this kind of awareness and sensitivity would help us better care for the membranes at all levels.

A personal soul issue, often called an identity crisis, may be indicative of a breakdown in the whole. A breakdown of a community often arises from clashing identities or a community soul issue. Healing one heals the other.

Remembering our interconnectivity through what is revealed in studying lifesystems and how they maintain themselves is useful for the care of the membranes.

Self-Organizing Systems Generate Their Own Membranes

Membrane work consciously attends to the membranes created by the autopoietic system. Remember: autopoiesis is self-creation, self-organization. This means the membrane is created by the autopoietic system itself.

A new definition of life arose in the 1980s that stated "an entity is alive if it creates and continually renews itself, including its defining boundary (read: cell wall, skin, membrane, bark)."[37]

Human beings and the cultural structures they create exist within lifesystems as well. They are not separate from them but embedded within them. Membrane work seeks to enhance, support,

---

[37] Sidney Liebes, et al. *A Walk Through Time: From Stardust to Us.* 38.

and tend to the systems and their boundaries at the bio-energetic level. The Medicine people do not create the membranes, they already exist, having emerged out of the self-organizing consciousness of the system that is housed within them.

These systems are self-organizing and interacting with each other as a whole. They maintain themselves and adapt to changes as needed while remaining in relationship to the other systems around and within them. The membrane plays a vital part in this adaptability. The membrane acts as a filter for what gets in and what stays outside. This intelligence is acquired through the sensing and awareness of both what is within and what is without.

"Cell membranes protect the molecules inside them and at the same time connect them to the outside world by selectively permitting some kinds of molecules to come in and others to pass outward through them. This soon makes the inside environment chemically different from the outside"[38]

This analogy can be extended through all the levels of membranes, from the micro to the macrophase. If we are going to truly hold and care for a village, it is wise to understand how lifesystems work, learn from them, and work with them from within. It is essential to understand that we are but a part of the system. From that point of view, we endeavor to allow our listening to become that acute and sensitive.

The medicine people tend to the membrane at the village level, interfacing with the spirits of place and keeping the village safe inside the membrane. The village is our town, city, neighborhood or location within which we work. (Define your village for yourself by using the *Getting Oriented* ritual in Chapter 12.) Medicine people

---

[38] Ibid., 42.

listen for anything dissonant or inharmonious, human or non, visible or non, embodied or spirit, within the membrane that needs tending to as well as an impending situation arriving from the outside that could cause harm or disturbance to the village membrane. In this way, it could be said that the medicine people are attending to the soul of their community by tending to the membrane that surrounds it.

It is impossible to separate the interiority of a thing from its membrane. Tending to one tends to the other.

This is the subtle truth we want to understand as we move forward in this book. There is the membrane, and there is the *interiority*, which the membrane encloses, protects, and informs. And yet, the interiority also creates and feeds the membrane. Although completely intertwined and interconnected with one another, they are not the same. You cannot have one without the other and you cannot care for one without caring for the other.

If we do not have healthy membranes at all levels of our community and villages, our communities are like the complex chemical interactions in the early sea, gathering and gaining form but continually washed away and dissolved by the chemistry of the sea itself. Without the membrane, there is not a held and strong center. Many of us experience this in our constant efforts to foster community again and again, only to have it disperse.

This is a big job but one of radical importance for restoring balance to our communities and the Earth. We begin this work slowly, by listening. If our intentions are in the right place and we have dedication and persistence, our communities and their healthy membranes will grow organically.

The Medicine People Care for the Village Membrane

Another reason it is so important for medicine people to hold the village membrane is that when someone is listening, the rest of the village can go about the business of living. "Someone is listening" means there are those who are interfacing with the nonvisible as well as visible aspects of the community and tending to what they hear through divination or other means. By trusting that someone is watching for and tending to what is happening both inside and outside the village membrane, the rest of the village can focus on other activities like growing food, tending children, and building houses.

When this is functioning well, the village medicine people can sense a tear in the fabric of their village's membrane and zero in on the place, person, or family in need. Unfortunately, the loss of the medicine people in modern Western culture has allowed these membranes to deteriorate. Dislocation, lack of intimacy with place, churches holding space for their "congregation" only and not uniting congregations through the tending of shared locations, loss of strong personal membranes, and the breakdown of family systems have allowed this disintegration to flourish.

Currently, many modern medicine people keep themselves outside the village they live in. There may be a medicine person working solo or disconnected from a place with no awareness of the importance of tending to the village membrane. It is time to correct this and return to becoming integrated members of our communities and tending to their membranes.

What Do Medicine People Need To Hold and Care for a Village Membrane?

* A strong personal membrane, including initiation into a medicine tradition or craft. If you have lost touch with your

birth lineage, try to find a lineage that resonates with you and do the training and initiation. You will eventually make it your own and it will grow but the training and the initiation are important.

❋ Strong membranes around their relationships to their guides maintained through their personal shrines and personal practice (this builds through time — be patient).

❋ A group of medicine people they work with that has its own healthy membrane held by the local trees. (This can be loosely affiliated and must not be held rigidly.)

Once a group of medicine people has established all of these, they can begin to tend to the spiritual membranes of the community at the village level.

When I first met Domenica in the cave, I had none of these. This is why I could not make sense of the wombs with wings. She guided me on the journey to acquire and develop them. Only when these were in place could I begin to understand.

For various reasons, many of us lost knowledge of how to care for the membranes when we lost the connection to our medicine lineages. For most of us, it's been a long story of separation and displacement, and the loss of our personal and family medicines. It's part of the Earth's story, one thing after another, too numerous to mention — the wars, the annihilation, colonization, the forced removal and fleeing of people, traditions, knowledge, and wisdom. But it is time now to find our way home, back to restoring this and caring once again for all the membranes for the sake of this planet and all of her beautiful, complex lifesystems.

Chapter 16

The Importance of Trees in Caring for the Village Membrane

"Ecological or systems thinking involves a shift away from tracing the evolution of individual species' lineage against environmental 'backdrops.' Increasingly scientists see evolution systemically and ecologically—as the simultaneous and intertwined co-evolution of all Earth's species. This way of seeing evolution brings it into new focus, resolving environments into ecosystems—complex webs of co-evolving, interdependent species. Each species helps shape every other and each is shaped by others....We amass evidence that Earth's rocky crust (the lithosphere), soils, waters (the hydrosphere), and atmosphere are permeated, altered, produced, and chemically regulated by living creatures (the biosphere), especially microbes."[39]

Trees as Keepers of the Village Membranes

The village membrane is also created and held in place by the root and canopy systems of the trees. Trees hold the

---

[39] Ibid., 23-24

membranes of communities and ecosystems through their connectivity to each other and the plethora of plants in the local bioregion. Coming into close communion with the local network of trees puts one automatically in communion with the membrane. Beginning to communicate and feed the network of trees helps one interact and participate in holding their membrane.

Trees are our wise elders and they must be appreciated as such. We can begin to identify trees throughout our ecosystem that want to be in relationship with us and connect them to one another through offerings and visits.

Careful, don't begin more relationships than you can attend to.

It is important to be able to attend to these relationships by making repeated visits to these trees. Listen to them and let them enter your dreams and daily life. If we befriend too many trees in this way we can become overwhelmed very quickly. You don't have to do it all. Assume others are doing it too. You tend to your grouping, others will tend to theirs. In this way, all the work gets done.

"A tree is not a forest. On its own, a tree cannot establish a consistent local climate. It is at the mercy of wind and weather. But together, many trees create an ecosystem that moderates extremes of heat and cold, stores a great deal of water, and generates a great deal of humidity. And in this protected environment, trees can live to be very old. To get to this point, the community must remain intact no matter what. If every tree was looking out only for itself, then quite a few of them would never reach old age. Regular fatalities would result in many large gaps in the tree canopy, which would make it easier for storms to get inside the forest and uproot more trees. The heat of summer would reach the forest floor and dry it out. Every tree would suffer.

Every tree, therefore, is valuable to the community and worth keeping around for as long as possible. And that is why even sick individuals are supported and nourished until they recover. Next time, perhaps it will be the other way around, and the supporting tree might be the one in need of assistance. When thick silver-gray beeches behave like this, they remind me of a herd of elephants. Like the herd, they too look after their own, and they help their sick and weak back up onto their feet. They are even reluctant to abandon their dead."[40]

I have many trees I work with. I was taught to do this by a tree I call the *Grandmother Oak*. She lives in the local park I walk in every day. I tell the story of meeting her in my book, *Teachings from the Trees*. Once I had established a relationship with her, she guided me to many more trees and taught me how to introduce her to them to form a network of trees that I now work with to assist them in maintaining the membrane of my village and community.

We can open connections between the trees and feed them and listen to them for guidance. Some fall, break, or die but remain important parts of the community in their changed state.

After working with the trees for a while, one becomes connected to the root system and can create much healing and communication in this way.

"...the roots are the most important part of a tree. Conceivably, this is where the tree equivalent of a brain is located. Brain? you ask. Isn't that a bit farfetched? Possibly, but now we know that trees can learn. This means they must store experience somewhere and therefore, there must be some kind of a storage mechanism inside the organism. Just where it is, no one knows, but the roots are the part of the tree best suited to the task. The old spruce in Sweden also shows that what grows underground is the most permanent part of the tree—and where else would it store important information over a long period of time? Moreover, current research shows that a tree's delicate root network is full of surprises.

---

[40] Peter Wohlleben. *The Hidden Life of Trees*. 4.

"It is now an accepted fact that the root network is in charge of all chemical activity in the tree. And there's nothing earth shattering about that. Many of our internal processes are also regulated by chemical messengers. Roots absorb substances and bring them into the tree. In the other direction they deliver the products of photosynthesis to the tree's fungal partners and even route warning signals to neighboring trees. But a brain? For there to be something we would recognize as a brain, neurological processes must be involved, and for these, in addition to chemical messages, you need electrical impulses. And these are precisely what we can measure in the tree, and we've been able to do so since as far back as the nineteenth century."[41]

Tending to these trees — meaning visiting them on a regular basis, sitting with them, listening to them, making offerings to them, including them in my invocations and healings, and accessing their medicines — is what I consider part of the general "housekeeping duties" of the work of caring for the village membrane. I have trees in my yard that I have connected to this web. I feel very supported and held by this network of trees. And I hope they feel the same from me. (For more information on how to work with trees, see my book, *Teachings from the Trees*.)

[41] Ibid., 82.

Chapter 17

Working With the Elemental Beings to Care for the Village Membrane

No one, but no one, knows place, land, water, Earth, trees, or even humans better than the elemental beings. The degree to which active and tended-to relationships with the elemental beings has become such an "out there," weird, and forgotten idea displays the importance they have to the medicine work and spiritual practices of this planet.

On Planet Earth, if we want to be a medicine worker or tend to the membranes at any level, we want to have a relationship with the elemental beings of place and Time. This bond was broken, destroyed, and lost so long ago because it was the only way to remove us from our medicine, to obstruct our power. But the elemental beings never forgot. They waited and they watched, they recorded and they hid, and they planned and they plotted... *When will those who can hear us return? Where are our humans?*

The elemental beings (the wedeme, kontomble, fairies, gnomes, elves, sprites) have been trivialized and demonized. Most humans are terrified of this relationship yet they also feel the inherent truth of it. And that terrifies them even more.

The elemental beings are ancient yet they have youth, joy and laughter, and playfulness. They love wordplay and riddles, quests and treasure hunts, and surprise! They love to evoke that in us, as well as our laughter, because it opens us back up to awe and wonder to which we are at risk of losing total connection. Mystery? Yes. Why? Because questions keep you wondering. Wondering is a place inside that allows you to become surprised. And what is surprise? A huge opening.

It's difficult for me to write about them. The relationship is so far beyond words and also filled with mystery, awe, tender connection, and vulnerability on both sides. So it should remain, but I would be remiss to not speak of them. It would be easy not to because even as they are woven so deeply into every piece of the medicine work, they also keep themselves out of the spotlight, so egoless and invisible that we can forget to mention them. They are small, so small that *nobody, not even the rain has such small hands.*[42]

Their brains are not like ours. Their consciousness is different than ours, which is why we so badly need them. Their consciousness is one with the Earth and the cosmos, one of intricate webbing and embeddedness. Disconnection and separation are not something they choose to entertain. This, for them, is illness. This, for them, is unhealthy. For and to them, everything is gloriously connected and they ardently show us that we must heal the breakages, the fraying, the shattering, the holes, the hardened. We must rip off the scars of defense and *hardening against,* under which healing is needed—underneath, inside, within, deep-down layers of hidden hurt and old wounds. We must dig them all out, display them, and soothe them.

They love us and they wish the best for us but truly it is Gaia

---

[42] Line from E.E. Cummings' poem, *Somewhere I have never traveled...*

they worry about, for she is their Mother and their home, and they see — they see what is happening and they know humans are the ones who can do something about it.

But it is not self-serving.

No. It is in service to life.

They are the defenders, the protectors of life. And yes, if we do something against life, they may not be kind to us for it hurts them physically and we shouldn't do it anyway. But at the same time, they need our protection and care. We are bigger than them, literally, and we have different skills, which they admire. And they need us…they have trusted us and we have not been kind to that trust.

In the Dagara tradition, one must *marry, merge* consciousness with an elemental being to be able to divine. I believe very strongly that this was a worldwide phenomenon of medicine people in all places — having different articulations, of course — but it was lost to most of us, and that is why the Dagara lineage can help restore so many others. They never lost this. This is of unimaginable importance. We owe a great debt to the Dagara lineage.

The understanding that a human being cannot divine alone — without the elemental beings, without a being with another consciousness guiding them; without collaborating with another species, a species that is one with the planet in every way and has a very different point of view — is actually an understanding that is impeccably astute and incredibly sane. Humans are flawed and we are flawed *by* our egos and *with* our arrogance. Relationships with the elemental beings guard against this.

"No," they tell us, "that is not how it is. That is just how you think it is because you're human. That is the way you want it to be or the way you think it should be because of all you cannot see."

They continually reveal to us our human minds, our own consciousness, our own points of view, pointing out the pitfalls. They help us remain humble, open, and aware of our blind spots. Of course, they brought this medicine to us and back to us. Of course, we need them. Look what has happened to the planet since we lost our connection to them. Oh my, do we *need* them.

The bonds are strong and can last through generations of a family lineage — multiple lifetimes. They wait for us when we die. They wait for us to come back or for someone new in the lineage to be born to take up the relationship again, to work together again. It is a symbiotic, mutually enhancing relationship.

Some humans say, "I must see them. They must give me proof." Ha! There is no faster way to send them away. If you say that, it is clear you have no use for the mystery or the quiet subtleties of the world and you have no tenderness for them. They require tenderness. They are so tender and fierce at the same time. But above all, the deepest truth about the elemental beings, one that must be understood and respected, is this: the elemental beings are very shy.

Would we but remember how to engage beings that are shy. Approach them slowly and tenderly. Giggle with them. Smile with them. Sit out in nature and commune with them. Leave them little tidbits of food and drink near trees. Listen for them. Remember them.

A Shrine for the Elemental Beings

For this shrine you will need:
* rocks, shells, coins, seeds, and nuts
* A place: a tree, a bush or if indoors, a plant or small fairy house

It's great to have a place to interact directly with the elemental beings and bring them gifts and food. Be warned — they are frisky. Things can begin to move around in your home. Conversely, you may suddenly find things you thought you lost.

Ultimately, this is a heart connection. Under these tricky deeds is a being wanting to know your heart. Wanting to trust you. A shy being that wishes to befriend you.

It is true, not all elemental beings like us or want to play with us but those won't come to the call. Some indeed want to be left alone and have nothing to do with humans. There is no need to interact with them unless you are bothering them and they let you know. Of course, you should listen to that but with this particular shrine and the following ritual, don't be afraid of calling the wrong kind because they simply won't come to an invitation of friendship.

Making the Shrine

* **Outdoors**
  * Put a small rock at the base of a tree or bush. Arrange it nicely with small ornamental shells around it or pretty stones, acorns, or pine cones.
* **Indoors**
  * A rock in a plant or fairy house will do.

* **Open the shrine**
    o They love metal, so when you open the shrine, offer a few coins under the rock or tucked into the Earth. Tap on the Earth with a stick or your fingers and call to them, telling them you want to be friends. You want to get to know them.
* **Ways to know that they have come and are around:**
    o Your garden seems happier, the plants seem stronger, there is more vibrancy and life.
    o You feel silly and giddy—dare I say, happy?
    o You find yourself wanting to play more, to dream more, to lollygag about.
    o You may begin to hear their voices or giggling or feel you intuit something from them.
* **Begin to leave them gifts:** honey, birdseed, more coins, milk at the shrine. You will feel them. They will come.

Ritual for Beginning to Form a Relationship with the Elemental Beings

For this ritual you will need:
* a coin

Beginning to understand and feel the presence of these beings all around you is the first step. Most notably present out in nature and wild places, by the water or on the mountain, they also inhabit our cities and suburbs.

* Simply begin to carry this intention: That you wish to connect with friendly elemental beings.

❋ Then add that intention to a quarter or coin, holding it in your hand and directing that intention into it.

❋ After carrying that quarter around for a bit, leave it at the base of a tree, under a rock, or offer it into the water.

❋ Release expectations. Be surprised.

Chapter 18

True Compatibility

What does it mean to work in a community and live in a village? This we want to reexamine.

In the middle of a group divination inquiring into the properties of oil, I stated aloud my belief that oil and water are not compatible and was given a big scolding by the wedeme. What they told me next was compelling and useful for anyone tending to a community membrane.

"Just because oil and water interact in a way that we define as incompatible does not make that the truth. Oil and water are perfectly made for one another. Their interaction and repulsion is perfect compatibility that actually allows life to happen. The fact that oil can repel water allows many lifesystems to exist. It is a necessary relationship. They are perfectly compatible," the wedeme corrected.

Okay, I was listening.

They continued, "It is your understanding of what it means to get along that is incorrect. Some things get along better when they are separated—when there is a barrier and they are each left whole."

They showed me life forms, cells, people inside their personal boundaries, and planets inside their magnetic fields, and called them each whole. They said each must exist in its wholeness, communicating through the membrane barrier using electric signaling and metabolic functioning. "They are completely whole with interiority and in communication and relationship with the other wholes around them. This is how life functions when it is healthy."

Being compatible does not mean being the same. If water and oil acted differently, they would penetrate each other and would no longer be whole. Rather, they are side by side and completely responsive to one another. We want to allow beings to be in their wholeness, witnessing them and responding to them as a whole while remaining in our own integrity and wholeness.

It is important to understand that there are different ways to communicate, and different ways we do communicate from within our wholeness, rather than demanding someone cut themselves in half and exist inside our wholeness in order to be in a relationship.

Sometimes we blend and meld well with others, other times we have to say, "Stay over there, give me more space." That is getting along perfectly.

Everything must be in its integrity. We must allow everything to exist in its integrity. That is getting along. That is perfection.

The wedeme pointed out that it has nothing to do with liking everyone and being liked. "What is this thing you humans have with wanting to be liked?" they asked. "It's not about that. It is about honoring each other's integrity." They asked, "Can you exist within the system holding up the integrity of the system above all else? It does not matter who likes you."

They showed the quantum realm, a whole field of discrete quanta that all exist as one community.

"This is the fractal reality of systems. You maintain your integrity and you allow others their wholeness. And it is not for you to judge whether another is in their integrity. Another's integrity is none of your business. It is not for you to police another's integrity.

It also does not matter if someone's wholeness is bigger than another's. You don't have to be the same, look the same. Some may be very large in their wholeness. That is none of your affair. You allow them their wholeness. What is important is the integrity of the system."

This teaching has stayed with me. I often try to meditate on it. We talk a lot about our own wholeness, our boundaries, but can we step back even a bit further to allow others theirs? Literally, getting out of each other's physical, emotional, and psychic space enough to allow each other to fully bloom? And can we apply this to all life forms, not just humans? What would happen if humans began to act like members of other lifesystems and actually did begin to put the welfare of the system above our own ego needs? Can we even begin to try? The wedeme are certainly encouraging us to.

Chapter 19

The Five Elements:
Crucial Relationships
for This Job

The Dagara tradition works with the five elements of Fire, Water, Earth, Mountain/Mineral, and Nature/Wildness. Acquainting yourself with these and developing an intimate relationship with each one will assist you as you move forward in this work. The elements are fundamental to any spiritual practice. They are essential components for doing medicine work here on Earth and for maintaining a healthy village membrane.

One creates relationship and intimacy with something by developing a sensitivity to it. An acquired sensitivity increases intimacy. Increased intimacy creates a deeper and more complex evolution of the relationship and the people/beings involved in it. One listens and responds, then listens some more. All of this work is developing an intimacy with the otherworld, the other dimensions, and the beings that inhabit them.

Consider this discovery of the five elements as a form of falling in love. When you fall in love with someone, you want to understand them and get to know them, to hear their stories and tell them yours. Fall in love with Fire, Water, Earth, Mineral, and Nature.

Your journey will not be the same as anyone else's. There is not one way to do this. The important thing is developing capacities — the capacity to hear, to listen, and the capacity for self-trust. If you wonder about something you think you heard from an elemental or ancestor, be patient with yourself and take the time to let things unfold. You will receive validation for sure if you have indeed heard correctly.

This work is not unlike other work. One builds confidence as they learn and grow. And it is equally true that, as with anything else, you can easily get in your own way.

The beings in the otherworld can use these elements in ways we cannot imagine. Trust that if they ask you for something, they know why they want it and what to do. We do not need to fully understand everything for it to work. Often reasons may be revealed to us later.

The Five Elements

Fire: Fire was first. Fire is the realm of the ancestors. It is the stars and the original flame. Fire is the origin of the universe. Fire is creation itself. Fire keeps things going. Heat purifies. Fire is something to be respected. It is fierce. Fire is transformation and transmutation.

Water: Water is that which heals and changes all. Water flows. Water is often used and offered for cleansing and clearing. It is an opener. Water is the element most often used for healing conflict.

It is good to be in intimate relationship with the water in your community. It is a way to take care of the All by taking care of the water. Medicine people are concerned with the general health of their community and water is the main barometer for this. Get to know your local watersheds. Find the creeks, visit the rivers, know the lakes and ponds. Go to the ocean. Sit and reflect.

Water is in everything. Hydrogen particles are found in all areas of the cosmos. Hydrogen was the first element created after the Big Bang, after fire. Fire and water created it all.

Water is the life-carrying element. It is widely accepted that there must be the presence of water for higher forms of life to evolve.

Another way to get to know an element is by observing what lives in it. Become intimate with the dolphins, whales, and fishes. Sit in it, swim in it, talk to it, look at it, drink it hot and cold. Sip the fog. Look at how water interacts with other things, with light, with dark. See how water is reflective. This is a special quality of water.

Earth: Often called Gaia after the Greek term for the Earth and the Earth goddess, Earth is a sovereign and coherent being. She has a special place in the solar system, the galaxy, and the universe. Earth is in sensitive relationship to the larger universe. More than we realize. But ancient people knew. They understood that the cycles of the planets, moon, and stars were in relationship to Earth and affected life on Earth. It is good to live in respect of Earth's intelligence and integrity, and to understand how she retains balance in all her systems to sustain and maintain life.

The iron crystal core at the center of the Earth and the liquid iron layer surrounding it create the heat and the electromagnetic fields that keep everything on Earth alive. This element also includes what is called the *telluric realm*—the underground caves, rivers, and volcanoes, the place between the center and the surface. This inner Earth realm is the realm of the gnomes and the elven race. There is a lot going on under the surface of this planet that is keeping it all alive. Some believe that the life codes for all beings that ever existed on Earth and all those yet to come are held in the center of the Earth[43]. She awaits notification from the surface that it is time to send up a certain pattern and life when the surface is ready for it. There is communication between the surface and the center. Earth is an actively alive being.

Earth is also an element into which things get buried for rebirth out of the Earth, initiation with and into a relationship with the Earth, and to connect with the ground, the land.

Earth feeds, grounds, and supports us.

Mountains/Mineral: The mountains. All of us have a "home mountain," a mountain or mountains we grew up "under." We may also have ancestral mountains from the places of our ancestors. These are important allies for us. They know us and hold our stories.

Mountains serve a holding function on Earth, like a boundary and a fence or barrier. Mountains are strong and lasting while at the same time always becoming the sea and the Earth beneath them. Ecosystems are in intimate relationship with the mountains as the mountains are constantly offering more minerals and elements to the system as a whole through rain, wind, and other forces of erosion.

Mountains and their fractal forms—rocks, stones, shells, and bones—hold all the memories. Minerals, gold, iron, copper, and silver are in the mountains. Mountains hold and store. They have caves and they are often places of pilgrimage. They are connected to dragons. Many mountains are volcanoes. Volcanoes are mountains with internal fires, still churning up internal process. Mountains offer so much richness to the Earth and to life, adding the elements as one adds spices to soup. Mountains can be depended on. Rocks too. Though they seem like they are not changing, they are.

It is essential to be in touch with the mountains in our

---

[43] Barbara Hand Clow and Gerry Clow. *Alchemy of Nine Dimensions.*

ecosystem. Acknowledge them, go to them, and work with them[44]. This is another important way to hold the village membrane. So have a mountain you reach toward, pray toward, hike, and leave offerings on.

Wild/Nature: Nature is created by the meeting of all the above. It is all the many forms of life, two-legged, four-legged, standing ones, flying ones, and crawling ones. Wild is the potentiality of life, of all the life forms. It is creativity itself. Honoring and supporting nature and wildness and staying in intimate relationship with it is extremely important to the health of the membranes. Find and go to the wild places in your village and near it. Know the wild animals and other life forms who live there, and honor them.

Shrines for the Village Membrane

The Village Ancestor Shrine

If a medicine person wishes to create an ancestor shrine for their village, they can follow the instructions given in "Creating and Tending to a Family Ancestor Shrine" in part three of this book. When they install and activate the shrine, they can extend its parameters to hold the ancestors of the village and villagers as well. If they feel so inclined, it is a great location to invite the public to do rituals for their ancestors or the general ancestors of place.

---

[44] Read more about how to work with mountains in my books *Teachings from the Trees* and *Notes from a Diviner in the Postmodern World.*

A Shrine to Hold and Care for the Village Membrane

If one feels inclined to take up the work of tending to the village membrane, the wedeme are recommending they do so at the medicine wheel that is described in Chapter 12. The medicine person can go to this shrine and intentionally set it up as the village shrine, tending to the soul and membrane of the village. It is to this shrine that the medicine person goes with the concerns of the village, and offers prayer and physical offerings for those concerns, entreating the shrine for help with and making offerings for these issues. By sitting with this shrine with that intention, they will be given information about holding the community and tending the membrane, and what is needed from the point of view of the entities associated with and the issues facing the village.

It is a place to have interaction around this. Issues like tragedy and crisis in the community are brought to this shrine as well as good news: births, unions, events, and celebrations. This is similar to the personal soul shrine but is extended out to the community/village level. Please see Chapter 25 for more on how to listen and how to ask.

Holding Objectivity

It is important to state that taking on the work of tending to the village membrane, divining, or any way of asking in on issues with a reach beyond ordinary forms of communication, does not give us permission to peer inside other people's private lives or act like we know what is best for others. It is very important, as a medicine person, to understand that just because we *can* look doesn't mean we *should*. In fact, looking without people asking or giving permission is not a good idea. This is outside of integrity and can reduce our access. For issues on the village level, we make offerings of water to clear the way for the best outcome or to help people find the way that leads to the highest good of all. We keep our requests open, knowing we do not know the best possible outcome but are only feeding the spirits to help those involved find their own best way. Any time we put our own intent onto prescriptions or offerings, especially those that have not been asked for, we are interfering with another's free will. And that really is not a good idea. We go to the shrine to offer support to the spiritual entities holding the village, to listen and interface but not to rule, dominate, manipulate or try to sway events in directions that our ego thinks is best.

It may be best to offer some illustration:

If there are issues of addiction in the community and also perceived evil deeds by those dealing drugs, we would not go to the shrine to ask for incarceration for the dealers and clean lifestyles for the addicts. That would be thinking we know how to best resolve this situation and putting our point of view on the outcome. What we want to ask for is healing for *all*, in whatever form that takes. We state that we do not know what is needed but know that the spirits in the other dimensions can see farther than us and have a more vast view to know how to help those in need.

Do you feel the difference between these two approaches to something plaguing many of our villages currently? The same goes for individuals: "I do not know what is best needed here but I am hoping you can lead them to the best way forward, to healing, or the best way to resolution."

We feed and we offer and we listen. We do not interfere unless the humans involved specifically ask for it.

If we have a divination with the parties and have permission from all to look and get specific rituals and prescriptions that all agree to, then of course, we do the specific rituals. But it is important to know that consent is crucial in this work, as in all others. Don't ask if you don't have permission and don't prescribe for those who didn't ask. If clients do not feel comfortable with what is being said or prescribed, advocate for them and with them.

We do not lose our free will, our voices, or our power with the spirits either. If you feel you cannot be clean in this way, that you are too invested emotionally in the community and want to have an impact on certain outcomes, then this shrine is not for you to hold and that is fine. You may approach your cause or your issue in other ways. But best to cede this shrine to someone else in your community who can hold it with objectivity and detachment. There is nothing wrong with having opinions and causes, and there are plenty of ways to engage with them and advocate for changes you want, but this is not the place.

How to Activate the Shrine

* ❊ Go to the medicine wheel you have already created with the intention of activating it as a shrine for the village membrane.
* ❊ Call in the entity that oversees the community. This is usually a sky being that shows up as a large white bird. Ask it to spread its wings of protection over your village and hold all in benevolence and grace.
* ❊ Offer one cup of milk in the middle of the medicine wheel as you do this.

A Shrine for Each Element for Better Holding the Village Membrane

Once one begins to take up the work of tending to the village membrane, it is powerful for them to have a shrine for each element in their yard or around their village. It is best if these shrines are easily accessible. If one has a yard, porch, or balcony, this is most ideal but one can also choose places in their local park or wild area. One will be making offerings to these shrines frequently, so if in public, it is best to put them somewhere where there is the opportunity for privacy.

A Shrine for Fire

It is helpful to have access to a fireplace or fire pit—a place where one can do fire rituals. If this is out of the question, then use a set location where there is always a strong candle available. It is crucial to be able to interact with fire and do fire rituals in a safe manner. Fire rituals are prescribed for issues of transformation, transition, transmutation, and release. These can be large, group rituals, or smaller personal healings.

Fires are also used to work with the ancestors: helping them cross, calling to them through the fire, and assisting them in transmuting karma.

A fire can be created for and to a specific entity. Offerings to the dragons are often made into a fire. Offerings can be made into or onto the fire. Fires can be made with special wood from medicine trees. When one builds a medicine fire, it is wise to surround the fire pit with a circle of ash and to invoke before starting the fire.

A Shrine for Water

A water shrine can be as simple as an abalone or other type of large shell that can hold water for a time after it is poured into it. Shells come from the water and so they are good representatives for water. If one is lucky enough to have water on their property or lives near a river or brook, these can be water shrines as well. The water shrine is a place to make offerings to and for the water. One can also make offerings to the kontomble (elemental beings of the water) here.

A Shrine for Earth

Earth shrines are generally trees but one can create a mound of Earth as well. At Earth shrines, we make offerings to the Earth and the land, the Earth of our ancestors, the Earth of the place we were born. We are also called to bury things in the Earth near the Earth shrine in a ritualistic way. It is a place to honor the Earth and the local land.

A Shrine for Mountain/Mineral

This shrine can simply be one or more stones. We make offerings at the mountain shrine to honor the mountains and to ask for strength and support for our clients, our village, and ourselves.

A Shrine for Nature/Wild

A wild place on one's land or a plant in your home with various crystals, rocks, and shells near it will do for a shrine to the wild. Shrines to the wild like to have mirrors hung on or placed within them. One can make a circle of stones in a wild area or place a statue of an elemental being or animal. It is nice to plant flowers here or put the shrine where there are lots of flowers. Here we make offerings to nature, wildness, and the wedeme/elemental beings.

Rituals to Hold the Village Membrane

Tending to the village membrane also means housekeeping of the spiritual and etheric fields of our villages. This means noticing where things are out of balance, what needs healing and repair, what needs activation, and what needs shoring-up. The work of tending to the membrane and the interiority involves constant, ongoing interaction with and tending to these shrines and entities to keep the relationship strong and alive.

Soul Washings for the Village

Soul washings can be done for the village using the instructions for the personal soul washing but extending it to the soul of the village.

A Basic Dompla or Sweep for the Village

Clearings of dirt from the village level are essential for the village membrane as well. One may sweep a main or mother tree of the village to rid the village of dirt following the same instructions as the basic *dompla* in Chapter 12.

Clearing and Tending to the Spaces Within Our Villages

Clearing a Home

Sometimes homes or yards need clearing. Signs are if a person feels uncomfortable in their home or things have been happening energetically that feel wrong to them, a consistent spell of bad luck, or fighting among family members. The first thing to do is identify if we are dealing with...

A ghost. The unhappy spirit of a human that has not crossed the transitional threshold to the ancestral realm. A ghost situation needs to be handled by contacting the spirit and asking what they need. They may need help crossing to the ancestral realm or help setting something right that they left unfinished so they can move on. Because this is a rather large job, it is advised to call in a diviner or spirit worker of another tradition for help in this situation.

Thoughtforms [45] left in the space that need clearing. If it is thoughtforms or energies that are stuck and need moving, one can use branches of trees, ferns, or herbs such as rosemary and sprinkle water throughout the home in a healing and cleansing manner.

---

[45] Thoughtforms are collections of thoughts or emotional states that have gathered enough density to acquire physical presence. They could generated by the person or persons living in the house or left by previous tenants, ancestors or the local community.

Bells can be rung while this is done, as sound can be very clearing. It moves energy in the form of sound waves. Drumming is useful here as well.

Stuck energies are another form of obstruction resulting from the lack of proper energetic flow. Energies can get physically stuck in corners or hallways, closets and entryways. Sometimes they get comfortable and take up residence or are created by a persistent behavior of the tenants. The more energy we give to emotions and feelings, especially if negative, the more power they have. We can actually create some of these stuck energies with our own persistent negative thoughts. That is why, as a practice, it is good to regularly open windows and doors, flush the house, and burn sage as a housekeeping chore.

Unexpressed emotions can also turn into a form of ghost — our unexpressed emotions haunting us. Grief and anger especially are candidates for energies that often need to be cleared from a space. I am not saying don't feel what we call the big negative emotions. One must simply be ready to clean up after oneself afterward, the same as if one spilled a physical substance. Offerings may need to be made to the energies that are present and needing attention, which can be notoriously stubborn. If the problem is extreme and persistent, I would recommend contacting a diviner to look into it.

Issues on the land that need healing. These include possible graves that have been unintentionally disrupted, mining, railroads, a sacred space being crossed unintentionally, or an unhappy tree or elemental being.

Clearing Places on the Land

Sometimes things happen in and to places, locations, and elements within the system and as with the personal membrane, clearings and cleanings need to be carried out for the good of all the residents of the village.

Many infractions and much disrespect have been perpetrated onto the land. For cases that are extreme and deeply embedded, I recommend contacting a diviner to look at it, but for general clearings and apologies, there are a few things you can do on your own.

❀ First, we must acknowledge that those of us who live in North America who are not Native American and were not brought here as slaves have been culpable of a great crime. The land is not ours yet we live on it. Great damage, chaos, and massacres were perpetrated on the first people of the North American continent when our ancestors came here and took over this land for themselves. It continues still. We want to be mindful, acknowledge this, and try to find a way to make amends and bring some kind of balance back to this situation.

❀ Being respectful of the history of the land is important. Research what has taken place where you live. Be respectful of the land and the life that lives upon it, including the ancestors and spirits of the people to whom the place belongs.

❀ Other transgressions have happened too: mining, extraction, railroads, paving. Many spirit beings have been displaced and have nowhere to live. These need to be fed and there is a debt to be paid.

❀ If you have recently moved to a home, town, or city, this is not the time to ask something of it. Take time to get to know a place and feed it for a while. Listen to it. Form a relationship with it. You are tending to it, which means listening carefully to what is there energetically. This may mean grief and it also may mean distrust. First we meet, then we court, then we build trust, then we can begin to interact in a way that has give and take.

A General Ritual to Clear Land

If one feels that there are difficult energies present on any parcel of land or place where they live, the following is a simple ritual to carry out.

* ❋ Determine a place in the land or in the wild suitable to dig a hole into the Earth and do a ritual asking for clearing. Dig the hole and surround it with a circle of wood ash.
* ❋ Take a whole, raw egg, and ask it to absorb and metabolize the negative or unhelpful energies that are present on and around the land and restore the place to wholeness.
* ❋ Place the egg into the earth.
* ❋ Pour two portions of hibiscus juice[46] over the egg once you have placed it inside the hole you have dug. This is a blood offering to the place, attempting to pay some of the energetic debt.
* ❋ Cover it all and let it do its work. Let the land absorb the offering and feel nourished by it. Let the egg slowly absorb any negative residue.

Feed, Feed, Feed

It is important to feed a place as well as the spirits and entities that are in it. This creates a reciprocal relationship of giving and taking. The more we give, the more we show up, the more the spirits trust us. Feeding them lets them know that we are aware of their presence and lets the land know that we appreciate all it gives to us. It shows general respect to show up with gifts.

---

[46] Steep 2 tablespoons of dry hibiscus leaves in 8oz of hot water. This is one portion.

Using Tree Resins to Feed the Elemental Beings and Village Membrane

Burning tree resins at a place is very healing and nourishing for that place and can be done by anyone quite easily. Here are some tips about this way of feeding for anyone interested in beginning the process.

Tree resins are fluids (hydrocarbons) secreted from trees. They release these fluids, which then turn into resins to protect and seal an injury. So in effect, they are a healing and sealing property secreted by the tree for the tree. The fact that we humans and beings in other dimensions can benefit from them (by eating them, using them in essential oils, and burning them for their smoke) is a gift from the trees. Though many people use resins, many easily forget this.

The wedeme tell us that tree resins and the smoke from burning them are great foods for the spirits in other dimensions and a great way to feed the elemental beings, most especially the wedeme, who live in the 2nd dimension—the telluric realm or inside of the Earth. This is good food for the elemental beings so they can do their work to aid the Earth in her recovery.

Trees have been on Earth a lot longer than humans. Humans evolved within the lifesystems created by the trees. Trees are our great friends and allies, and indeed, our elders. Trees created many of the hormones in our bodies and so can provide a lot of healing energy and medicines for us. That is why humans respond so well to tree medicines. Burning tree resins and inhaling the smoke helps strengthen our village membranes. The wedeme say: "It gives them substance." If your community is engaged in a new idea, project, or is trying to embrace a new energetic field, tree resins are very helpful for this.

You can use resins to feed the allies you have in the spiritual dimensions and most especially to feed the wedeme of a place.

Burning these in the wild (when the risk of fire is not present or burning responsibly when it is) feeds the elemental beings of the place. This is an important thing to do at this time on the planet as the elemental beings have been neglected for so long.

The offering can be made by burning the resin on charcoal and offering the aromatic smoke it produces, or by offering the resins as they are to a place, shrine, or in a ritual. The resins can also be offered to fire in fire rituals, offered in water, or crushed up and rubbed onto body parts.

A Community Labyrinth

A great way to tend to the membrane of your village, as well as its precious interior, is through the use of a labyrinth[47] — one you create yourself or one already in your community that can be used by the public, both individually and as a group.

There are varying designs for labyrinths but they are all spiraling foot pathways that lead the user to a central place and focal point, from which they exit along the same pathway. Labyrinths can be made as elaborate or as simple, as big or small as you wish. For a more permanent installation, some use river stones or bricks to mark the outlines of the path on a flat, grassy area. Other designs utilize hay bales as the guiding edges, or large sticks or logs. For temporary labyrinths, the pathways can be drawn into the sand at the beach or on a riverbank, or marked on a large, heavy cloth that can be moved around to events. Many communities now have permanent installations of labyrinths on public property. They are a center and focal point that can also be seen as the umbilicus of the community or village. They can be walked at seasonal events, moon cycles, and on holidays. There is no limit to the gift and place a

---

[47] For online resources of how to build and maintain a labyrinth see veriditas.org.

labyrinth can hold for a community.

Labyrinths offer us a place to go to with a question, thought, hope, or aspiration. I was taught to hold the question or aspiration on the way in, receive the answer or confirmation in the center, and unwind it all on the way out.

Labyrinths can be walked at times of stress, celebration, contemplation, or when a community needs to come together to settle a dispute. Before beginning to discuss the dispute, have all the participants walk the labyrinth in a meditative way, making their way into the still center where they can listen for an answer to the question they have carried in, or make an offering or prayer for outcome. Some participants can stand on the outside drumming, chanting, or simply silently holding space while others walk. Others can be stationed at the entryway to meet the person going in and greet them again on the way out.

Other Rituals to Maintain the Health of the Village Membrane

There are many rituals that can be offered at the group and village levels to support healthy membranes — far too many to include in this book, but here is a list of a few. Let the rituals arise organically from and in the place where you live. Also note that one medicine person cannot do everything, thus the need for a medicine community. Some in the community will be more suited to host group events, others better suited for solitary tending, and others for working with individuals or families. Let each find their own and do what suits them most to avoid burnout. You do not need to be of the same tradition to share these responsibilities.

* *Village Soul Washing* — Collective soul washing dealing with the collective shadow
* *Grief rituals* — A place for community members to

metabolize grief
* *Ancestralization* — A place for community members to help ancestors who have not crossed well
* Seasonal Quarter and Cross-quarter Day Celebrations
* Full Moon and New Moon rituals
* Rituals honoring the waters
* Rituals honoring the land/wild places
* Fire rituals — for transformation, transmutation, and release
* Mountain journeys
* Journey through the underworld
* Initiation rites for young people entering adulthood

Chapter 20

Story

The following story illustrates the power of a medicine woman holding space for her community and the healing that flows out of that. The setting is Bronze Age Britain at Silbury Hill. It illustrates a time when humans crossed dimensional thresholds regularly, shape-shifted into animals, and shared consciousness with animals and their ecosystem. Each had a role and this kept the membrane strong.

Notes on the Setting

Silbury Hill has been called the largest prehistoric structure in Britain. It is located on the Wiltshire Downs and is part of a group of sites that make up the Avebury Henge and stone circle. The building of Silbury Hill began in 2750 BCE and took generations to complete. It was raised by human hands and is composed of chalk blocks.

Silbury Hill is not a burial mound as was originally thought. Indeed, mounds of this sort are scattered across the planet. They were built with intention and painstaking precision, and their placements were chosen with great care. They clearly served a ritual function but what that might have been escapes the modern

mind. It is, however, commonly accepted that early people celebrated the quarter and cross-quarter days of the year. Many of the
mounds have a particular alignment to these natural phenomena —
Silbury Hill to the spring equinoctial event.

Silbury Hill is surrounded by a human-made, deep, chalk-lined
ditch. Even as the ancient builders raised the hill, they dug a deep
trench down. This trench, in Neolithic times, contained water. The
Swallowhead Spring, which is the base of the River Kennet, sits at
the base of Silbury Hill. Many Neolithic sites are built on or near
the origins of their local water source. In November, the water dried
up. In the spring, especially near the equinox, when the snow was
melting and the land thawing, the spring bubbled to overflowing.
At spring equinox, the moat was filled high with water, giving the
illusion of the mound of Earth remerging out of the wetness, rising
again from the depths of the primordial waters.[48]

Celebrating Equinox
Silbury Hill, 2485 BCE
Britain

She arrives at the edge of the forest silently so that I know not
from where she comes, and appears suddenly before me. Her hill
spreads its flat top powerfully behind her, carving its curve into the
sky. The wind blows her pelts apart, raising her hair into two tall
peaks upon her head.

"I need antlers for equinox," she says. "Could you gather me

---

[48] Information gathered from: Michael Dames, *The Silbury Treasure: The
Great Goddess Rediscovered,* and Peg Streep, *Sanctuaries of the Goddess.*

some?"

I nod my head. "Yes." Does she not know I would do anything for her?

It is cold but not winter's cold. It is only the cold of the wind blowing the wetness off the melting snow. It is cold but winter is ending. Waters flow everywhere.

She has seen me carry deer upon my shoulders down into the village, presenting my people with offerings of food. She knows I am a man of the deer. She knows they will give me their antlers.

The winter was long, bringing with it much snow. The snow buried food as She slumbered, making my work more necessary. So much snow means so much water, assuring good crops. Long, restful moons await as the Goddess offers Herself in plants dripping ripe with food.

The branching antlers that grew into fullness at harvest, now no longer useful, shed—new nubs of growth already protruding underneath. It is necessary for me to find the antlers soon after the deer shed them, lest they become food. I travel the forest silently behind the deer, the trickling water breaking the silence around me. I arrive at their sleeping places as soon as they leave them. I explore their daylight feeding grounds at the sun's setting, finding fine, firm, freshly shed horns. I gather them into a pile within my shelter at the edge of the forest, tossing them gently upon one another. Their meetings send a clapping noise through the cool, damp air.

There are many antlers. The snow, being so deep, pushed the deer down more and more from the hills into this rich river valley. The trees offered bark, for many moons their only food.

The Earth oozes moisture beneath my feet, pulling them in sucking movement downward as I walk upon Her, returning up smells of muddy ripeness. I travel the same tracks over and over. I venture out to explore new ones. I walk the walk until I am sure every antler that has fallen shall be hers.

When she returns to collect them, the pile reaches above her womb.

"Such a pile I have never seen," she says. She looks up at me with her big brown doe eyes.

I look at her looking up at me. There is a large difference in our height.

"I am longing for you," she says, not moving her eyes from mine. "I wish for you to lie with me."

What is in those eyes I wish to be. "I am not worthy," I say.

She lowers her eyes and begins to gather antlers into her arms. I bend to help her.

"No," she says, extending her arm toward mine to stop me. "It is I who must carry."

I say nothing and I back away from her. I sit on the edge of the forest and watch her — muffled pulsing beneath the thick, hardened ice surrounding me.

I have seen her tripping through the forest in the summer, traveling as silently as sunlight through the trees. I have followed her quiet rustling; her feet landing upon soft flowers whose long stems bounce back, unharmed, purple and white heads reaching.

Gushing water opens the Earth in places it is not normally open, creating streams and rivers through the forest; floods in the fields. The deer disperse, traveling farther and farther, the food becoming abundant everywhere.

The offerings the deer made of themselves left more food for their own. Their offerings more sacred, themselves needing food. The parts we cannot eat I requested back, returning to them offerings of offerings. From my hands, I feed the deer the brown grasses now emerging from beneath the frozen ground, offering them back some of what they gave. So hungry were we.

She has been washing the antlers in the place at the base of the hill where the spring bubbles into a frothy stream at equinox. I sit where the trees edge the forest behind her, watching. Her full body of water surrounds the hill, which rises roundly and swollen, wet from the Earth. She squats before it, mud covering her legs, and leaning toward the water, immerses an antler into the sacred water, speaking soft prayer.

I am the mud between those legs. I am the strong, hardened bone she fondles. I am fur pressing warmly against her nipples.

She stands and removes her clothing, showing herself to me. Water drips fast drops behind me as I explore her hills and ravines in adoration; travel her jutting peaks and dipping valleys with my eyes.

Though I am always among them, I will not take a deer until she has offered herself to me. I sit for three days before, my weapon in my hand, asking. On the third day, I become the hunter. Hunter I remain until one of them presents herself; emerging suddenly from the thickets, white breast expanding in deep breath, saying, "Take me."

After I have taken her life, I thank her for offering herself as the gift of food.

The rains have been falling. I warm myself inside my shelter. A fire crackles and burns before me. She appears on the other side of it, startling me.

"Why is it that you carry no sound?" I ask.

"Perhaps it is you who knows not how to hear."

"That cannot be true," I say. "I am a man of the deer. Hearing is our greatest gift."

"Then why is it that you cannot hear me?"

"You are not a deer."

"Perhaps," she says. She kneels before the fire. Water drips everywhere upon her. Her white chest heaves in slow, deep breaths. She folds her hands together. "You do everything well," she says, admiring it. Her deep brown eyes peer at me between the flames, which dance, shimmering within them. She slowly blinks. Magic.

"The Goddess will be most pleased with the offering you have made Her."

"I gathered not for the Goddess," I say. "I gathered for you."

"Anything you do for me, you do for Her," she says. She shakes her dark, wet head so that the fire sparks and crackles with the moisture it has released. "Even burning this fire is a prayer."

I lift my eyes to look at her but she is gone. From my doorway, I watch her running gracefully back across the field.

In the morning, I find a deer mask and skirt, placed beside me during slumber. The mask, large and elaborate, displays the largest pair of antlers I had found. I know the deer who wore this crown. I stand in my doorway and look across the field covered with the cool morning fog. There stands the hill that my people built, laboring for years that we may celebrate, dancing upon the grassy womb of the Goddess; that we may see Her only by opening our eyes.

On the third day, I walk, carrying the mask to the base of the hill. Inside Her frothy, bubbling depths I cleanse myself and whisper a soft prayer. On the water's edge, I sleep, letting the equinoctial sun warm me. In a dream, the Goddess comes to me. Her tall antlers reach high into the sky, sunlight filtering through them blindingly bright. Chest forward, nostrils puffing clouds of air through coolness, she says, "In every drop of moisture am I found. In every wish and desire."

Later, I join the parade of people climbing Her grassy womb toward the fire, which burns powerfully at Her center. The furry skirt hugs me closer as I find her standing within the group of people waiting to become deer. From a hoof, she feeds broth into me. Musky and fragrant, she whispers into my ear, "Wear the mask."

The mask I have been carrying for three days I lift finally to its place upon my head. My eyes look out from within the dark warmth. The weight of the antlers tips me slightly forward as they pull, reaching powerfully up.

I look down to find her eyes buried deep. She bows her antlered head briefly before disappearing into the crowd of deer. I cannot locate her, though I try to. She could be any one of these deer

160

dancing around the fire in circling frenzy as light meets dark in perfect equinox.

Twigs crackle only slightly beneath hoofed feet
meeting grass I stop to eat
tearing freshness close to the ground
bottom teeth
top teeth
pound pound
crunching grass within me – Earth and sky
within its moisture released; within my mouth are they
grass am I: Earth and sky.

I turn to find her eyes, mask off, looking at me. I look at her but it is myself I see reflected back, along with the flames of the flickering fire behind me.

I know where to find her. She is sleeping, curled beneath a stone at the henge. She sits up suddenly when she hears me, rising to her knees as I approach her. I remove my clothing and stand myself tall and firm before her. Her arms wrap around my legs as her tears water me, offering me growth inside her warm, enveloping mouth.

Part Five

The Importance of Oil as an Offering to Life and the Membranes that Contain It

Chapter 21

Oil as an Offering for the Membranes

"Boar and deer are extremely partial to beechnuts and acorns, both of which help them put on a protective layer of fat for winter. They seek out these nuts because they contain up to 50 percent oil and starch—more than any other food."[49]

"Lipids give cell membranes a fluid character, with a consistency approaching that of a light oil. The fatty-acid chains allow many small, fat-soluble molecules, such as oxygen, to permeate the membrane, but they repel large, water-soluble molecules, such as sugar, and electrically charged ions, such as calcium."[50]

"Each cell of your body is encased in a tiny bubble of membrane. This membrane has about the consistency of...salad oil. The first time I read that factoid, I didn't find it very reassuring! Salad oil seems like an awfully fragile boundary to place between a cell and

---

[49] Peter Wohlleben. *The Hidden Life of Trees.* 20.
[50] "Membrane." *Encyclopædia Britannica,* 25 Sept. 2019, https://www.britannica.com/science/membrane-biology.

the rest of the world. Luckily, the plasma membrane turns out to be very well-suited to its job, salad oil texture and all.

What exactly is its job? The plasma membrane not only defines the borders of the cell, but also allows the cell to interact with its environment in a controlled way. Cells must be able to exclude, take in, and excrete various substances, all in specific amounts. In addition, they must able to communicate with other cells, identifying themselves and sharing information.

To perform these roles, the plasma membrane needs lipids, which make a semi-permeable barrier between the cell and its environment."[51]

"The lipid bilayer is a universal component of all cell membranes. Its role is critical because its structural components provide the barrier that marks the boundaries of a cell. The structure is called a "lipid bilayer" because it is composed of two layers of fat cells organized in two sheets. The lipid bilayer is typically about five nanometers thick and surrounds all cells providing the cell membrane structure."[52]

In the teachings about the membranes of life—the physical membranes around cells, the wombs, and uteri gestating life; the membranes around our families, villages, and Earth—the wedeme tell us that oil is an appropriate offering for their care. To reiterate:

[51] "Structure of the Plasma Membrane." *Khan Academy*, https://www.khanacademy.org/science/high-school-biology/hs-cells/hs-the-cell-membrane/a/structure-of-the-plasma-membrane.
[52] *SparkNotes*, https://www.sparknotes.com/biology/cellstructure/cellmembranes/section1/.

When we speak of the membranes, we speak of the actual 3D mem-branes that surround and support all levels of life, from the micro to the macro scale. We speak of the physical boundaries that create an inside and outside, allowing a being to have an interiority and remain in integrity within a system full of outside influences. We also speak of the spiritual membranes that surround the etheric bodies of all forms of life.

Oil is an appropriate offering for both the physical and spiritual membranes. While we understood that oil provides an important function for the physical structures of membranes, we wanted to understand how oil, as an offering, could help. To learn that, Strega Tree diviners carried out a divination to learn more about oil as an offering and we were met with a complex set of responses, which I try to convey below.

It is fair to say that oil is hugely important for reasons we had never considered. This information came in divination from the wedeme, the elemental beings of the wild. I was the diviner and the translator of what they were telling and showing me in this inquiry. I try to leave some of it in their language so the reader can also make any connections to what the wedeme have to say for themselves. I also try not to explain or augment what they say so as to not distort the message coming through. That is who the "they" in "they said," is in the following.

Divination Time

The Qualities of Oil

Oil creates a barrier. Oil is what helps build a membrane. It keeps the membrane healthy, porous, and permeable. The oil helps the membrane retain its shape and creates elasticity. Oil can help things be elastic and non-elastic, stick together or repel—both are necessary at certain times.

Your brain cannot think without oil. Things would crash and come to a grinding halt without it. Oil makes you think. Oil makes things flow.

The Importance of Pits, Seeds, and Nuts to the Lifesystems

Pits, seeds, and nuts contain precious oils. Seeds and the oils within them hold the concentrated essence of that which created them. They are embryonic forms. Inside the seed, nut, or pit are all the instructions and components needed to grow into another form of that life. These allow the seed or nut to grow into a new tree, plant, or bush. They are potentialities waiting to be activated. This is contained within the oil derived from said nuts, seeds, and pits as well.

Seeds contain the life force — the "pre-codes" of life. Raw potentiality is contained inside a nut or seed and oils carry this.

As *ash is that which remains of fire,*[53] *oil is that which remains of life.* Oil holds the life codes within it. It is essential. Oil is rendered out of life and life processes. If life conserves what works in order to ensure the continuation of life, oil (fat) seems to be one of the properties used to do this.

Oil Holds the Field of Potentiality

In the early universe was a field of potentiality that the wedeme likened to oil. I was shown it as something golden and glowing inside a seed or kernel. The wedeme prefer seed or egg stories to define creation, something bursting with potential and opening to it —

---

[53] A reference to an earlier teaching given to us by the wedeme. See: *Notes from a Diviner in the Postmodern World: A Handbook for Spirit Workers*, Chapter 4.

rather than an explosion (the Big Bang), it was a blossoming.

"That's oil also," the wedeme said, showing the "golden elixir" at the beginning of time. "It's a field of potentiality. Thought was there too, in the early universe."

According to the wedeme, "the universe is a golden field of potentiality enlivened by thought." The seed or kernel is concentrated thought. It is so concentrated, so ripe, that it has to open.

"The seed is really ripe, it is heavy. Isn't it funny that you call the quantum vacuum empty when it is really so ripe, full, and heavy?[54] It is not light either. It is dark. When something becomes light, it is releasing the energy. Light is expression. The little seed is so heavy, unexpressed, fecund, it must burst open."

Anointing with Oil

This raw potentiality inside the seeds, nuts, and pits that their oils are derived from is very potent and can activate other potentialities, meaning, bring them forward into form or activity. This is why oil is used for anointing. To anoint someone is to activate something inside them. A role or purpose that has been dormant is being brought to life by the anointing. Where you place the oil on their body is important too. You can activate the third eye in the middle of your forehead to increase your inner and intuitive vision by applying the anointing oil there, the heart to open or offer it protection by placing it there, and so on. The qualities of the oil used for the anointing are important too. Rose or spikenard oil evoke different potentialities. Rose is used to activate love and a love energy, spikenard is used to activate inherent spiritual abilities or gifts, such as healing or prophecy, and is used in initiation.

---

[54] The wedeme are referring to the quantum vacuum of physics that is also often called an emptiness or a nothingness because the particles that exist there are virtual.

How to Offer Oil

Sometimes, high-quality vegetable oils are asked for in a ritual. We can offer it directly onto the Earth. "Oil is good for the soil," the wedeme said. "If you want your brains to think, get some oil in the soil."

But more than this, the wedeme wanted to talk about an important part of the life cycle that produces oil and generates it for the Earth herself, and how that part of the life cycle is being eliminated and therefore denying the Earth her oil.

"Instead of offering refined oil you buy at the store," the wedeme suggest, "allow some things to rot. Bury some oil-bearing nuts and seeds into the Earth. Instead of picking and gathering all the walnuts off the tree, bury some inside the Earth. Allow trees to rot back into the Earth. Allow seeds and nuts to remain on the ground and rot. You are denying Earth this part of the life cycle, which is essential to her health. You clear everything away, gather everything, collect everything. Leave some nuts for the Earth. They are her nuts anyway."

They want us to pay attention to the whole story of oil. Oil is part of a life process that the Earth needs. There are many components involved in the creation of oil that need to be paid attention to. Oil is essential for life but how oil is rendered is a crucial thing to understand. Merely offering a lot of purchased, refined oil is not the solution. Instead, we must pay attention to the life cycles that create oil, and how we are or are not in right relationship with this for true healing. By life cycles, the wedeme mean the entire process that it takes to create oil in all its many forms on the planet.

"Pay attention to the pollinators," they said. "The pollinators are essential for the production of oil. You must see the whole picture," they warned. "Do not begin offering a whole bunch of purchased, refined oil but preserve the lifesystems of the planet by honoring all the processes and stages they go through to become and remain a life system and care for those beings like pollinators that allow them to prosper."

They showed the reality of circulation. The life cycles of plants. The life cycle of oil. The life cycle of the planet. "Stop depleting the Earth and interrupting a vital process. **Stop interrupting the process.**"

What the wedeme were getting at here is the way humans have interfered with and interrupted the organic, natural, and inherent processes of lifesystems.

"Although most people know that honeybees pollinate plants, few are aware that there are hundreds of thousands of plant pollinators, many of whom have coevolved over millions of years with specific plants. Less than 6 percent of them are known to researchers. They range from bats, to mosquitoes, to mice, to ants, to opossums, to bees, to monkeys, to beetles, to lizards, to flies, to birds, to butterflies, to flying foxes. There are at least 1,500 bird species, 15,000 wasps, 40,000 bees, 20,000 butterflies and moths, 14,000 flies, 200,000 beetles, 165 bats, and 300 other mammals that pollinate plants. Perhaps 80 percent of all the flowering plants are pollinated by beetles. Forty percent of the angiosperms have a primary dominant pollinator with a number of other, less regular pollinators. Some plants have only one. The 700 to 900 fig species in the world (including the Indian Banyan), for the past 40 million years, have each been pollinated by its own individual kind of fig wasp. Their lives are often mutually interdependent; neither can survive without the other."[55]

Carbon, Coal, Oil, and Gas

When the wedeme spoke of oil as an offering and as an

---

[55] Stephen Harrod Buhner. *The Lost Language of Plants: the Ecological Importance of Plant Medicines to Life on Earth.* 191.

important part of the life cycle and systems of the planet, I had not made the connection to the kind of oil we know as petroleum. The fossil fuels we extract and burn are not a small subject. And under all this information on oil as an offering, it looms. The oil, coal, and gas that we extract from the Earth to power our lives are also indicated in this discussion and yes, make the subject much more sobering.

Oil, as we all know, is a precious resource but to understand the spiritual implications of oil in our lives and add the spiritual dimensions of oil to this fossil fuel reality is even more chilling.

Oil was created by the decay of ancient sea life. Coal was formed by the decay of ancient trees and plant life. What we use to power our engines, our computers, our homes, our businesses, and shopping centers, is the decay of ancient life.

"Today's deposits of [these] fossil fuels come from trees that died about 300 million years ago. They looked a bit different—more like 100-foot-tall ferns or horsetail—but with trunk diameters of about 6 feet, they rivaled today's species in size. Most trees grew in swamps, and when they died of old age, their trunks splashed down into stagnant water, where they hardly rotted at all. Over the course of thousands of years, they turned into thick layers of peat that were then overlain with rocky debris, and pressure gradually turned the peat to coal. Thus, large conventional power plants today are burning fossil forests. Wouldn't it be beautiful and meaningful if we allowed our trees to follow in the footsteps of their ancestors by giving them the opportunity to recapture at least some of the carbon dioxide released by power plants and store it in the ground once again?"[56]

The oil belongs to the Earth. It creates barriers for her lifesystems, supports her membranes, and keeps things running

---

[56] Wohlleben, 94.

smoothly. What does it mean that we extract it and burn it, and in the burning of it damage the very membrane Earth created to safely host biological life — the ozone layer — one of the membranes we have weakened with our own human actions?

To contemplate the fact that most of the wars and tensions that currently exist between nations are, at the core, over the subject of where oil is located and who has control over it adds another layer to the warning the wedeme gave about interrupting the processes of the life cycle. We need to honor the life cycle of carbon.[57]

Oil and Membranes

Oil is a very important subject indeed, as are the membranes. We must care for both of these and yet, currently, I think it is fair to say we are failing in that task. Our survival as a species definitely hinges on these two concepts: oil and membranes.

Being medicine people at this time on the planet is no small feat. How do we keep the oil and the membranes healthy with all of this going on? Political interests and corporations are currently in control. As spiritual leaders, we must find a way to address this situation for the good of the planet and all life.

In truth, it should not be that difficult for us to begin to pay attention to and be more honoring of the life cycles that generate oil; to bury seeds and nuts, a portion of all that we harvest, as an offering back to the Earth; to allow more trees and plants to go through the natural process of rot and return; and to stop extracting so much oil, coal, and gas from the inside of the Earth. This oil, coal, and gas

---

[57] The carbon cycle refers to the natural, biological pathways through which carbon is transferred from non-living substances to living organisms and from one living organism to another. The entire cycle, however, begins with plants. See: "The Carbon Cycle." *Petroleum*, http://www.petroleum.co.uk/carbon-cycle.

took millions of years to form and the Earth needs it for her own continued health.

We have many forms of alternative energy now that do not disrupt the natural life cycle of the planet and do not burn the membranes. But we need to *want* to do this. We need to *want* to focus our will there if we want to continue to live on the planet and attempt to restore balance. If we can truly understand that we must care for the membranes of every living creature, including the planet, would it be possible for us to make this shift?

Ah, but to care. Caring, we were told, is another offering to the membranes.

Prayer is a Form of Concentrated Care

At this point in the divination, the Earth piece was selected to speak. The divination kit contains entities who speak when they are chosen by the stick. Another offering that can be made to strengthen the membranes, we were told by Earth, is care. To care. To care is an offering to the membranes. "Care is like oil," Earth said. She did not mean *tending to*. She meant to *care about*. To be concerned with, to think about and notice and wish the membranes well. To take time to consider them. That kind of care.

We must offer our care to the membranes—our thoughts, our time, our energy. That is healing for the membranes.

Then the wedeme added, "Prayer is a concentrated form of care. It is very good for the membranes. It can be any kind of prayer. If the intention is for caring, no matter what style the praying, understand that your prayer is care and it is a way to feed the membranes. Pray for all the membranes Earth created that are fraying. Pray for all the membranes."

Chapter 22

When the Center Cannot Hold

"What we do know is that life began with membranes, with boundaries that created cells by separating them from everything else.

"Inside that container, possibilities arise—complex interactions that create different and sophisticated functions. The membrane is semi-permeable, letting in energy and matter in continual exchanges with its environment. Without that permeability, nothing new could be created, and, like all closed systems, the young life form would quickly wear down and die.

"Life cannot be sustained when the boundary becomes rigid. Nor can it generate new capacities and adapt to its environment if the boundary is too open"[58]

In the course of the divination inquiring into oil, the wedeme also made the connection between seeds and what lies within them

---

[58] Margaret J. Wheatley. *Who Do We Choose to Be?* 64.

and the atom and what lies within it: the nucleus and the weak nuclear force that holds it together (weakly).

There is a strong nuclear force and a weak nuclear force. It is
the weak nuclear force, or the weak force, that allows for what we
call "radioactive decay." When radioactivity is released from the
disintegration and decay of an atom of heavy metal, this is radioactive decay.

Sometimes things fall apart and that breakdown can be toxic to
other beings in the area or environment. But sometimes things have
to break apart and release one articulation so that they can transmute into another. When this happens, if the membranes are held
and strong, they will serve as protection or at least minimize the
destructive force that has been released by this change and transformation. When strong membranes are not in place, this breakdown can wreak havoc and cause more destruction than is necessary. There may be no coming back from such an event. We want
to tend to the membranes and keep them strong at all levels to minimize and contain these potentially toxic forms of transmutation
and rebirth. We can help manage, mitigate, and contain them by
tending to and shoring-up the membranes.

The atoms that create radioactive decay, while they transmute
their interiors, are called "unstable." It is also unstable forces, persons, or situations in our families, groups or communities that can
cause this kind of toxic release. It is wise to watch for these and
perhaps sequester them while they are having their transformation
to keep others safe. We are encouraged to be on the lookout for
them to protect ourselves the same way we are asked to protect
ourselves from the sun.

Some Scientific Background

Fission is the division of the nucleus of an atom, which is heavy
and has an unstable nucleus, into two. This is the process set into

action in nuclear weapons and power plants. Some atomic bombs use a combination of fission and fusion. Fusion is a combination of two lighter atoms into one larger one. This happens inside the sun. Again, this is the nucleus, the interior space that is disintegrating and undergoing change. It is important to understand that, in the case of nuclear decay that creates dangerous radioactivity, it is the interior of the atom that is decaying. Some of this happens organically and makes people and other living beings ill because it bypasses the integrity of the membranes and begins to break down the interiors of other membranes.

The nuclear weapons we have created seize on this process and weaponize them. The intentional release of this power as a weapon to harm and destroy is lengthened due to the half-lives of these atoms. It takes a long time for some of them to complete their toxic disintegration.

Firstly, the wedeme say on this topic, "Just stop making these weapons"—which, for most of us, is common sense, yet as political entities and countries, we have not stopped. In fact, a briefcase follows the president of the United States around always and everywhere in case he needs to unlock the codes to deploy such absolute destruction on the Earth. There are many nuclear weapons stockpiled inside the Earth, waiting to be deployed and currently, there are many being built.

Power plants that use the same process to create what is called "safe energy" are not safe at all. They are extremely unstable. Nuclear accidents and spills damage lifesystems for many generations, infiltrating the reproductive capacities of the life cycle and compromising the future.

The Breakdown of Village Systems

On an emotional and psychological level, within our family systems and community systems, humans can have this kind of toxic breakdown of their interiority—meaning that the stability of the mental, emotional, or psychic interior is breaking apart, damaging the membrane packet that was holding them, and causing harm to the entire system. The wedeme say these radioactive, emotional, mental, or relational breakdowns can be mitigated by healthy membranes.

Sometimes things break apart. Marriages break apart, destroying the interior of a family system, but if the membrane is strong around the system and all parties work to keep it that way, the breakdown can be less toxic for those in the system. Sometimes, crisis in one person can cause a subsequent crisis in a family, workplace, or village but again, if the membranes are strong, it can be mitigated and the breakdown can be withstood without damage to the whole system.

Even after an unexpected breakdown, if we work to repair the membranes by first tending to our personal membranes, then up the scale through family, village, Earth, and beyond, we can reach a healthy conclusion. Often these breakdowns can create much-needed change or transformation if handled properly. Paying attention to and caring about the membranes is crucial in all these circumstances.

"Whenever a living system changes, it is attempting to save itself, to preserve its identity"[59]

Margaret J. Wheatley writes about these breakdown moments in her book, *Who Do We Choose To Be?* When things fall apart and the center cannot hold, it is up to the leader of the group to reassert the identity of the whole group. The identity is what holds groups together. This idea equates with what the wedeme call *original*

---

[59] Ibid., 65.

patterns (discussed in Part Seven of this book) and the *soul origin pattern* (discussed in Part Two). As medicine people, when a being or element is in trouble, we can do the work of calling back the original pattern of that being to help it remember itself, reaffirming its soul identity and allowing it to reformulate around that. This is crucial work we have been doing at Strega Tree for a while now—calling the original pattern of Earth, of water, individuals, and more, to help them remember themselves and regenerate the truth of who they are.

Shrines Help Support the Membranes

Membranes can be attended to at corresponding levels of the shrines, meaning the personal membrane at the personal soul shrine, the family and village and their attending shrines, and so forth. Creating a shrine for each level is, in essence, a shrine for the membrane. Shrines are very essential membrane work.

Rituals to Return Original Patterns and Help Contain the Membrane When Things Fall Apart

A Ritual to Help Return the Oceans to Their Original Pattern

In a community theme divination carried out by the Strega Tree collective, the wedeme told us the oceans are experiencing severe blockage of their natural flow. We need to help with this. One of the rituals given was this simple ritual listed below.

Human actions have interfered with the patterns of the oceans.

This ritual will help eliminate the pattern of blockage from the oceans by returning them to their original pattern. The oceans form and contribute to Earth's most important membranes. The health of the oceans is important to the health of the membranes.

We all know the oceans are in trouble. The wedeme accentuate: "Don't dwell on what has gone wrong. Rather, focus on what can be done to help and get to work." The point here is to hold the oceans in their highest articulation.

This reminder from the wedeme is concerned with which way we focus our energy. It is not to say things have not happened that were wrong and out of alignment, and that there are not those to blame, but frankly, we only have time to move forward. Medicine people should take notice of this. Spending energy on what went wrong or who has done us wrong is truly a waste of our gifts, and even a distraction. Instead, we want to get down to the work of restoring balance. For a medicine person, that means on the energetic planes.

For this ritual you will need:
* Two shells (Before doing the ritual, clean and clear these shells by leaving them out in water in the sunlight for a number of hours.)
* Water from the ocean (Apologies to those who do not live near an ocean but it does need to be actual ocean water for this ritual. If you don't live near an ocean but are near a river, lake, pond, or creek, you may change the ritual to a healing for the body of water of your choice using your local water source.)
* Two small bowls that can nest within one another
* Fresh or rainwater. (If you do not have fresh or rainwater, you can clean water by leaving it out in the sun for eight hours.)
* In this ritual, the two shells will become the ancient

ancestors of all shells. These two shells will be called upon to hold the pattern of the oceans before there was a blockage. We are going to call on the ancient ancestors of all shells that have never known the pattern of blockage.

The Ritual

❋ When you are ready to do the ritual, take the shells and call the pattern of "no blockage" into them. You do this by holding them in your two hands and calling on the ancient ancestors of all shells. Really hold this intention as you call these ancient ancestors into the shells. Speak this into the shells: "I am calling on the ancient ancestors of these shells that never knew the pattern of blockage. I am calling you into these shells to come and help heal this pattern in the oceans."

❋ The inside (smaller) bowl contains fresh water. Place the two shells that now have the original pattern in them into this water. Place that bowl inside the larger bowl and add the ocean water to the outside bowl. The shells in the fresh water will imprint the ocean water with this healthy, original pattern. Water is "coherent," meaning that what happens to water anywhere, all water feels. By returning this healthy pattern back into this little bit of ocean water, all water will receive this blessing.

❋ Leave for a complete 24 hours on a shrine you already care for. If you do not have a shrine, designate a place for this bowl to sit while the ancestor shells do their work of healing.

* After 24 hours, you may offer the water to the Earth in a place you feel drawn to.
* Do this ritual seven times (you can take a break between each) using the same shells. When you are finished, you may clean and clear the shells again and return them to their previous use, or offer them to the Earth by burying them.
* You may find, as I did, that you receive a healing as well when you carry out this ritual.

Ritual for a Group, Family, or Village System That Has Suffered a Breakdown

For a village or family system that has suffered a toxic break-down, Margaret J. Wheatley recommends that the leaders help the group remember their identity or who they are, the common value, or what in this book is being referred to as the soul. And help the membrane rebuild around that.

"This is a critical leadership responsibility as the organization moves through crisis and even in calm times (if these even exist now). It is the leader's role to make visible the stories, usually un-conscious, that people are acting from. And then to consciously name a more empowering story linked to the identity. There are many images for the role that a shared story plays in self-organiz-ing: it is a shared perceptual filter; it creates coherence at the core; it is the reference point for individual actions; it is an aspiration of who we choose to be."[60]

For this ritual, it is not always appropriate to call in the original pattern of the group as the breakdown may be indicating that a change was needed. A new identity or identities may be emerging and this is what needs to be recognized and honored.

---

[60] Ibid., 206.

Ritual:

❁ Gather the members of the group together, or representatives if it is too large to include all. Have them each write out what the group means to them, including expectations, what they love about the group, and what is not working for them. This is the identity they hold of the group.

❁ Share one at a time with the whole group.

❁ Reframe: Come to a coherent combination of all the identities to form the new identity, or more than one identity if a split in the group is to follow. If discussion is needed here, allow it. Use a timer if you need to. If the conclusion is to reassert the original identity, that is important too.

❁ Reassert the original identity or assert the new identities of the group with all agreeing and understanding. As Wheatley says, often the breakdown comes from different sectors having developed different identities. Then they are acting out of these different identities and confusion develops or communication becomes challenged. Often a fracture happens resulting in two separate identities that have developed over time that need to make space for each other to go their own way. They may want to be connected but more loosely affiliated. It may be time to grow and often this means a splinter, which does not have to be painful if it is consciously recognized and honored rather than seen as threatening. If it is openly discussed and identified, it can be worked with in a constructive manner. All of this must be held open as possibilities.

❁ Go into this ritual with the intention to listen, and encourage others to as well. Visions grow and evolve, movements grow and evolve. It is not a failure if groups fracture or splinter. It is *how* this happens that determines if it is accomplished in a healthy or toxic way.

✹ The leader may want to include silent reflective time with a candle lighting and intention setting, drumming, singing, or other activities that can help cohere group focus.

Chapter 23

Story

In the following story, a breach of trust has happened between the dominant wild animal species — the snow leopard — and the humans who inhabit a village within their ecosystem. A priestess from the Shrine of the Leopard attends to this tear in the membrane.

Notes on the Setting

Çatal Hüyük is a Neolithic settlement in Anatolia that some scholars date to as early as the 8th millennia BCE. Çatal Hüyük is located on the Konya Plain, in what is now Turkey.

The ancient settlement of Çatal Hüyük was a city of honeycombed rooms and courtyards, a self-contained unit with interconnecting walls. There were no separate buildings and no doors between dwellings. With the use of ladders, the people of Çatal Hüyük entered their homes through the roof. The city housed as many as 7,000-10,000 residents.

The people of Çatal Hüyük were agriculturalists and horticulturalists. They engaged in extensive trade. The homes were kept meticulously clean. Within these dwellings were many large wall paintings and plaster reliefs. Many of the rooms within this hive-like village have been identified as shrines.

In one shrine room there is a plaster relief of twin leopards standing face to face between two torches, their bodies adorned with a rosette pattern. The snow leopard is the top predator in this area and, as with any indigenous culture, must have been held in high regard by these early inhabitants.[61]

In the Lair of the Leopardess
Çatal Hüyük, Anatolia, 5916 BCE

We were scared that morning. We worried for our safety. And so we entered the shrine of the leopard. We danced her dance. I knew it was not enough, so I went up into the mountains. I followed her trail (stalking the stalker) to try to see what it was we were missing.

She who kills, hiding her kill in a tree, dragging the dead body up, up (from her jaw, hanging flesh-filled fur—fresh blood running, as she leaps with it), safely tucking it within protective branches.

She who so cleverly, most thoughtfully, stalks her prey (following them in crouched silence, calmly observing) watching for the perfect moment to sneak up from behind and, with one swift blow, (teeth sinking into the soft edges at the back of the neck) stop the breath which flows within them.

There have been killings—in the village—three early mornings,

---

[61] See Marija Gimbutas' *The Language of the Goddess* and *The Civilization of the Goddess* as well as James Mellaart's *Çatal Hüyük: A Neolithic Town in Anatolia.*

(not consecutive, not close together in time, but three). A ruckus, at the border of the village a screaming (shattering the silence of dawn) as she enters our village — as she takes one of our sheep.

The trails of her bloody footprints leave obvious evidence of her violation (the breaking of the understanding we have between us), leaving open questions as to what she will do next.

On the third morning, the people of the village refuse to leave their shelters. Within these shelters, accessible only through ladders leading to openings in the roofs, they stay (clustered-together rooms whose adjoining walls touch each other), pulling thick skins over roof openings, closing themselves within. Beneath thick membranes, they huddle in groups, children safe in the space between them.

After the dance inside the shrine, we walk through the empty fields to the edge of the village — to where the sheep are kept. I see the bloody footprints, the trail leading away from the village. I take them as a call to action.

— *We must have a community dance, outside, around the fire.*

— *They will be afraid to perform it.*

— *We cannot possibly fit them all into the shrine. We must convene and it must be all of us.*

— *Perhaps in daylight?*

— *At sun's set?*

— *I shall go to her. Tell them. Tell them I have gone to her.*

— *Do not go to her. Going to her now when she is so obviously hungry is only an invitation.*

— *Tell them. Tell them I have gone to her. They shall find solace in that.*

My right foot I place on her lead footstep, letting her print impress me. Left foot to left hind, hands becoming paws (tail extending up), I crawl away.

She is resting when I discover her (sniffing along after her, following her strong scent as I had so long ago in initiation when I came to know her), the kill stored in a tree above her.

I stand behind a row of trees and peer into the space that encompasses her. A sunlit opening; low green grasses chewed down by something ruminating. She stretches herself in the sun, wind blows through thick layers of her spotted yellow coat. Eyes closed to the warmth, half-smile upon her face, she rolls herself pleasurably upon the Earth, belly up; legs splayed open, back arcing—front and hind legs reaching. She stops. (Resting in stillness.) Her tail moves around her in slow, swinging gesture. She laps herself lovingly.

This quality of leopard I have long admired. Her ability to be satisfied, I have observed, tried to emulate (myself always leaning toward forward in longing). This ability to violate, however, this is something I have never paid respect to.

Back at the lair, she drops the kill onto the grass and (head up, body stretching back, wide mouth open) performs a loud, roaring meeeeow. Three small cubs, so small they have no spots, come running toward this sound. They pounce eagerly (paws and faces smeared bloody), eat ravenously at the sheep while she paces, circling around them and the kill; watching.

From high in a tree above them, I watch, my long body stretched out along a firm, moist, unbending branch as I rest, my long, spotted tail hanging within the leafy branches beneath me.

As a priestess in the shrine of the leopard, it is my job to help others process fear. Leopard power should be invoked only when needed; used most sparingly. It is reserved for times of intense stress and serious danger. To Her we bring the unimaginable, unacceptable.

Inside Her shrine, in front of the wall sculpture of one fearless leopard face to face with another fearless leopard, fire bending light on either side of them, we dance Her dance. Within our leopard masks (pointed ears, pant legs of spotted coats stretching to our knees, tails suspended down before arcing — in a half circle, up), we spiral, jump, dance.

Then, the sparring begins.

After her cubs have picked the bones clean, they move together deeper into the lair. The cubs' clumsy bodies lope along happily after her. Soon, they will grow into those large, ambling feet. Those coats (will grow perfect — black outlining deeper brown rosettes, proving their very leopardness), which hang in vulnerable sheets of slackness, shall someday enclose them exactly.

Within this large, grassy clearing she has marked off and claimed as her own through persistent roaming of the perimeters, they will live with her and her only for 24 moons.

(During the sparring, eye contact is maintained, deepening sight.)

They, all energy now, from the meal she has brought them, engage her in play; biting at her, pouncing on her, locking open jaws. She flips them, playfully bites back. This game lasts a long time until she, finally tiring of it, whacks them away roughly with her front paw. *"Enough!"*

They cuddle themselves near and upon her — curling themselves into slumber. She curves her body around them; in sleep, surrounds them.

There is the occasional villager who comes to us, requesting assistance. But mostly, it is we who go to them (having noticed their eyes widening before sinking deeper into themselves) — after the silence has enveloped them — offering a hand.

It is a rare person who understands it is fear which has overtaken them.

She will mother her cubs fiercely (feeding them, protecting

189

them, sparring with them), teaching them well how to be leopards. After 24 moons, she will release them into the wild, and they will be ready. (Then, and only then, will she accept a male into her lair.)

After a few days of my observing her, she sets out again on a hunt. She marks off a smaller territory within the lair for the cubs. There they shall stay, as she has directed them, playing with each other (loping and groping), awaiting her return.

I follow her out into the woodlands of these mountains, watching her independent hips swaying, her confident shoulder blades rising and falling lucidly within the sleek fur that protects them. She stops to drink from clear streams cutting furiously through steep, angling rocks; her body (leaning in toward the water) does not get wet.

These mountains, lush and dense, full of caves and underground waters, she has always lived in. In the tallest parts of them, she has always stayed. We have traveled to see her. It is we (making ourselves a question) who enter her domain, until now.

These recent transgressions startle.

I follow after her, carefully placing each paw (turned inward for silence), leaping over wide divides, stopping to pick thorns from between my paw pads with my short, straight, tearing teeth.

As the sparring progresses, two leopards face each other, circle on all fours, fall into each other's eyes — looking. The priestess challenges the participant to keep looking (to go in deeper, into it go) as around them, other priestesses and participants dance a circle, circling off a space.

Fear, like a predator's prey, gains more power when looked away from. Unlike the leopard, we want to look away. We do not want to see what it is we are about to kill.

In the tall, blowing grasses within which she hunts, I stand myself. Their tall tips brush coarse against the soft skin of my human, female breasts. I stand (still) on my hind legs; tail behind me, ears twitching with listening. I wait until I hear it. From behind, the landing thud of her most deadly pounce. Face forward, body tall, I wait for it (longingly yearn), the back of my neck tingling in anticipation.

She circles me, tail lowered, brushing over and over against my soft fur as she fast paces. Her body tense with waiting, eyes deep in the trance of focused hunting.

She stoops, listening ears twitch, first one then the other; grass grows high around her as she crouches (front legs forward and down, head up, shoulders back and ready, rear-end raised) — sudden, swift sprint into the meadow before us.

I recognize it when I hear it, the scream of instant death unexpected.

In the distance in front of me, she stands tall, turning herself toward me, a young deer hanging from her jaw. She looks at me; placing her eyes against mine, which lower to the challenge.

As a priestess, the one in control of the ritual, it is my job to pounce when eye contact is dropped. I jump, pouncing fiercely on the other leopard, scaring them even further. Above them I tower, myself holding them firmly against the floor that supports them. Into their eyes, which looked away, I push myself. (Look at it. Look at it. Take back your power.)

They must, they will, perform it again.

Into the lair I walk, wearing only my human nakedness. It does not take me long to find her leopard face peering through the tall grasses at me. The strong and seeking nose, the gray and silent eyes, I approach.

"Why do you take our sheep?"

"I am hungry," she casually responds, "and sometimes I get the taste for sheep."

"Those were our sheep," I say, feeling it surge up within me, my body wanting to tighten itself around it. "My people now have fear."

"Fear they shall have," she says, then more urgently. "Fear they must have."

Into her eyes, I look. Back into mine, they push, deeper challenging. I look back meeting the challenge, letting my anger surge in wave after wave until I fear it will overcome me (eyes want to weaken). Into that I push, entering the dark abyss of her black pupils, falling forward into it until it moves, turning over into unquestionable, human ferocity.

"Move out of my way," comes the voice of the hungry cat within me, "lest I devour you."

She lowers her eyes.

In the morning, I descend the mountain to my village. In a grassy clearing between the river and Her mountain of molten liquids, I see it.

In a circle stand our interlocking, connected buildings (full of deep, dug-out rooms and burning fires) around which wrap deeply plowed, dark fields — the work of human hands.

(We must move the sheep in closer.)

Out scattered in the fields, I see my cubs, so young they have not their spots (we must for a while pull more tightly together).

Closer within, we shall move things — ourselves — a smaller enclosure we must create, around which I shall circle (pacing, watching) and for as many moons as it takes, mark off safe space.

Part Six

Tending to the Many Layered
Membranes of Planet Earth

Chapter 24

The Multilayered, Multileveled Reality of Ensoulment

"We are held within countless containers of safety. The Earth, our mother, created a variety of systems to enclose us within layers of protection while remaining interactive with our local solar system. The atmosphere and magnetosphere are but two examples of systems created by the Earth that repel asteroids and other space debris, as well as harmful radiation, while allowing other beneficial matter and light in. Similarly, the heliosphere of the sun encloses and holds the solar system within a contained, protected space, while interacting with the galaxy as a whole and so on. Layer upon layer of membranes that are permeable, yet protective."[62]

When I set out to write this book, I certainly didn't think I was writing about the soul. I thought I was writing a book about the membranes. Only upon writing this book did I come to

---

[62] Dintino, *Notes from a Diviner in the Post Modern World*. 113.

understand that what Domenica is doing in the cave is tending to the multilayered, multileveled reality of "ensoulment" that "is somehow keeping it all alive." Most importantly, she is tending to the soul of the planet.

In Dagara cosmology, if you dream of someone naked, it is a "*siura* dream" and it means they are at risk of death. As stated earlier, the *siura* can be thought of as the membrane. The person in the dream is not just naked—the dream is all about naked. The dream continuously makes the point "naked, nude, unprotected, at risk." That's its only point. The dream is not sexual in any way—it's not about that. I only understood while writing this book that it means the person's soul is naked because their membrane (*siura*) is weakened. I write to figure things out. This was proving to be true once again. The push for us to work with the membranes is because of this: The souls of things are at risk.

All of life is alive and ensouled. And the Earth is as well. She has many membranes that surround and protect her interiority, her soul. By tending to and caring for her soul, we support and strengthen her membranes.

soul (n.1)

"A substantial entity believed to be that in each person which lives, feels, thinks and wills" [Century Dictionary]; Old English, *sawol:* "spiritual and emotional part of a person, animate existence; life, living being"; from Proto-Germanic *saiwalo* (source also of Old Saxon seola, Old Norse *sala,* Old Frisian *sele,* Middle Dutch *siele,* Dutch *ziel,* Old High German *seula,* German *seele,* Gothic *saiwala*) of uncertain origin."[63]

---

[63] *Online Etymology Dictionary,* https://www.etymonline.com/.

Earth is Alive and Has a Soul

"Viewed from the distance of the moon, the astonishing thing about the Earth, catching the breath, is that it is alive. The photographs show the dry, pounded surface of the moon in the foreground, dead as an old bone. Aloft, floating free beneath the moist, gleaming membrane of bright blue sky, is the rising Earth, the only exuberant things in this part of the cosmos. If you could look long enough, you would see the swirling of the great drifts of white cloud, covering and uncovering the half-hidden masses of land. If you had been looking a very long, geologic time, you could have seen the continents themselves in motion, drifting apart on their crustal plates, held aloft by the fire beneath. It has the organized, self-contained look of a live creature, full of information, marvelously skilled in handling the sun."[64]

Earth is an alive being, self-organizing and self-regenerating, with a type of consciousness we might call intelligence. We can think of her as one whole ecosystem having the same qualities of self-organization and self-regulation as ecosystems previously discussed in the village membrane chapter.

Earth holds and protects all the membranes of the village, ecosystems, humans, and animals within her own membranes and she, in turn, is nested within the cosmic membranes that surround and enclose her: her magnetosphere and the sun's magnetosphere moving out to the galactic membranes.

If Earth is alive, she is ensouled. Tending to the membranes of the Earth tends to her soul and tending to her soul tends to her membranes.

---

[64] Lewis Thomas. *The Lives of a Cell.* 144.

The Many Spheres or Membranes of Earth

Earth's most important relationships are with the sun and the moon. The sun enlivens the Earth. Shining its light on her, it allows the Earth to come alive. "Earth is a darkness that agreed to be enlivened by the light."[65] The most profound light-bringer to Earth is the sun. The sun is the fundamental source of energy for the planet. She needs this life-giving light and yet, she must protect herself from it as well. She protects herself from it with her many self-generated, self-created membranes. These include the intricately layered membranes of the lithosphere, atmosphere, stratosphere (ozone), hydrosphere, magnetosphere, and more.

To support these membranes, we support the Earth in her natural processes, which support and create the membranes. We have been failing in this task, allowing the Earth's natural membranes to become compromised and frayed, leaving all who live on Earth in a state of constant overexposure. In this neglect, we are failing to care for life itself.

Caring for life itself is the job of the medicine people. It's why the medicine exists: tender care for the precious interiors and the membranes that enclose them.

The spheres (membranes) of the Earth can be broken down into four categories:

* The lithosphere — the crust or mantle
* The hydrosphere — all the water on the Earth
* The biosphere — the life forms of Earth
* The atmosphere — which contains the troposphere, the stratosphere, the mesosphere, the thermosphere, the exosphere, and ionosphere, which contain the magnetosphere. The ozone layer occurs in the troposphere and the stratosphere.

---

[65] The wedeme in a Group Theme Divination.

The ozone layer was formed two billion years ago when blue-green algae were so successful at reproducing that they created an excess of oxygen in Earth's atmosphere, making it toxic for many other forms of life. This excess oxygen eventually combined with the sun's UV rays to create ozone molecules, which are effective at absorbing UV rays. The creation of this layer served to protect the Earth from the sun's UV rays as well as use up the excess oxygen. Functions and organic processes of the biosphere created this protective membrane. It arose organically from the interior experience.

"Most scientists today recognize that Earth's lithosphere, hydrosphere, atmosphere and biosphere are dynamic systems—self-organizing and inseparably interconnected."[66]

Consider for a moment all these membranes Earth created to protect herself and all life upon her from the sun and the outside environment.

---

[66] Sidney Liebes, et al. *A Walk Through Time: from Stardust to Us.* 24.

Chapter 25

Being a Medicine Worker on a Planet in Crisis

Fundamental Protocols for Diviners and Medicine People

The subject of tending to the Earth is one that can be extremely painful at this time. Many of us find ourselves in a state of despair over what has been happening to the planet and not knowing how to act. It is important to assert certain teachings here to help the medicine person who wants to stay engaged despite the annihilation and collapse of lifesystems that is currently occurring on our planet. We can be activists and engage in all kinds of ecological solutions from a science-based perspective. We can work toward legislation on the political level to offer much-needed protections. All of these activities are critically important. From the point of view of this book, we are engaging with the spiritual dimensions of this subject.

The medicine is to protect life. It is to nurture and help the membranes that protect and support lifesystems, but the damage to the Earth is so severe at this point, we may be beyond the tipping point as far as climate change goes. Because of this reality, many of our current efforts might feel futile. What can pouring hibiscus do to help with the climate crisis and extinction rates that are upon us?

First, we must admit that we do not have the solutions but we can listen and respond to what we hear no matter how subtle, painful, or upsetting. I do not have any definitives about what will happen with regard to this crisis nor would I ever be so arrogant as to think I did. But I am often told in divination that there is not a lot of time and we must get to work.

It is important as medicine workers to acknowledge that we do not see the whole picture from our human perspective. Therefore, it is ever essential for us to stay open and able to listen to messages from entities who do have a larger perspective than us.

Another point to understand is what is needed *now*, meaning the moment you are reading this book. Divination is a snapshot of a moment. A ritual I prescribe today may not be relevant for the Earth when you read this book. What is needed today may not be needed tomorrow, especially in times of crisis. The medicine is not a stagnant, set-in-place tool. It is ever-changing and adapting to situations that need healing and help. Since we need all hands on deck when it comes to the Earth crisis, I offer you this following instruction to help stay engaged with the active present you are alive in, whether or not you are a diviner.

Protocol for Divining

One of the main things we can do as medicine people is make offerings to the Earth, letting her know that we care, and perform rituals to support her in her own processes. We can also do rituals and make offerings to begin to offer some repair and remuneration for all the disregard and disrespect that has been afflicted on her by humans. Some examples of these are listed at the end of this chapter. But most importantly, we must be able to listen and ask what is needed without preconceptions. That is where divination comes in. The following are the basics of divining.

The Essentials of Divining Are Who, What, Where, Why, and When?

These are the questions to direct any inquiry we enter into. It is also helpful to return to them when we feel overwhelmed. Each medicine person is schooled in their own particular way to ask questions and receive answers. This is what I mean when I speak of divination and divining. If you have absolutely no training but still want to help, listen in your own way. There are also rituals and ways to participate listed in the second half of this chapter that do not require divination tools and skills. You could also take this question to a diviner, asking what you can do to help the Earth and her membranes and carry out the rituals prescribed to you. Or you could enroll yourself in training that gives you the tools you desire. The following is a basic guide for carrying out divination.

Who: When we are divining, we are entering into an inquiry. In this case, we are inquiring about the Earth, the planet we live on, and how to care for her membranes. This is the *who*.

What: We want to know if there is an issue that needs tending to and listen for what issues need attending to *today*. This is the *what* of divining. Once that is determined, the next question is always: Are offerings needed? If a yes is received[67], go down the list of common offerings in Chapter 11. Remember, the offerings that are needed (once we become familiar with their qualities and what they are usually called in for) provide insight into the feel, importance, and quality of the next category.

Why: Is there a ritual to go with it? What is our intention when

---

[67] If a no is received when we ask about offerings, it may be that nothing is needed at the time. We must respect that as well. But it could mean something else is needed that is not an offering, or that we are being asked to be still and come to a deeper understanding of the situation before we act. We can ask for a dream to help with this, or a message to come to us. We keep listening as listening is our primary job.

we make these offerings or carry out this ritual? Perhaps we are asking for healing, apologizing, sending love, strengthening the membranes or counteracting negative thought forms, or offering a cleansing or a clearing. This is the *why.*

When: When shall this happen? Immediately? The next full moon? A week from now?

Where: Most important: *Where* are the offerings to be made? The *where* indicates to us which entity we are calling in to carry out this work because it is not us. We are the intermediaries and facilitators. We want to remember this or we will become overwhelmed thinking *we* have to "save" and "cure" and "heal." We offer physical materials to help those we are calling upon to carry out the "saving" and the "curing" and the "healing." Keeping this in mind keeps us grounded and understanding our place in the arrangement of things. It helps us remember our own sphere of influence and stops us from taking on too much or doing too little. We have great influence as human medicine people on this planet. This is not to be undermined or underestimated but we must also know who we are working with and *who* to go to for *what* situation for the greatest effect.

Earth has many allies, as does every medicine worker. Calling on the right entity for the job is crucial. Surrender the work to them and remain in humility.

For issues of the magnitude of the Earth Crisis, some are more fitting than others. Here is a list of entities with their "job titles."

Hierarchy of Beings[68]

The following hierarchy of beings is one that has been shown to me through years of divination. Most of these entities are cross-

---

[68] For more detailed information on all these entities, see my book, *Notes from a Diviner in the Postmodern World.*

cultural but go by different names and identities in different cultures and belief systems. If you have an active practice, I am sure you will recognize where the entities you work with fit into this template. If you don't yet have an active practice, use the template as presented, allowing yourself to see correspondences that fit your worldview over time.

The word *hierarchy* can be difficult for those of us who yearn to live in cultures with decentralized centers of power and wish for less stratification, ranking, and inequality in our communities. I too dislike the idea of hierarchies when they mean power over, absolute authority, and status by race, gender, or resources. I use it here because it is relevant to the concept I wish to convey. By *hierarchy*, I mean sphere of influence, not greater or lesser.

Certain beings have a sphere of influence that is larger than others. This does not make them better or more important, they simply have different ranges of influence. Understanding this helps us determine who is the right entity for which job. As a human medicine person, I cannot singlehandedly take on the issues that Earth is facing. It's too big for my sphere of influence. The Earth has her own sovereignty and intelligence that has nothing to do with me, but I can call on those with more influence to help me help her, and I can listen to them as well, for I trust they have a bigger picture view than me.

The Hierarchy of Beings[69]

Cosmic Source Entities

Sphere of Influence: Entire Cosmos

Source: God, Goddess, the All, Uni, the One, Nyame, Great Spirit

The World Tree: Structure upholding cosmos and creating Time

Nyur*: The web of connectedness

Nyamping*: Ancient ones, gatekeepers of the ancestral fires, wise sages, saints

❋ ❋ ❋

 The Elemental Forces

Sphere of Influence: layer below Cosmic Source, intergalactic and galactic, solar system and planetary

Cosmic Justice: Thunderbird, lightning, storms, ocean, vulture, owl, Kali, Durga, Ma'at, archangels

Underworld Goddess: Berew*, inner earth being, dark goddess, horned god

Sun

Moon

❋ ❋ ❋

Beings from the Space Above

Sphere of Influence: sky, above Earth, galactic, solar system, planetary, stars

Saazumwin*: angels, light beings, star beings, stars.

❋ ❋ ❋

_____

[69] Words with stars are words I was taught or learned on my own as part of the Dagara Cosmology of Stick Divination.

Connecting and Filtering Entity
Sphere of Influence: interdimensional, thresholds and boundaries
Siura*/Sie*: membrane/soul, Ba/Ka

❋ ❋ ❋

Village Level
Sphere of Influence: Surface of Earth, villages, eco & life systems on Earth
Elements of Earth[70] -Medicine Wheel: Fire (ancestors), water, Earth, mountain/mineral, nature/wild
Humans

❋ ❋ ❋

Transdimensional Beings
Sphere of Influence: intercommunication between all entities and realms, inner Earth, surface of Earth, Humans
Elemental Beings: wedeme*, kontomble*, and various names from other traditions
Spirit Animals: archetypal and Earthly forms

For issues of the Earth crisis, the Elemental Forces (addressed in Chapter 26), beings from the space above, *Nyur*, wedeme/kontomble, and animal spirits listed above are most helpful. To follow is more detailed information about each of them and corresponding shrines if the reader wishes to create them.

---

[70] These five elements come from the Dagara cosmology.

Shrines for Entities to Help Care for the Earth Membranes

The Saazumwin

In the Dagara tradition, the *saazumwin* are the ones who stretch between the stars and the Earth. They have much love for and investment in the evolution of life on Earth. They are benevolent and can be called upon for working with the water, the stars, and general care for the Earth. I highly recommend working with these beings if you want to implement care for the Earth and her lifesystems. In other traditions, they are known as angels (not archangels), light beings, star beings. They can show up as white birds as well. By "working with them," I mean divining with them by using the protocol listed in the previous chapter.

If you wish to form a relationship with the saazumwin...

* Begin by making an offering of milk (any kind) to running water. In a stream or river, simply pour the milk (one cup) into the water, telling the *saazumwin* you are ready to begin a relationship with them for the greater good of the planet.
* Wait for a sign that your message has been received. This can come in a dream, by seeing a white bird, tall beings in white robes, light tunnels, or many other means. You will know when you receive a response.
* Water sources will always be the best places to work with the *saazumwin* and continuing to do so is a good idea, but you might want to create a shrine to them as well, for more focused and intensive work.

Theresa C. Dintino

A Shrine to the Saazumwin

For this shrine you will need:
* A medium or large clear glass bowl (so the light can get in)
* Rainwater

Installing and Activating the Shrine

* When you install this shrine, put an ash circle around the bowl. This shrine can be inside or outside but in a location that gets tended to frequently to make sure the water level stays consistent and it is not neglected. The water will become stale and dirty. You will need to clean it from time to time. When you clean it, keep a bit of the old water and add it back into the bowl with the new. The reason for this is that though it looks dirty to us, it has acquired medicinal properties worth keeping and these can be transferred in a "homeopathic" dose with the small amount of the older water.
* When you install the shrine, tap on the floor or Earth, calling on the *saazumwin,* telling them you are ready to open a deeper relationship with them and what your intentions are.
* Then offer one portion of hibiscus to activate the shrine. You may offer this onto the Earth or into the bowl of water, or set it beside the bowl of water.
* Offerings can be made into the water, onto the Earth beside it, or, if inside, set next to the bowl of water.

Common Offerings to Saazumwin

❋ Milk is a common offering for these entities.

❋ Crystals (put your intention into the crystal before offering by speaking the words into it softly)

❋ Gold and colloidal gold

❋ Flowers. The flowers and *saazumwin* are in deep connection. You can access one through interacting with the other. You can create star water by leaving water out under the stars and offer it to the flowers.

❋ Let yourself listen and tune in. A whole world will open up. You can also tune in to the *saazumwin* through the trees.

Nyur

Nyur is the entity in the Dagara tradition that oversees soul rootedness and connection through the webbed network of roots on the planet. *Nyur* calls us back into the web of connectedness and belonging. The wedeme say that the Earth has a "nyural network" that keeps us all always connected. If we stay tapped into the nyural network, we are always fed and nurtured, we feel we belong, know our life's purpose, and can listen to the overall health of Gaia.

Connect with *Nyur* and the nyural network through the trees, making offerings at their bases and connecting them up to one another.

Theresa C. Dintino

A Shrine to Nyur

* Place a small, conjoined root at the base of a tree.
* Tap on the Earth, calling on *Nyur* to come and inhabit this place as a shrine.
* Make offerings to *Nyur* onto this conjoined root.
* Common offerings: See "Top 5 Offerings" in Chapter 11.

A Note About Humans and Our Place

"I will say, from my own belief and experience, that imagination thrives on contact, on tangible connection. For humans to have a responsible relationship to the world, they must imagine their places in it. To have a place, to live and belong in a place, to live from a place without destroying it, we must imagine it. By imagination we see it illuminated by its own unique character and by our love for it. By imagination we recognize with sympathy the fellow members, human and nonhuman, with whom we share our place. By that local experience we see the need to grant a sort of preemptive sympathy to all the fellow members, the neighbors, with whom we share the world. As imagination enables sympathy, sympathy enables affection. And it is in affection that we find the possibility of a neighborly, kind, and conserving economy."[73]

Wendell Berry reminds us that "we can only save what we love and we can only love what we know."[74] Humans are indeed most

---

[73] "Wendell E. Berry." *National Endowment for the Humanities (NEH)*, https://www.neh.gov/about/awards/jefferson-lecture/wendell-e-berry-biography.
[74] Ibid.

210

effective when they put their energy into matters at the local level. Movements can grow out of these that call in more humans to work at their local level in the same way. Groups can have a larger effect. This is how we can be most effective — all working at our local level creating networks between us and strengthening the work in this way.

We now have technology that allows us to create online "villages" with people across the planet. Again, strengthening the network between these groups is essential. Humans can also accomplish a lot by calling upon entities and guides for the larger spheres of interest, as stated earlier.

Transdimensional Beings

The wedeme, kontombe, and all elemental beings have a lot to say about the health and well-being of the Earth. They live within her interior and in her waters. They are the primary ones to listen to for this job for they can facilitate conversation between all beings in the hierarchy. Their realities are deeply woven into the web of the Earth and they can network and tell us what is needed, where, when, and who to call in. They can see what needs to be reconnected that has been disconnected, and places that require care and restitution. Rely on the elemental beings for many issues about tending to Gaia and her lifesystems. To create a shrine to the elemental beings, see Chapter 17.

Animal Spirits

Animal spirits and guides that humans work with derive from overarching archetypal animal spirits that exist on a cosmic level. We can call on the archetypal forms of these allies to assist with matters of concern to the Earth. We can assume that the qualities found in the domestic or wild animals we are familiar with also exist at a higher and more powerful level with the archetype. We can work with the animal allies at all levels to assist with matters of the Earth.

Shrines to Animal Spirits

* A simple shrine to an animal spirit or guide is a figurine of the animal or animals or something from their being, such as antlers for a deer shrine, teeth of animals, jawbones, or fur.
* Make an offering of one portion of hibiscus onto it to activate the shrine.
* Common offerings: See Top 5 offerings in Chapter 11.

Chapter 26

Restoring the Dark/Light Balance to Heal Earth's Membranes

When we carried out the divination inquiring about the sun (mentioned in Chapter 4), the sun also gave us this message: "When things are out of balance, you don't have protection. When there is no justice, it's anyone's game."

The membrane work helps uphold balance. Organic justice arises out of things being put back into proper alignment. We can try to impose balance and justice onto our systems as they are, but as hard as we try, it won't work if things are off at the deeper levels. One of the huge imbalances currently plaguing this planet and human consciousness is our imbalanced relationship with darkness and light. For this, we must call upon the entity *Berew* from the elemental forces listed in Chapter 25 and her corresponding entities in other traditions: the inner Earth goddess, the dark goddesses, black Madonnas, dark mother, the horned god, and the dragons. These are the ones who bring the dreams. They are the keepers of the soul of Gaia.

What indeed is the soul of the planet? The interiority of Gaia?

The soul of the planet lives in darkness. Her interiority is black. Her core is iron. She generates heat at this center — a life-giving, life-nourishing heat different from sunlight.

When we are out of balance with the dark/light, so is the Earth. Earth needs us to sustain this balance to help herself sustain it as well. In this way, we help tend to her membrane (siura) as well as her soul. We can listen to her soul in the darkness and collaborate with it. We can rest and help her rest. We can synch with her, dream with her, and come into intimate relationship with her evolutionary processes.

Making Friends with Darkness to Connect with the Soul of Gaia

Humans have fallen in love with visible light. In this "enlightened" endeavor, we have blinded ourselves to the truth: the universe is 96% dark. It is not visible light that deceives, it is its interaction with the human eye and the magic of "sight" that co-conspire in this deception. Add the modern lifestyle of constant artificial light and the ruse is complete. Though our eyes may tell us otherwise, the darkness is with us always.

The current agreement in physics is that the universe is made up of 74% dark energy, 22% dark matter, and 4% luminous matter. If 96% of the universe is dark, then it might be worth our while to try to develop some kind of relationship with this grand presence once again.

Sight is a relatively new technology. It took almost four billion years of Earth's evolution for the eye to emerge. There were beings who felt the light of the sun, sensed it, and responded to it. Photosynthetic cells learned how to eat it but no one "saw" it. For all that time, there was no seeing.

According to fossil records, an ancestor of the trilobite appears with the first eye 540 million years ago. In a universe 16 billion years old, that is only in the last billion years. The first eye had multiple lenses, like a dragonfly, and was made out of calcite. Thanks to this prehistoric trilobite, humans and other creatures continue to use this technology to see.

When Earth turns away from the sun's light, we are met with the rest of the universe, which is mostly dark. This reality is not only there at night. It is there all the time. For half of our planet's rotation, we are bathed in the sun's light, which blinds us, literally, to the rest of the cosmos.

There is darkness all around us. Within us, it is dark. The roots of plants and trees are stretched into the dark soil. The center of the Earth is always dark. The bottom of the ocean is completely dark — so dark that some of the creatures, like viperfish, produce their own light in response to that darkness.

Before humans invented artificial light, we interacted with the darkness more often. When the sun set each day, we stopped working. We circled the fire outside together in the darkness, watching the stars, noticing phases of the moon, telling our village stories. The darkness mattered. It revealed things unseen in daylight.

Visible light is one part of the electromagnetic spectrum. Visible light is electromagnetic energy. There is also dark electromagnetism — electromagnetism that we cannot see with our eyes; electromagnetism that we forget is there simply because we cannot see it. We interact with these nonvisible waves of electromagnetism all the time. Dark waves of electromagnetism power our cell phones, our computers, and our microwaves. Don't be deceived by thinking that if you cannot see something or it is "dark" that you are not interacting with it.

Membrane work includes working with the darkness, with that which we cannot see or perceive with our ordinary senses — seeing beyond event horizons, moving through membranes into other realities and dimensions, permeating other worlds. There is so much more than what we can see with our eyes that also needs tending to. Tending to the inside of Gaia, her soul, is one of them.

From a scientific perspective, the Earth's interior is composed of four layers.

* The deepest layer is a solid iron ball whose temperature is between 9,000-13,000 degrees Fahrenheit.
* Next is the outer core, a shell of liquid iron 7,200-9,000 degrees Fahrenheit. This layer creates the Earth's magnetic field and is 1,400 miles thick.[75]

"All forms of life on the planet are in deep connection with the Earth's magnetic field, especially our reproductive, endocrine, central nervous system, and immune system. The planet has a pulse, a heartbeat so to speak; an Earthbeat. It is a very low-level electromagnetic rhythm that our bodies are synchronized with.

"The Earth's large magnetic field is generated from its iron and nickel core. This field acts as a sort of shield protecting Earth from oncoming loose dirt and debris in the cosmos. Without the magnetic field, biological life would not have formed on Earth.

"The human body possesses an ancient analog system of direct-current energy, which responds to the Earth's field. The electromagnetic pulsations of our brains match those of the Earth. These are very low-level, electromagnetic pulsations that our bodies sense and stay in rhythm with. As much as our bodies are tuned into the dark/light 24-hour circadian rhythm, they are also aligned to the daily electromagnetic rhythm. The analog system in our bodies receives messages from the electromagnetic fields it encounters."[76]

---

[75] Earth's Interior. *National Geographic,* https://www.nationalgeographic.com/science/earth/surface-of-the-earth/earths-interior/.
[76] Dintino, *Notes from a Diviner,* 103 and see Robert O. Becker, *The Body Electric* and *Cross Currents.*

"Our planet is an 'electromagnetic event' which creates a field called the magnetosphere. The magnetosphere, discovered in 1958 by Explorer 1, extends far beyond the atmosphere into the larger solar system. Earth's spinning molten core of iron and nickel is its 'electromagnetic event.' This powerful electric charge creates this magnetic field around the planet. We are contained and protected from galactic space by this magnetosphere created by Earth. It is the protective womb within which Earth holds us.

"We are not wildly unprotected beings on the surface of a vulnerable planet in the middle of cold, unfriendly space. We are cradled within this womb-like field. Earth's field interacts closely with the cycles of the sun and the moon. The electromagnetic field of the sun, the heliosphere, blows against Earth's magnetosphere, causing it to form a tail behind Earth, which trails into space.

"The pulsations of the sun's field affect Earth's magnetosphere. They are in relationship to each other, forming a web-like matrix of interwoven fields. The heliosphere is larger, and embraces the entire solar system."[77]

Woven together, these pulsing, vibrating fields, enclose us, hold us, surround us.

It is important to pause here and understand that the magnetosphere is created by the outer core of the center of the Earth. This inside space generates that outer membrane. Going along with the thesis of this book, the health of that interior space affects the health of the exterior membrane. This is an important understanding for us.

---

[77] Dintino, *Notes from a Diviner*, 136.

If we can support the interior of the Earth, her soul, we can help her maintain her membranes that are so vital to the health of the planet and all life upon it.

❋ Next is the mantle, 1,800 miles thick, which has two layers, the upper and lower mantle. Then there is the crust, the outermost layer, which is the layer upon which we live, containing rock, , and seabed.[78]

❋ The last layer is called the lithosphere. This is the rocky crust, mantle, "skin" or bones of the planet—the hard outer crust including mountains, caves, and fissures. There are also underwater mountains and caves. The lithosphere is also under the ocean. This layer, or membrane of Earth, is important to interact with.

Our forebears interacted with caves in a remarkable way. Some of our oldest artwork as humans is inside caves. Interacting with this level of the Earth is important. This level is closest to the interior of the Earth. Much of it is the interior of the Earth come to the surface. The Dagara belief teaches that the stones and rocks hold memories. At this level of working with Earth, we could consider memory being held here—Earth memory. It is interesting that very early humans left messages in caves as though they knew the stones would hold the memories for future generations. Going inside caves is like entering the inside body of the Earth. As we saw in the previous story set in Malta, humans went into the deep caverns of the Earth to dream and to connect with her darkness.

---

[78] "Earth's Interior." *National Geographic*
https://www.nationalgeographic.com/science/earth/surface-of-the-earth/earths-interior/.

"Imagine yourself in the center of the Earth, in a womb-like space, in total darkness. What sounds and feels like the steady beating of a drum is coming from this warm, dark core. The waves emanating from this drumbeat wash over you, and your being begins to beat in time with it. It is a primal beat, a pulse of waves keeping you alive. You are reminded of being within the body of your mother before you were born, and being in intimate connection with the rhythmic beating of her heart. This electromagnetic pulsation is your umbilical cord to the Earth.

"Our planet has a beat, an Earth beat; a very low-level electromagnetic rhythm that its lifesystems have evolved with and synchronized with. Studies have shown that being cut off from this pulse upsets the 'clocks'—the rhythms and biocycles a lifesystem uses to regulate itself—in plants, animals, and humans. Earth is an organism, a being, a system that has, through a process of creativity that took 4.5 billion years, made the space for every lifesystem on the planet to emerge, including the humans species. Evolution is a process of interacting, adapting, and aligning. The electromagnetic fields on Earth played a crucial part in the process of the evolution of life on Earth, and continue to inform it at all times."[79]

The molten outer core of the Earth plays a vital part in sustaining the temperature and supporting life on the planet, and was a key factor in Earth becoming a living planet. Planets without this molten, generative outer core do not go on to create and sustain life. This type of heat is qualitatively different than that generated from solar rays. This is the most interior, most holy center of the planet. Her generative core and outer core.

---

[79] Dintino, *Notes from a Diviner*, 134.

Communing with Darkness and Collective Dreaming As Ways to Care For the Soul of Gaia

"The world rests in the night. Trees, mountains, fields, and faces are released from the prison of shape and the burden of exposure. Each thing creeps back into its own nature within the shelter of the dark. Darkness is the ancient womb. Nighttime is womb-time. Our souls come out to play. The darkness absolves everything; the struggle for identity and impression falls away. We rest in the night."[80]

In the temples of Isis, dream incubation within one of the dark inner chambers was one of the initiation rites. It was believed that Isis would come to you in a dream, providing information, answers to questions, and divination. Temples of dreaming were prevalent among early Goddess-worshipping cultures where the darkness was honored as being equally important to the light, as we saw in our previous story set in Malta. The Goddess, associated with the moon and lunar consciousness, held you within the darkness, which was a safe place not to be feared.

Honoring darkness seems to go hand in hand with recognition and respect for the Goddess, which translates into overall value for women and the female mysteries at the cultural, political, and socio-economic levels. As stated in Chapter 13, on the islands of Malta (circa 4000 BCE) where great colossal statues of the Goddess still stand, is the underground hypogeum. In this deep, subterranean temple dug out by antler picks was found the famous *Dreaming Goddess:* a large woman asleep or dreaming on a small boat-like structure. She wears typical priestess attire, breasts exposed, and a bell-shaped skirt.

Isis was also associated with ships and boats. There was a

---

[80] John O'Donohue. *Anam Cara: A Book of Celtic Wisdom.* 2.

spring festival in which she was placed in a boat and libations were thrown to the sea, washing the Soul of the Earth, this soft, vulnerable interior getting that kind of care.

In Minoan Crete, where the Snake Goddess ruled supreme (6000-1500 BCE), the temples had rooms that archaeologists labeled "pillar-crypts"—deep, sunken rooms, completely dark, with one pillar running up the center—used for ritual and initiatory purposes. A place to interact with the darkness, the soul of ourselves, and the planet.

I believe that humans entered the caves to commune with the soul of the planet. There they formed a deep relationship with the planet and were guided in ways to live. It's time to do that again. We can enter virtual caves now and do the same.

The Importance of Sleep and Dreaming

Let us retreat to the cave of dreams. Dreams are integrations—time for integration on all the dimensional levels. Sleep is time for deep rest but most importantly, dreams. In sleep and dreaming, our bone marrow is replenished. There is re-infusion. Digestion. Integration. Sleep helps T cells fight disease.

In a recent shamanic journey, I approached a tree with humility and bowed before it. A door opened to a cave-like space within it. I lay down in the fetal position in golden light and dreamt. I felt a deep reweaving inside my bones, the marrow of my bones—a healing, a boost, a stem-cell rejuvenation through dreaming. In dreaming, there is a dark feeding, an inner knitting.

Dreaming is a deeply healing and transformative space we humans are no longer making use of. All current healing modalities operate in "waking" time.

In his book *Why We Sleep*, Matthew Walker, PhD, states that the increase in dreaming and REM sleep in which we do most of our active dreaming contributed to homo sapiens developing sociocultural complexity and cognitive intelligence.

"The second evolutionary contribution that the REM-sleep dreaming state fuels is creativity. NREM sleep helps transfer and make safe newly learned information into long-term storage sites of the brain. But it is REM sleep that takes these freshly minted memories and begins colliding them with the entire back catalog of your life's autobiography. These mnemonic collisions during REM sleep spark new creative insights as novel links are forged between unrelated pieces of information. Sleep cycle by sleep cycle, REM sleep helps construct vast associative networks of information within the brain. REM sleep can even take a step back, so to speak, and divine overarching insights and gist: something akin to general knowledge—that is, what a collection of information means as a whole, not just an inert back catalogue of facts. We can awake the next morning with new solutions to previously intractable problems or even be infused with radically new and original ideas."[81]

If dreaming is an evolutionary tool, is it one we can use to consciously engage with the planet and co-evolve with her? The answer is yes.

The Earth needs our dreaming. Our brains fall into a rhythm during dreaming that feeds the Earth. Humans used to dream collectively. The animals would co-dream with us, especially dogs. During the dreaming phase, the community slept in a circle. This form acted as a membrane for those that existed within the community and protected the dreamers.

I was given this image of collective dreaming in divination, an image that remains with me: a group of humans in a cave, wearing

---

[81] Matthew Walker. *Why We Sleep: The New Science of Sleep and Dreams.* 74-75.

white, sleeping in a circle together in the company of dogs. The dogs are also dreaming. I watch their astral bodies as they travel, yet the physical bodies stay as a circle. The circle of dreamers is surrounded by large, otherworldly birds; guardians of the dreams and the dreamers.

For me, to even return to a place where we believe there are beings in the universe that guard our dreams is transformative.

When medicine groups start to work collectively, they begin to dream collectively. The dreams are seen to belong to everyone in the community and are interpreted in this way. Information comes through to the whole through individual dreamers. The dreams are guarded and protected, valued and listened to.

As medicine people, we can re-learn how to dream with this planet, collaborate with her, be co-creators with her, and remember that we are in relationship with Earth. At this time, it is more essential than ever to focus on listening to her soul, her dark interior. If we can support her soul, her holy of holies, perhaps this can help her repair the membranes, which she is in control of. The Soul of the Earth can speak to us in this way and we can listen together.

A Shrine to the Soul of Gaia

* Make an offering of water onto the Earth, asking her to guide you to what she would like the shrine to her soul to look like. Begin to listen for it.
* One suggestion is a meteorite or a large dark stone. Obsidian or tektite can work as well.
* If you keep the shrine inside, put it on a plate so you can make offerings onto it.
* Once you make it, please pour one portion of 8oz of hibiscus

on it to activate it. If you have never done an offering of hibiscus, know that this is a substitute for a blood offering. Acquire some dry hibiscus leaves (about 2 tablespoons) and steep them in 8oz of water. You can also use a teabag. As you make this offering of hibiscus onto the shrine, speak to the inner Earth, telling her you wish to co-dream with her to see what is needed at this time on the planet to help support her lifesystems and processes.

Ritual

Co-dreaming with the Soul of Gaia

You may do this actively, in a group or alone.

* First, create the shrine to the soul of the planet (listed previously).
* Second, do the guided visualization, *Journey to the Soul of Gaia* (in the next chapter).
* Now, move into active dreaming with the Earth. Dedicate 10 days for this intentional dreaming in which you are not stressed and can be sure to have at least three nights of eight hours of sleep.
* Make an offering onto the shrine to the soul of Gaia before you enter into this phase, letting her know you are moving into conscious collaboration through dreams with her. Tell her what you wish to learn or invite her to share what she feels you need to learn.
* In your journal, record dreams and the experiences of your journey and this active dreaming time.
* If in a group, make time at the end of the 10 days of active

dreaming to share your experiences.

❋ I recommend not talking during the active phase of dreaming as this could interfere with the process.

❋ Once you share and collect your data, you may wish to go back into active dreaming to ask for refinement of the messages coming through.

❋ You may wish to divine on the material coming through.

❋ Enter into this as a time to commune deeply with the soul of the planet and listen deeply.

Chapter 27

Journey to the Soul of Gaia

Y ou may access the free recorded version of this visualization on the Strega Tree website, stregatree.com under the *Guided Meditation Journeys* tab. Below is a transcript of the recording for those who need it.

This is a guided visualization and meditation to commune with the soul of the planet. Please find a comfortable place to sit or recline. You may want to have a notebook near you to take notes after. If you are unfamiliar with this type of journey, the instructions are simple: Follow the prompts as much as you feel comfortable but if at any time you feel yourself being pulled into another direction or experience in the shamanic realms, go with it. Don't stop yourself because of the instructions or prompts being given. Allow your subconscious and spirit to take you where they want you to go, even if it is different than what is being suggested, and especially if it is different than what you expected. Everything that comes to you in the journey—images, information, words, knowing—is what wants to be there. Often messages will only become clear later. Allow your imagination and right brain to take over. Refrain from judging yourself or what you are seeing. Relax and let the experience unfold.

Welcome to the Journey to the Soul of Gaia

In case anyone is unfamiliar with the term, "Gaia" is the name the ancient Greeks bestowed upon the Earth and the Earth goddess. We will call her Gaia often throughout this journey.

Take some time to set the intention to listen deeply to what Gaia wants to say to you.

Now, breathe in a deep, cleansing breath, filling your lungs. Exhale completely. Inhale again and feel the air swirling around your heart as it enters your body. Exhale, releasing all of the stress and tension you might be holding.

You may find that there is still something distracting your relaxation. It is safe to set this aside for the duration of the journey, knowing you can pick it up again at another time when you are ready.

Allow yourself to notice a golden, glowing light illuminating the crown of your head. As the light moves down the body, you feel yourself relax deeply. The light washes over your forehead, touches on your cheeks, and rolls down your chin to your neck, bringing deep relaxation. The golden light reaches your shoulders, your chest, and back. As it moves through your belly area you may sigh a deep exhale of release. The golden light washes over your hips, relaxes your thighs, and continues to flow down your legs until it reaches your feet and rolls off of your toes. You have entered an even deeper place of calm.

You are ready to begin the journey. Take a few moments to notice any guides or helpers that have arrived or invite in any you wish to have support you.

You now find yourself in a forest, thick with fir trees and rich with moisture. There is a narrow footpath surrounded by a golden glow pulsing before you. You begin to walk down this path. You walk until you see a small clearing and blue sky up ahead. You continue walking until you come to the edge of a body of water. A small boat made out of tree bark waits for you. The gentle waves lap the shore and move the boat slightly. You know that you are to get into this boat but you are not sure where you are going.

Now a guide emerges out of the forest. This is the guide who will row the boat and escort you on this journey. The guide may be part animal or a hooded being. This is the psychopomp who will escort you and bring you back.

Acknowledge this guide and thank them. This is your guide for this specific journey. This guide waits for those who wish to make this journey.

You now enter the boat, sitting on the small seat prepared for you. The guide gets in and begins to row.

You travel a long time in this boat, over many waters. Waters blue and green, green-brown, blue blues, and at night, endless black. The waters slap a slow rhythm against the boat's edges. *Slap...slap...slap...* You lie within its bark-covered roundness, listening. *Slap...slap...slap...* You and the boat rock together upon the waves.

In the dark, the moon is above you, shining its light down into the water and making a path of beauty.

Day breaks and you see islands rising in curving shadows of hills from the waters that everywhere surround them. Enormous stone temples stand tall upon them.

On shore, a priestess greets you. Her exposed breasts curve freely over a bell-shaped skirt, which sways below her knees. You notice a necklace of stones hung between tiny, delicate shells.

The priestess leads you into the hypogeum, the large group of moon-shaped chambers dug into Gaia's depths. You follow the bowl of fire she holds in her hands, descending a ramp deeper and deeper into her womb tomb. You become aware of a presence—a deep, dark energy; the flow of moisture and inner welling. The deeper you descend, the stronger it becomes. You continue to walk through many interconnecting, rounded chambers. Many of the chambers are at different levels, connected by steep wooden ramps. The atmosphere is cool but thick with dampness that envelops the body in a blanket of sticky dew. The bowl of burning light makes uneven flashes upon the glistening stone walls surrounding you.

The priestess leads you into a large oval hall with a high, vaulted ceiling. The ceiling is painted with a red, curling pattern. Many people are lying on mats on the floor. She motions to an un-occupied mat with folded blankets beside it. You sit on the mat. The far end of the room has a carved lintel design creating three mock doorways reminiscent of the temple above.

Are these only false passageways or something more? The priestess walks away, taking her light with her. In the blackness, you unfold your blanket and pull it over yourself. Reclining, you silently greet the inner Earth goddess, the soul of the planet. "I am here. I am listening. I care deeply about you. Speak to me. Return to me."

There are memories within these rocks. Figures begin to move upon the walls. The walls begin to pulse with swirling motions moving with the energy that is present in a flowing, lucid dance.

Only human work can transform this pain.
Gather her many pieces
Make her whole
Free the bird of your soul
Transform shadows into light

(Take at least 10 minutes to be in silence here.)
It is time to return now. Ready yourself to leave this place. Bid

farewell to the inner Earth goddess, the soul of the planet, for now.

A priestess approaches you with a bowl of light. You follow her slowly up out of the chamber. You reach the top of the temple and emerge into the daylight. It is early morning, so the sky is overcast and the light is not yet bright. Your psychopomp is there waiting for you.

They lead you to the water and you again sit inside the small bark boat. You travel back over water until you land on shore, where you bid the psychopomp farewell. You return to the forest and follow the path back to your home. You are now home. Become aware of the room you are in, of your body, which is here waiting for you.

Take a few long, deep breaths here.

As you begin to return to waking consciousness, slowly begin to move parts of your body and stretch. Take a few more deep breaths as you acclimate to the room around you and remember where you are.

Take a moment to express gratitude to the healing temples, the psychopomp, and the inner Earth. Collect the main message into one feeling or thought.

Close your eyes and give yourself a hug, then offer it to the Earth as well.

Take a few more breaths.

Your Journey to the Soul of Gaia is now over.

Chapter 28

Story

Notes on the Setting

Newgrange is an ancient temple located 2.8 miles north of Dublin, Ireland, dedicated to the sun of the midwinter solstice. It dates to 3200 BCE and is part of a larger complex of megalithic structures in the Boyne River Valley aligned to certain celestial events such as lunar movements and seasonal shifts. These structures precede the pyramids by 500 years and Stonehenge by 1,000. Newgrange is an earthen mound built-up over a stone structure with a corbelled roof design so sturdy that to this day, it has never leaked. It has a narrow, tunnel-like passage that opens to an inner chamber with three rooms surrounding a central one. At the time Newgrange was active, it was covered with quartz crystal.

What is remarkable about Newgrange is an opening called a "roofbox" in the front of the building that perfectly captures the light of the midwinter solstice sunrise, directs it down the passage, and into the central chamber which, when illuminated, reveals itself to be covered with images of the spiral and triple spiral.

Indeed, it has often been called a *womb tomb*. With its vagina-like entry to the uterine-shaped chamber, it quite mimics a return to the womb. In this ancient community at the midwinter solstice, you could actually walk back into the womb and receive the life-giving power and nurturance of the solstice light on these three spirals. You could participate in the creative process of the universe: birthing light from the darkness.

Yes, Virginia, There is a Newgrange

Virginia Woolf
London, 1941

Because we forgot how to console ourselves—because we forgot our connection to the Earth, to the sky, to the smallest cell within us, the most encompassing black hole surrounding us—because of this, we know despair.

Once, we walked to Newgrange. Once we knew, the snow crunching for miles beneath our feet, we knew how important it is to remember—to remind ourselves, to experience rebirth and so, believe again.

I laughed when I wrote this. I, who had only just decided to walk into the river. I who was so cold, so cold—so alone—that to me, the water felt warm.

County Meath, Ireland
2400 BCE

It is cold and there is nothing to do. Imagine! Nothing to do? We have stored all our food, stacked all our wood, set ourselves up for the darkness. All there is to do is wait for the snow to become so deep that we cannot think of moving about. The days are becoming shorter and shorter. "The sun is leaving us," I say.

"To Newgrange," you say, speaking with light in your eyes of our place of pilgrimage at each solstice of winter—the place we all hope to journey to, hope to complete our work in time to take days to walk to, to be reborn within Her womb, to be reborn through the darkness into the light. Each solstice of winter, those in the village who are healthy and willing journey to Newgrange.

"I went every year with my mother," I say. "My mother."

"Your mother," you smile.

I love you so.

The work in our newly-formed home has gone so well. We are quite pleased with ourselves. You say I have big feet.

"Big feet are good," I say.

"Yes. We will travel quickly."

"Have you ever seen it?" I ask.

"No. Always a date late."

"So with me," I say. "We'll leave early for plenty of time."

"We'll travel alone, you and I, not to be held back by the group," you suggest.

"But the group—the group is safer," I respond.

"No, no. Don't want to miss the solstice again," you insist.

I close the door to our shelter and box it in tightly with twigs and branches. When we return, it will be difficult to find at first, with the snow—the winter—concealing it. But inside will be dry; ready for the time within.

The snow arcs and crests on the hills around us. The wind has blown it smooth and the sun reflects off its vast, shiny surface. Twinkling. Glimmering. Shimmering. In our darkest season, so much brightness, so much whiteness, surrounds us.

The snow is so thick, in some places the paths are blown over, the snowdrifts covering footprints. Our feet sink deep to the knee for long distances, our legs lifting, lifting, heavy, hurting, only to meet our own knee-deep prints again—only to realize we have circled back and around.

London, 1941

The war, this most awful Second World War, was raging. I was raging. I know I was about to fall apart. I knew I needed to let myself fall apart—the layer upon layer of affectation. In order to rebuild myself, I needed to let the glued-together pieces finally expand; burst open. The anger. I needed to go beneath the anger; under. There was something down there, black and shining. I had only begun to glimpse it. But I could not bear the look on all of your faces. Your worry. Your disappointment. I could not take one more pill.

You see, I wanted to feel it. I *wanted* to know it, as difficult as it would have been, exhausting. To *experience* it was the solution—the key to it all.

While the biggest part of me was being pulled in like a magnet, I fought to keep myself from dropping deeper and deeper for you. The resistance was killing me. All my being was grappling and grappling. My mind was losing ground. I was losing ground. Then, I realized, there is another way to get at it—to free this thing black and shining, rotating, at my core.

County Meath, 2400 BCE

"Hurry. Hurry."

You rush me. I have never been a fast walker. It was always I who held my mother back. I want to keep up. I move. I push forward. I keep thinking, *Big feet. Big feet.* You are big. Your footsteps are twice as long as mine. I point that out to you. "Look," I say, "I must move my feet two times as much as you. Only to keep up, I must do double the work. Please, slow down. I am growing tired."

London, 1941

"Why are you writing such things?" you, Leonard, asked.

The sight of my own anger on the page—how it chilled me. I asked myself: How could anyone react to the things I was seeing, reading about, hearing about with anything but anger? I know, I know. Ultimately, it makes no difference to my feelings whether or not they are ladylike. I cannot help but feel it. How is it that you do not feel it?

You told me, with your eyes and looks and sideways glances. You said to me, "Everyone already has enough to worry about. Pull yourself together, Virginia." But it is not the self that will not pull together. It is the selves; it is these that seem to want to split and scatter. Of course, I could not tell you that.

County Meath, 2400 BCE

My mother went slow for me. I was always looking around, feeling everything. After a few days, she would drop her frustration and tell the group to go on ahead of us. A resigned sigh, with the words, "Should have left earlier. We'll miss it again." Then—hands on hips, looking forward—watching our group of people trudge in a straight line ahead of us, "The solstice will come whether we're there or not. If only to *see* it."

I stood beside her, looking where she looked, toward the hills of frozen white Earth, curving. I listened to the leafless trees around us. I could hear them reaching, breathing, in spite of the cold. Swaying. I listened to their tall, exposed bodies creaking—loud popping—as though expanding, ready to burst open, break apart—yet they do not. They remain whole.

The sun was dipping orange behind one of those hills, spreading itself in pinks and yellows upon the snow.

"I see it," I said. "I see the solstice, Mother. It is always around us; in the light that flickers off the snow in pinks and yellows; in the sun, though distant, ever present. I see it, Mother. I see the solstice. It is within us."

"Yes," she answered. "Because you see, you walk slowly. Perhaps next year, I shall come alone."

She never did. We continued to go, every year, together. She

stopped pushing and, I think, even stopped wishing. The journey —
the journey became the thing.

But you, your will is so strong and I, for some reason, cannot
fight you. I can feel how it is killing me — this rushing, this doing
things only for the joy of having them done. *I am missing out on what
feeds me.* The shadows on the morning ice, the clouds drifting
slowly by, the smoke of an early fire. I look at the piles of wood and
think, *I don't remember stacking them. I only remember how late we
worked — how fast. I do not remember the precise feel of the actual stacking:
the feel of the wood beneath my axe, the sound of the blade on living wood,
the smell of freshly cut tree spirit, released, released, released by the force
of the axe.*

The feeling of you loving me, I remember — the pride in your
eyes when we accomplish, the excitement in your voice at the
thought of doing more. It is the love — the you loving me — that I am
feeling now. It is this I am savoring.

London, 1941

In the book, I wrote, "Life for both sexes — and I looked at them,
shouldering their way along the pavement — is arduous, difficult, a
perpetual struggle. It calls for gigantic courage and strength. More
than anything, perhaps, creatures of illusions as we are, it calls for
confidence in oneself. Without self-confidence, we are babes in the
cradle. And how can we generate this imponderable quality? By
thinking that other people are inferior to oneself... Women have
served all these centuries as looking-glasses, possessing the magic
and delicious power of reflecting the figure of man at twice its natural size."[82]

You scoffed when you read this but it was the scoff of recognition. Recognition, I know now, is not enough. Even in recognition

---

[82] Virginia Woolf. *A Room of One's Own.* 35.

will some—most—close their eyes to others; the inflated image in the looking glass too important to let go of.

County Meath, 2400 BCE

Still, my mother and I were happy when we arrived. When, from a distance, we could finally see the circle of stones, we would smile, the joy stretching between our cold, separate bodies, and walk faster. The shared vision of light flickering off the domed, quartz surface unified us—bringing the rhythm of our feet into unison.

Upon arriving, we would circle around it slowly, observe the carvings and deep incisions on the large stones of the outer wall, and lay our hands upon them, our fingers fondling the thick grooves of moving spirals and spinning wheels. Within Her sacred triangle, we planted our prayer of hope for the sun's return.

Mother peered longingly between the two boulders pushed together in front of and closing the entrance—the ones that only a few days earlier had opened to receive solstice.

"I'm sorry, Mother."

"No, no. It's all right," she said. "I've grown to like it this way. The mystery. Come." Her hand extended out toward mine. "We circle back now, to home."

We both know my feet are not big. You push me even so.

I see you, I see you betting on me, calculating with your head. Your head saying, *She can take more. I can push her further.*

I am already dying and I know it. It is this—the spark of fire before death—that you see in me and mistake for strength.

I do not correct you.

London, 1941

"Let me add a dream, for it may refer to the incident of the looking glass. I dreamt that I was looking in a glass when a horrible face—the face of an animal—suddenly showed over my shoulder. I cannot be sure if this was a dream or if it happened. Was I looking in the glass one day when something in the background moved and seemed to me alive? I cannot be sure. But I have always remembered the other face in the glass, whether it was a dream or a fact, and that it frightened me."[83]

And now, I feel almost certain. It seems more than evidently clear that it is *this*—this precise fear, the fear of the animal in the looking glass—it is this which is generating all the hate, the destruction; it is this which is tearing our world apart—scattering our *selves*.

County Meath, 2400 BCE

"What have I done?" you say when it is already too late. "What, oh what?" Your scream echoes off the cold around us.

You carry me the rest of the way. I understand it then, watching you force your tired body to carry all that extra weight. It is yourself you have been loving in me—your own weak self you are pushing. It has nothing to do with me. I could have been anyone. You get me to Newgrange on time for the solstice. What my mother never saw—what she gave up because she could see me—you let me see.

I am scared until we get there. Frightened. I never liked the darkness and being so close to it.

You walk quickly toward the opening, right past the entryway.

"Slow down. Slow down," I say, pointing to that beautifully carved stone that stands in front of, almost in the way of, the entrance—the rock my mother and I prayed over every year. You take me back. You hold me before its face full of smiling, triple spirals. I breathe in the wide, arcing wings of creation expanding on the surface before me. Even now, I can feel your impatience. After all, we

---

[83] Virginia Woolf. *Moments of Being*. 69.

have come for the inner chamber. We are not there yet.

"Perhaps the solstice, seeing the solstice, will make you better," you say.

"I have seen the solstice," I say. "It is always around us. This is only a symbol. It is not magic. Symbols are for people like you, to remind you of what you forgot."

You look at me. I think, for a moment, you almost see me.

London, 1941

Will the women of the future know different? Will they finally dig down and claim that thing, black and shining — their essence, their essential power? Will they recognize the other face in the mirror as their own? It will be difficult to dig out from under all those centuries of rage.

County Meath, 2400 BCE

We move down the tunnel together. You burrow me through except for the places where I have to crawl. The last of my energy is spent slithering myself between two tight, squeezing walls of stone; crawling back in. The chamber is as I remember it, as my fingers had memorized it in the grooves engraved on the stone out front every year — three round, bulging, interconnected rooms — the triple spiral — regenerating. We had felt it every year, my mother and I, the spirals traced longingly by our fingers creating the deep movement of spirals within. It is there, out front — it has always been there — displayed for all to see.

The solstice is near. The light of the lamps is extinguished. We sit in the darkness with the others, waiting.

London, 1941

I know. I am not deluding myself. I know there will come a time when I will have to do this work, the work I am turning my back on this time. I will return, someday, to do it. Here's hoping for an easier place.

County Meath, 2400 BCE

The light comes into the chamber with startling brightness. The solstice floods the interior around us with a whiteness, exposing a stone room covered with engravings we could not, in the darkness, perceive.

You grab my arm. You can see it. The pain is overwhelming you.

"It's all right," I say. "I can see darkness only the other side of light. Light only possible because of darkness. Nothing separate. Look at the ceiling above us. See these circles, separate but one? I will go but I will not be gone. The two that you see, two parts of that same one."

You look at me. I am you. I will go now. You hear me. You hear me say it with your eyes.

The spirals above take me in. I feel myself swirling, whirling, whooshing, swooshing. Weight leaves me. I am light. I am darkness. I am always…

Part Seven

The Cosmic Membranes

The Golden Womb

She searched the sky
Without a sigh
Without a whim
About what she was to win.
What were these images?
What did they mean?
But most of all she wondered:
"Why has she chosen me?"

She searched all night
Until she realized:
She did not need to search the sky;
She simply needed to open her eyes.
She gasped, for there it was
The beauty more than heaven above.
It spun in circles,
A golden womb.
With wings of a blood-red shade
She had not expected a message so soon.

"You have been chosen
To carry on
My unfinished business
Come, chosen one."
She followed blindly down
One of those blood-red tubes
And as she to an opening came
A golden light was upon her lain.
"Now go," said the voice,
"You have no choice."

So she wandered
Unknowingly through that place
It seemed in an alternate
Time and space.
And answers then flooded her mind
Solutions the world was yet to find.
And stumbling desperately for a way out
Her head did find the birth canal.
And when again she opened her eyes
She slowly began to realize
That out of that golden womb's girth
She had experienced a second birth.

And all the solutions fresh in her head
Only thought she, "I must be dead."
But then another answer said,
"When we are born we hold all the answers.
We forget them by the time we learn
To talk, to walk.
We are all former philosophers.
If only some could be reborn
At an older age: a different morn.
Then all the answers we would
Find.
If only we would search our
Minds."

She smiled now
Because she knew
She now
Had all the answers and solutions
If only she could learn to use them.

And flying high
In the air
Solutions flowing through her hair
She flew around the world three times
Raining down solutions in golden clouds
And uttered a phrase aloud:
"The golden womb must be found."
And then she quietly closed her
Eyes
And flew to Crete
Where she died.

—Mia Szarvas[84]
Age 13
2/17/06

---

[84] Mia is my daughter and she wrote this poem on an international flight
after I told her a bit about my meetings in the cave with Domenica.

Chapter 29

Working with the Patterns on the Holographic Skins of the Cosmos

Original Patterns

"Don Juan contended that our world, which we believe to be unique and absolute, is only one in a cluster of consecutive worlds, arranged like the layers of an onion. He asserted that even though we have been energetically conditioned to perceive solely our world, we still have the capability of entering into those other realms, which are as real, unique, absolute, and engulfing as our own world is."[85]

The wedeme often speak about "original patterns." When they refer to this, they mean the pattern something or someone started with that contains the original intent behind its

---

[85] Carlos Castaneda. *The Art of Dreaming.* viii.

manifestation in 3D reality. These etheric intentions move through the outer dimensions, then come into full physical manifestation in the 3D. This is a complicated concept that I will try to explain in more detail.

Original patterns exist for everything: human beings, ideals, collective agreements, values, belief systems as well as for all of biological life. Water has an original pattern as well as the planet as a whole. The grasses, the organs of our bodies, the mountains, and the minerals all have an original pattern that holds their original intention and purpose. It goes on and on. When patterns get muddled, confused, or overwritten, it is time to return to the original pattern for a reset.

Returning to patterns of origin is an important practice. It is worthwhile to examine any artificial imprinting we may have adopted that is not our true pattern. Cultural conditioning and life experience can interfere with our patterns of origin. Original patterns of water and other elements on Earth can be changed by events that take place here. However, examining beliefs is not enough. Re-patterning is the work of the 6th dimension. When I speak of the 6th dimension, I am working within the template of the Nine Dimensions of the World Tree as articulated by Barbara Hand Clow in her book, *Alchemy of Nine Dimensions* and detailed in the front matter of this book.

The Dimensional Membranes

What is a dimension? I conceptualize dimensions as different layers of reality that exist simultaneously but are vibrating at different frequencies. Because of this, they are not perceived by our standard forms of perception. Like Don Juan in the quote at the beginning of this chapter, I often use the illustration of concentric circles (layers of an onion) to describe them but only to offer a conceptual feel. Truly, the dimensions are overlaid, intertwined, and deeply conjoined, as is Time. Everything is right here, right now, but for our human brains to comprehend we need to reduce and separate.

Each dimension has a membrane separating it and enfolding it within the other dimensions. The skins or membranes are what must be traversed to cross into the other-dimensional reality. Again, as with all other membranes in our model, the "within" of the dimension—the soul—generates the membrane. The membrane is an "intelligent barrier" that is alive and able to discern. This is true for the cosmic membranes as well. This is why when humans "travel" through the dimensions they often meet guardian-like beings or encounter prohibitions (you need a key or password or magical phrases to unlock the portal) to passage or entrance. When this happens, the human travelers are encountering the membrane itself which, with its intelligence, discernment, and filtering ability, will allow them access or not, determine readiness or not. This is often based on how they respond when they meet the membrane or barrier. These guardians will appear and speak to us in language and images we can understand. Some may be particular to the membrane itself generated by the contents of the "within" and who "lives there" or set there by those who tend to these particular membranes.

Time is also a part of dimensional differences. We perceive other dimensions and other realities by coming into sympathetic vibration or resonance with the frequency of the vibratory field encasing them. Time is created and perceived by frequency. A different dimension having a different frequency could be operating on a different timescale. That is how they can be right here, right now, but beyond our own perceptive capabilities. It is also why drums or repetitive sounds are often used to open portals to access other dimensions.

We always exist in different dimensions. It is where we place our perception that we experience. With practice, one can become skilled in crossing the dimensional lenses or membranes and per-ceive other levels of reality, which are other dimensions.

In Hand Clow's *Alchemy of Nine Dimensions*, the 6th dimension is the realm of geometric forms and patterns. Patterns and geomet-ric forms allow light and sound from the outer dimensions to man-ifest into concrete, physical matter in the 3D. The light from the 9D and beyond comes through the 7D lens of sound (vibration), which creates geometric forms in the 6D to birth the material world we live in.

The 6D can hold general patterns—human, dog, etc.—but also individual patterns. Indeed, the pattern of our soul is alive in the 6th dimension. By keeping a healthy relationship with the 6D, we can remain united to our Source soul and the intentions we came into this physical life with from the outer dimensions.

Conversely, we have created and set patterns through our col-lective actions here on Earth that are now held in the 6D. We must address the patterns we wish to change here on Earth in the 3D by working with those we have set in the 6D either deliberately or un-consciously. A pattern of war is one example. Patterns of abuse and violence are others. How about patterns of extraction and consum-erism, patriarchy and slavery? Those are all being held for us in the 6D like a program we saved to our hard drive. We must remove them at that level if we really want change.

The patterns and forms are held on the skin or membrane of the 6D. The light moves through them like playdough moving through cookie-cutter shapes and patterns in the "Magic Dough Machine." We have the capacity to change these forms or return others and ourselves to the patterns of origin by working consciously with the 6D. This can change our experiences here on Earth.

What is important to understand is that we have set many of the patterns there with our actions and intentions, some collec-tively, some individually. Some we wish to return to and others we may wish to reset.

Sometimes I see patterns as archetypal figures, other times as forms and geometries held with a circle. It is complicated and I am simplifying it in an attempt to communicate the concept so you can take in this idea and feel into it for yourself. The wedeme offer many rituals that include this concept.

A medicine person may wish to address the pattern of punishment that we, as a collective, have agreed to and helped to stamp onto the 6D that many of us feel repressed by. They may offer rituals for those who feel disconnected from their own pattern of origin and want to realign with it. These are two very different ways to work with the forms and patterns being held in the 6D.

Working to make changes in the 3D through the lens of the 6D is a very important concept for us to embrace. We can try all we want to make changes in the 3D but if the pattern remains in the 6D, it cannot change. We must work at the level of the 6D to truly change the 3D and restore life to its original patterns.

I was shown this with the pattern of "lack of sisterhood" among women here on Earth. During a ritual with a group of women, I was shown the goddesses, classical Greek, fighting in the 6D. This pattern of women not getting along is stamped there; fighting for power from a place of disempowerment. I understood that this issue was one that needed addressing at that level. For all our efforts, human women are never going to succeed until we address it at that level. In this case, I was shown the archetypes rather than a pattern within a circle.

The 6th Dimension: Divination Time

To come to a better understanding of the 6th dimension, Strega Tree diviners carried out a group divination on the subject. I was the diviner for this particular inquiry. In asking about the 6D, I was shown a skin or membrane (a translucent, curved surface with a thickness like the covering of a driver's license) with patterns on it.

These patterns looked like geometric shapes held within a circle—a stamp-like image. The coating was also called a lens. The wedeme spoke of how light moves through that lens and how the patterns and forms set there create what we perceive to be reality—the light holograms that we are and encounter every day.

"Don't you see?" they said to me. "The lens is like a membrane and you can change its focus and change its pattern." They showed the light going through it as having rainbow colors. They were adjusting the light by how they turned the lens and when they turned it. Sometimes it appeared to be a series of layered lenses, one in front of the other, like in the ophthalmologist's office. They were affecting the patterns on Earth by what light they were allowing through the lens. Then they showed what looked like an old-fashioned embroidery hoop (two parts) attaching to the skin or membrane inside and outside, and the patterns being sewn or "stitched" into that. They said, "You have to have a membrane or skin to imprint onto and project through. The form has to go through or plant into a skin." The skin looked like a permeable membrane.

They said, "Don't think of the 6D as local to one place. Rather, it is wherever there are membranes. Anywhere a membrane is, it is being held by the 6D. The 6D is the membrane." They repeated, "Stop thinking the 6D is in one place at one time. It is everywhere, even in the 9D is the 6D. Also, even inside a body. You carry the 6D inside of you." They showed cells, then went right to women and ovaries, follicles and egg sacs.

This was a new understanding for me, that the 6D is the membrane—that all the membranes are the 6D and to not locate it in one time and space. It is everywhere.

This vision and view of what they gave me and give me constantly of the skin or membrane with patterns and light going through it has a striking consistency with what is called the Holographic Principle in physics. In reading about string theory and quantum gravity to try to understand other things the wedeme were showing me—stitched and woven together light in the cosmos, a tapestry, structures similar to the stitching on the back of a Persian carpet that resemble a computer motherboard, forms and original patterns—I found the Holographic Principle. The Holographic Principle, this mechanism, possibly exists as a function of how the universe works. A hologram is not a human. We are much more complex than that but this repeated information about forms on skins projecting certain patterns with light moving through them is something to pursue as a way to be more effective in our collaborations with the universe and life in general. Conceivably, there are patterns/forms on each concentric, nested membrane informing what is within.

The Second Coming

Turning and turning in the widening gyre
The falcon cannot hear the falconer;
Things fall apart; the centre cannot hold;
Mere anarchy is loosed upon the world,
The blood-dimmed tide is loosed, and everywhere
The ceremony of innocence is drowned;
The best lack all conviction, while the worst
Are full of passionate intensity.

Surely some revelation is at hand;
Surely the Second Coming is at hand.
The Second Coming! Hardly are those words out
When a vast image out of Spiritus Mundi
Troubles my sight: somewhere in sands of the desert
A shape with lion body and the head of a man,
A gaze blank and pitiless as the sun,
Is moving its slow thighs, while all about it
Reel shadows of the indignant desert birds.
The darkness drops again; but now I know
That twenty centuries of stony sleep
Were vexed to nightmare by a rocking cradle,
And what rough beast, its hour come round at last,
Slouches towards Bethlehem to be born?

—William Butler Yeats

Divination time continued...

The wedeme show the forms in the 6D as cookie-cutter shapes and the light coming through the forms. Then they show a woman with a cookie cutter, saying to the dough, "Now, you stay in the little shape and be good." After which they show what we might call "chaos" — when things do not obey the form. When things fall apart. *When the center cannot hold.*

Each dimension has an opposing force that keeps it in balance. For 6D, it is chaos. "When the *shit hits the fan*," they say, laughing as they show multiple forms or cookie-cutter shapes going into an electric fan and breaking apart. "There must be the crashing down," they say, "otherwise, nothing can breathe. Life needs form but if the form is too rigid, it cannot breathe, meaning it cannot achieve its full potential." This relates to the weak nuclear force discussed in Part 5 and the destructive capacities found at the root of life as well.

"This is not to instill fear," they say. "It's like the old saying, *you can chart your course but then you have to navigate the waters*. It is up to you to remain permeable to change, *adaptable*, and not get too fixed and rigid. Because then you are shutting down creativity and that will not be tolerated."

They flash to the soul origin pattern. They said, "The form is a guide, a roadmap. Like a reference. It *in-forms*. Form is a guide and is not to be DOMINATED with your will."

This felt like a scolding to humans.

"Just stay out of there, the force of your will is restrictive."

They continue, "You have a very limited understanding. Your will needs to stay soft like the chameleon. Human force and aggressiveness," they say, "they force themselves into things instead of sensing and listening. And responding."

Humans are in a habit of pushing against, forcing against: "give me," "tell me."

"This creates a rigidity in the membrane, which makes it easy to shatter, like glass. It is bad for the membranes. You need to speak into it slowly and gently so that it gradually opens. You are just slamming around and then the glass shatters and you say, *Why isn't anything working out?"*

They are showing that it is more like the dilation of the cervix.

"If you would just breathe and listen, things would slowly unfold. Instead, you shatter the glass."

It is almost as though our insistence on "knowing" makes it fragile. The insistence on knowing, *being sure*—this thing called a "guarantee." They are outraged. This idea of *guarantee* angers them. They show warranties and contracts and how ridiculous humans are in their need to almost self-soothe. "Can you promise me?" They show humans saying this to each other. "Even marriage," they say. "You are setting up a thin sheet of glass. Relationships are also forms."

We humans have become like this because we have lost the practice of caring for the membranes, the wedeme say. We have created a situation where no one feels safe.

"Humans need to go back and start over by setting up the membranes."

We need to have respect for the way it works. They show the cosmos.

"You need to have respect for the way the cosmos works." Then they laugh and say again, "Because things do not always go according to plan."

They think we are utterly ridiculous. Then they show contractual documents again. Things locked up in safes and families fighting for generations about what is written on the paper in the safe-deposit box. They show the playdough machine again and there is huge, raucous laughter about how humans think they can "play" with genetics.

They show conditions that have arisen in the postmodern world. They say: fixation, OCD, depression, and anxiety are "the plagues of your time and are because of this imbalance."

"Being rigid, creating things that are too fragile because the center cannot hold, that is a symptom of the lack of healthy membranes."

It is a symptom, not the cause. "Get back to the root," they say. They show the root chakra. "Get the membranes going there. Get the membranes going in every dimension of your bodies, of your communities, of your psyches. Again, you cannot create it from the top down. You cannot create it from the outside in. A government is not going to do this for you. And neither is some force coming from the outside going to land here and do this. No. This is from the inside out. And it is done with extreme care. It is done with care. Care. Care for the vulnerability of every potentiality."

Learning how to work in a responsive and sensitive way with the 6D is the work of the care for the cosmic membranes.

Chapter 30

The Holographic Principle

From the equations of string theory emerged the Holographic Principle. The theory that reality "may take place on a distant boundary surface, while everything we witness on three common spatial dimensions is a projection of that far away unfolding. Reality, that is, may be akin to a hologram. Or, really, a holographic movie."[86]

Theoretical physicist Brian Greene explains: "The journey to this particular possibility combines developments deep and far flung—insights from general relativity; from research on black holes; from thermodynamics; quantum mechanics; and, most recently, string theory. The thread linking these diverse areas is the nature of information in a quantum universe."[87]

When Greene asked his mentor, John Wheeler, what he saw as the most important subject physics would be exploring in the future, he answered: "Information."

"Traditionally, physics focuses on *things*—planets, rocks,

---

[86] Brian Greene. *The Hidden Reality: Parallel Universes and the Deep Laws of the Cosmos.* 272.
[87] Ibid.

atoms, particles, fields—and investigates the forces that affect their behavior and govern their interactions. Wheeler was suggesting that *things*—matter and radiation—should be viewed as secondary, as carriers of a more abstract and fundamental entity: information… That such information instantiated in real particles, occupying real positions, having definite spins and charges, is something like an architect's drawings being realized as a skyscraper. The fundamental information is in the blueprints. The skyscraper is but a physical realization of the information contained in the architect's design."[88]

This harks back to the original patterns shown to me by the wedeme and the ongoing teachings I receive from them on how to work with these forms and patterns to effect change in the 3D. At this level of the membranes—the cosmic level, which may extend to the far reaches of the universe and our participation in creating it—we are only at the beginning stages of understanding that we can and we do.

For the purposes of what can be safely and responsibly covered in this book, beginning to tune in to this understanding is probably a good place to start. We can be that big and we can be that small and what we do at the small affects the large—as above so below. Opening ourselves to understanding the mechanisms and workings on this level unveils a whole new set of questions. Can human medicine workers be effective at this level of the cosmos, attending to the cosmic membranes and collaborating consciously with the universe or multi-verse as a whole? I believe we can, but an expansion of our minds and beliefs is required.

Information

A large battle was waged in the world of physics between

---

[88] Ibid., 273.

cosmologist Stephen Hawking and quantum physicists Gerald 't Hooft and Leonard Susskind over whether information can be lost in a black hole. The answer proved to be no. The battle itself is what led to the answer, with Hawking finally conceding.

Information "falling into" the gravitational force of a black hole remains on the outside, on the event horizon of the black hole—the membrane, the skin. Though it falls in, it is also recorded on the surface. Information is never lost. It is against the laws of quantum physics. This fight helped to further the research that created mathematical equations that point to the reality of the Holographic Principle.

We must understand that when physicists mention information, they are not thinking in the same way as regular humans—as in a definition from an encyclopedia, a manual for a grill we just bought, or to learn something by googling it. They speak in terms of bits (binary yes or no), many of which can indeed add up to complex patterns and forms but not quite the language we tend to think of.

Greene again: "So you start to ponder. What actually is information, and what does it do? Your response is simple and direct. Information answers questions. Years of research by mathematicians, physicists, and computer scientists have made this precise. Their investigations have established that the most useful measure of information content is the *number of distinct yes-no questions the information can answer...* A datum that can answer a simple yes-no question is called a *bit*— a familiar computer-age term that is short for *binary digit*, meaning a 0 or a 1, which you can think of as a numerical representation of *yes or no.*"[89]

Often in divination, I open what I call "holographic packets of information." I see an image or a pattern inside a circle and the

---

[89] Ibid., 288-289.

longer I poke at it with the stick or by asking questions, the more it begins to open and downloads large amounts of information being held in that holographic form. The soul origin pattern is like this, as are memories stored in Time or on the membranes, even archetypes and lineages. We open these holographic packets with the yes or no movement of the stick. The stick literally speaks to stick diviners in binary answers. It has a language by how it moves. A yes or no. It answers our questions with a yes or no. To confirm, we ask, "Are you sure?" Yes or no. To increase the banter and keep the pace of the inquiry going we ask again, "Are you sure?" Yes or no. Then another question. Yes or no. Slowly, we unpack the information in the packets with these series of yes or no questions.

I was advised by my mentor and continue to guide students, "If you get stuck or lost following the information coming through in a divination, return to the binary. Go back to where you got lost and begin with yes or no." Unpacking information is accomplished in the same way that it was "packed." *Bit by bit.*

The skill of an accomplished diviner is knowing how to ask the right questions. As when using an internet search engine, it matters what question you put into it, what terms you use, and how you string them together. You know when you've gotten it right because the whole world opens to you when you do. And you know when you've gotten it wrong because nothing is turning up with your searches.

Each holographic packet contains different quantities of information. Some have so much, as in hidden and broken medicine lineages, that multiple divinations are needed to slowly open them and receive their information. As with the membrane divinations and teachings that have become this book, sometimes we are unpacking the bundles of information over years. But to understand that these information packets are stored in the membranes was new. Is storing information in this way a universal given?

Back to Greene: "...since the information required to describe physical phenomena within *any* given region of space can be fully encoded by data on a surface that surrounds the region, then there's reason to think that the surface is where the fundamental physical processes actually happen. Our familiar three-dimensional reality, these bold thinkers suggested, would then be likened to a holographic projection of those distant two-dimensional physical processes.

"If this line of reasoning is correct, then there are physical processes taking place on some distant surface that, much like a puppeteer pulls strings, are fully linked to the processes taking place in my fingers, arms, and brain as I type these words at my desk. Our experiences here, and that distant reality there, would form the most interlocked of parallel worlds. Phenomena in the two — I'll call them *Holographic Parallel Universes* — would be so fully joined that their respective evolutions would be as connected as me and my shadow.

"That familiar reality may be mirrored, or perhaps even produced, by phenomena taking place on a faraway, lower-dimensional surface ranks among the most unexpected developments in all of theoretical physics."[90]

Not that any theoretical physicists would care, but this is definitely confirmed by the stick divinations I have done.

The subject of information and how it is stored continues to be compelling outside of physics and divination as well because, in our human anthropocentric reality, information seems to be the thing to watch for and pay attention to in the near future — how much of it there is, how we interact with it, information overload, AI and the like. Perhaps we are ready to make an evolutionary leap on all fronts with understanding information: what it is, how it is

---

[90] Ibid., 298-299.

stored, how we access it consciously or unconsciously, how it informs our world and reality. *In-forms*.

What is information in its purest form? Light waves, sound waves, dark waves, memories of electrons interacting, nuclei decaying, stars dying, the universe expanding. Information is not what we think, yet we think this to understand information, to comprehend, to make meaning, to make sense, to create further articulations of that information, more complex forms, and compound information. Do we begin to see how a whole new world is opening just by asking: *What is information?*

2005

"The universal womb enables the galactic womb, solar system womb, solar and Earth womb, ocean womb, community and village womb, mother womb, daughter womb, cellular and quantum womb."[91]

When I next saw Domenica in her cave, she hugged me and welcomed me. As I hugged her, I saw something hanging off a clothes-drying line behind her. It was a womb with wings. Golden, with gold dripping from it as though she had dipped it in liquid gold—liquid gold that never dries, never hardens but remains porous, eternal. It was hanging on the line from the wings, which were also gold, to dry. The gold contained many colors within it: yellow, red, even silver. The colors swirled around and within each other like oils. I let go of her embrace and approached it. I said, "This is mine, isn't it?"

She agreed.

I took the womb with wings off the line and into my hands, and it took off, carrying me, flying, dangling from it. I was scared, flying

---

[91] Dintino, *Notes from a Diviner*, 112.

through space, my hands holding on to the womb with wings, flying to where, I didn't know. There was darkness and there were stars. It was the night sky as we know it. I felt cold and then realized I should climb up into the womb. It was dark inside but not like the darkness outside. Here it was warm and embracing and safe, and it held me like a seedpod flying through space.

Chapter 31

Thought as Packets of Information

The wedeme tell us *thought was there at the beginning of the universe too.* Thought. What is thought? Is thought when two pieces of information come together and create something new? When we think a thought, are we transmuting light into something new out of two or more previous somethings? Or putting two separate thoughts together—combining two bits of information to make a new one? Is thought a creative act? Does it have a cost? Yes, I think so.

Do we understand that evolutionary development means that humans can think, deduce, decide, arrive at conclusions, think new thoughts, have realizations, and experience enlightenment? If we break it down scientifically, it is all quite fascinating. How do elements born in a star become a human, and how do humans take these elements and form a brain that can think? And as this brain thinks, it can think new thoughts, and as these new thoughts occur, they create new realities and...wow! *Think about it!* Thought and thinking are part of the evolutionary process of the universe, the cosmos.

Our thoughts thinking—is this some sort of cosmic destiny? If this is so, should we be more aware of what thoughts we think? This is what the spiritual teachers from all times have been trying to teach us as they encourage us to turn our thoughts into prayers, mantras, and invocations. From a scientific perspective, it seems to be true that thoughts are pretty important. And from a technological point of view as well, since we are teaching computers how to think.

"You create your own reality" is too watered down and simplified. It is not all that simple and this overused phrase is actually doing us a disservice. The problem is, it is not just us thinking individually that can change the world. We must think *together*, collectively · change collective patterns, look at what we have created thus far as humans and have stamped onto the 6D, and perhaps consider an overhaul.

Let's consider what thoughts really are: One thought is a complex collection of information. Information is made up of binary bits of yes or no. We do not really create our own reality; it is all those eons of creating over and over again by thinking complex thoughts. One thought is already incomprehensibly complex. Many people become frustrated when they try to change their thoughts to change reality. When it doesn't happen, they feel they have done something wrong. Nothing is wrong except that even that thought needs a bit of an evolutionary tweaking. If you really want to change your reality, begin to understand where thoughts and thought patterns arise from.

We arise and have arisen out of the quantum vacuum over and over and we have added unbelievable complexity to the cosmos by doing that.

There is a wise sage from the Dagara lineage with whom I work in divination. One day, I asked him, "What is real?"

He said, "Thought."

The reason I asked the question is because he was showing me a ritual to do by putting someone in the middle of a triangular

265

shape. I asked him what was so important about the middle of the triangle and he responded, "What is in the middle of the triangle is real." That is why I asked, "What is real?" and he answered that thought is real. *Thought is real.* Not quite the answer I was expecting.

"Meaning it has density, it has some kind of mass to it?" I asked.

"Yes."

"So, it can change things in the 3D?"

"Yes. If the thought is strong enough and if the intention is clear and you put it inside a triangle..."

Ah, now we are getting somewhere.

Prayer is concentrated thought. The wedeme say prayer is care. Prayer is a form of care. Care is healing for the membranes. Prayer, incantation, invocation, poetry that repeats and is repeated, language spoken with intention, thoughts thought with clarity — these are real.

I have written over and over that the membranes guard and protect but they also hold information/patterns/bits. Would we dare to call this a brain? Maybe not but definitely intelligence, consciousness.

The universe seems to be composed of skins that contain an inside and the information on the skin determines what is experienced inside: *within.* But as we have learned so far in this book, what is inside also informs and "controls" the condition of the skin or membrane. These are not separate events. They are collaborating and co-evolving.

If we live inside the matrix, do we also understand that we are running the matrix and that it is all information and stored information? Yes, indeed. This does not imply meaninglessness but it can shift things if we learn better how to unpack and interact with what we are held by and how we are telling it to hold us. AI should change its name. Information is information. When you run it through a human, you get stories and myth because humans can feel, and feelings need these kinds of containers. And that will never change.

Divination Time: Earth Speaks

At the advice of the wedeme, I ran my own co-dreaming with the Soul of the Planet Program in October of 2019. (This is recommended in Part 6 of this book.) The program was rich and all the participants received many dreams and much information from the soul of the planet. At the end of the program, we did a group divination, pulling together all the information that had come through from the Earth. What we were told was similar to the information I had received in that journey so long ago in 2005, when I went to Dominica's cave and set up my own space in the otherworld.

In the divination, the Earth spoke to us about how her life will continue regardless of what happens to humans. The issue is whether or not humans will continue to inhabit the Earth. The Earth told us that it is the lifesystems of the planet that enable, sustain, and nurture biological life that are in danger and if we want to stay alive on this planet, we need to learn to run information through our hearts.

Running Information Through Our Hearts

To finally ascend and move forward, we must learn to run information through our hearts. We have become very good at moving it through our heads, our brains, and machines but running information through our hearts is the next phase for humans.

Humans are not taking advantage of this technology within us that is unique and underused. The heart gives us access to the universe. Learning how to run information through our hearts will give us a better understanding of the information from a universal perspective. The human heart emerged out of our ability to feel.

This capacity to feel was new to lifesystems and the heart has continued to evolve out of that. Millennia of human experience have led to a refinement of our hearts and now it is time to go the next step. This is the new frontier, running information through our hearts; using this essential filter to think new thoughts. Heart Speak.

Also in the divination, the Earth spoke to us of memories. The Earth said, "The memories will live on," and when she said that, she showed her iron core. "The memories will live on," she said, long after the solar system is gone, which it will be because we have a middle-aged star that is supporting the solar system. When that life cycle ends, the memories will live on into the cosmos. What she meant by this is that the information of everything that ever lived and thought would live on. When she said the word *thought*, she meant the creative power of information. The Earth told us the creative power of information is thought and that doesn't mean it's only human thought — it's information that is taken and made use of. That is what thought is. And she showed me again what the wedeme had shown me previously, how in the very beginning of the cosmos thought was there. When she said this, she showed particles coming together and making use of information in a new way.

That is what thought is for these beings that I work with. Thought is the amazing capacity for information of any kind — a particle meeting another particle, a human talking to a human, an animal sniffing another animal's butt — then taking that information and coming up with a new piece of information. That is thought and that is the most creative force in the universe because it is a combination that creates something new. And that is birth. Earth is saying thought will live on because all of these interactions, all of the memories, everything that has happened on Earth, will go back into the cosmos and be available to be picked up and turned into thought again by something or somewho.

This soup of information we are all swimming in has the

capacity to meet others and create something new out of that inter-action. That is thought, that is creativity, and that is what will con-tinue. The place where we are right now on this planet, "this ful-crum point," she called it—this point, this moment...it is so ready to have a new thought and become something else, if only we could find a way to spark that fire. If we do, we will create a different memory (story) that gets conserved. But it does not mean all is lost if we don't.

There will be other opportunities in the cosmos for this partic-ular expression of information that has been the human experiment to come back together and re-form itself. But if we do want to try to ascend Humanity, it is not the Earth that needs to ascend but Hu-manity, with a capital H, and when she says that the animals are right there—all the beings we share the living biosystems with are there—they will ascend with us and it will be a different moment. But there is no judgment either way. Things die and are reborn and memory is what is retained.

Memory is what is retained. Information is retained. And that is what memory is. It's not local to a human brain. Memory is a universal way to conserve everything that has happened and help it build on itself. Memory is information that is in some kind of se-quence that can be built on right where it left off. Memory is also a universal force. If we could understand it, we could reactivate it. All of this is so valuable to us but we have to get out of this place we are stuck in as humanity. And when she says this, she just shows war. "It's just the worst thing," she is saying. "You've got to get rid of war. It just sticks humans into grief and pain and holds them there for generations."

Earth wants us to know she is a sovereign being and she has her own evolution regardless of what humans decide to do.

In Conclusion

All of this information and thought, and how it is held on the membranes in all the fractal layers, is the work of tending to the cosmic membranes and what is held within them. Accessing the membranes at this level and running the information through our hearts is the work of the medicine people. All of the work and rituals given throughout the pages of this book can be applied by a crafty and imaginative medicine person.

The membranes are alive. They are sentient. They have a consciousness. When working at the cosmic level, we must approach them in this way.

A Shrine for the Cosmic Membranes

The One-Breasted Woman

There is a shrine in the Dagara tradition that falls under the category of the *saazumwin*. She is called the *One-Breasted Woman*.[92]

The *saazumwin* are the ones who stretch between Earth and the stars. They are the beings from the space above, the light-bringers, the star beings. They are cosmic and benevolent and can often be seen as what many call angels.

I was told very little about this shrine when I was instructed to make it. I was told to make a *saazumwin* shrine with the form of a seated woman holding a child — to make her whole and complete but then, after I completed it, to cut off half of her body. *Do not cut*

---

[92] Jack Goody. *Death, Property and the Ancestors: a Study of the Mortuary Customs of the Lodagaa of West Africa.* 372.

the child, only the woman. Cut off one breast, one arm, one half of her body. I thought this was very strange. When I inquired about why this shrine needed to be cut, the person who gave me this prescription said he did not know — that was just the way she was always made. He had very little information on this entity and did not understand her, but I was being asked to make her nonetheless.

In this tradition, when a diviner makes a shrine, it is considered a very big ritual. The diviner gathers all the "ingredients" that will go in the shrine, then sits in ritual space and invokes, offering their hands to the entity that will be housed on the shrine — the one who has asked for the shrine. The diviner allows them to use their hands to build the shrine.

The shrines are made of clay dug from the earth. Once created and activated, they become powerful energy portals in the shrine room where the diviner goes to interact with the entities housed there, making offerings and prayers in this space.

I had learned through my experiences with previous shrines that I would understand more about the entity residing on the shrine as I went through the process of building it, and I would learn even more as I continued to interact with it. So, knowing very little about the *One-Breasted Woman*, I embarked on this request with an open mind and heart.

I was prompted to include many seashells and a necklace I had procured years before that features the Goddess Inanna. My grand-mother's rosary was requested as well.

As I worked the clay, I was guided to make the head of both the woman and child in the shape of a star. Onto the edges of these star points, I was told to put golden glitter. The seashells on and around her body and star head evoked the feeling of a star emerging from the deep ocean, a star emerging from the primordial waters of the cosmos. She was a star being that was also part of the ocean in a compelling way — a star with the briny smell of the ocean, like the womb. My *One-Breasted Woman* was built as a star woman with a star child.

To cut into the figure of a woman was very difficult for me. It brought to mind many associations that were disturbing. I could not bring myself to cut the head or face but gently cut into her body. I succeeded in cutting off one breast, one arm, and half of her torso. It was an odd feeling. I sat holding the parts of clay I had cut off, wondering what to do with them. I offered them back to Source. As I did this, I understood why I was cutting part of her off, because the other part of her always remained with the stars. The removal of half of her body was an ever-present reminder that this was not a mortal woman. This was the Archetypal Star Mother.

I settled her into my shrine room and activated her as I had been instructed, then went about my business. But when the midwinter solstice came around, the *One-Breasted Woman* began to speak more loudly. She wanted to be moved to the center of the shrine room and be adorned with small white lights and boughs from evergreen trees.

Then this *One-Breasted Woman* began to show me who she truly was: the one who births light from Source through the darkness to the Earth. She is the one many cultures celebrate at the winter solstice, the time of utter darkness in the Northern Hemisphere in the turn of the planet's year. In our most dark time is birthed the light. This was a dark goddess in my shrine room holding the light deep within her body. This is the *Cosmic Womb Mother*, the one who births us from Source into embodied form. The midwife to light and life.

As I have moved along in this tradition, I have learned that the *One-Breasted Woman*, this *Cosmic Mother*, holds all the codes and patterns of our souls within her. She knows who we are, what our potentialities are, and what we chose to do when we came into this life. She holds the memory of us, for us, within her womb, as all mothers do. When we die, we return to her womb to be reborn again as whomever and whatever we wish to be next. She is a kind and compassionate mother and is one with the stars. She has the memory of us all stamped into her womb.

If you feel compelled to work at this level of the membranes, begin by creating this shrine. Then listen. Ask her to teach you...

Ritual for Working With the Cosmic Membranes

Accessing Portals and Traversing the Cosmic Membrane

Certain places on Earth have or are portals and access routes for crossing dimensional boundaries, and interacting with the cosmic membranes and what is held within them—alternate worlds and realities. Some are naturally occurring, others have been created and tended to for millennia—Stonehenge, Avebury, and other stone circles or Earthworks; temples or outcroppings, caves, waterfalls, confluences of waterways, mounds, stargates...many that we call sacred sites, canyons, trees, forests, and mountains. Many were tended to by our ancestors or the ancestors of the place in which we now reside.

When we discover one, we must approach it with caution as there are more than likely guardians set there by humans who previously accessed these magical openings. If they had to flee under unfortunate circumstances, they may have set protection there that, if you are not mindful and respectful, you will meet in an unpleasant way. Do not walk forcefully into these portals or places saying "give me." If you do so, it is at your own peril. Remember, membranes are also protective. They can be barriers to keep certain energies out. You may not be granted access immediately or when you want it. It may come later—or never—but trust that the membrane has intelligence and can determine your readiness. If you are refused, you will eventually be called back when the membrane perceives your readiness.

When you meet a cosmic membrane's opening or doorway...

❋ Sit and listen.

❋ Proceed with caution and care, using the tools I have offered you throughout this book.

❋ Your #1 tool is always humility. Do not forget to take this tool with you always, in all of the dimensional layers.

❋ Your second tool is inquiry. Ask who, what, where, why, when, and how.

❋ Listen, then respond. Do not react. Respond.

❋ Make offerings. Listen with your heart.

❋ Beginning to work at this level of the membrane care, with the cosmic dimensions, is something that takes time and maturity. It will evolve and develop for you through time.

❋ When you travel, always take your guides with you.

Chapter 32

Story

For My Daughter: A Roadmap to the Passionate Universe

#1

Assume there is no such thing as control. Then it will be less surprising when cars swerve off the road or planes fall from the sky. Instead, cultivate awe for the fact that cars stay on the road at all, that drivers agree to keep to their side of the yellow line and stop at red lights. We are on a planet that is spinning within a solar system, which is spiraling through space at 180 miles per second, every minute of every day. In the midst of all this wild movement, isn't it a miracle that we can stand up?

#2

Don't argue over whether life is meaningful or random. It is most elegantly both. Within the deepest, most chaotic meaningless-ness there are patterns; patterns that repeat themselves. Within these patterns exist crazy-quilt randomness.

In a museum in Florence, Italy, you, my eight-year-old daughter, and I looked at paintings of Christ from the Middle Ages. You were not a Christian girl. You were a secular girl. I had told you a few things. You knew you had been created by the Earth, by a process called "evolution," that you are turned-over stardust churned over millions of years, that the universe began with what some called the *Big Bang*, that time and space were created in that original moment, and that before that, there was nothing. Still, you often asked me what came before.

This was not the first time you had seen pictures of Christ hanging on the cross. These were simply the worst ever. His skin, pale gray, hung slack around his protruding bones. Blood spurted from a cut above his right breast.

"Why are there so many pictures of him dying on the cross?" you asked.

"They believed," I replied, "and many still do, that through his death he saved the Earth or humanity — us. They believed that he died for us so that we could live, so that we could enter what they called 'The Gates of Heaven.'"

"Well, that's stupid," you said. Your little face was scrunched up into a knot, like it got when you were angry about something. Your legs coming out of your cotton yellow shorts were tanned and skinny. You wore a gray T-shirt with colorful flowers on it, and a star necklace your friend had given you. Your bare feet sat upon your red cloth flip-flops. "I do not believe that."

"They believed he was their savior."

"Why?"

I frowned. "There had been signs," I said. "Certain omens."

"What's an omen?" You looked back at the picture. "Is there an omen there?" you asked. Your long, curly hair hung down your back, reaching the bottom of your shirt. It was almost white around your hairline where the sun had bleached the small, new-forming curls. Against the tanned skin of your face, it looked like a halo.

At the foot of the cross were two women, crying with their heads bowed. There were angels flying around. They looked like

276

bugs with heads. One of them held up a cup to collect the spurting blood. Two others held the Sacred Heart of Christ forward toward the observer as an offering.

"Yuck, Mom. Look," you said, pointing. "What are they going to do with that?"

"It's all symbolic, honey. Don't take it so seriously."

"I don't understand what the symbol of someone dead and bleeding could be."

"Try to appreciate them for the art, not the meaning," I said.

You looked up at me. I was tired of your questions, yet could feel that you wanted to ask so many more. You didn't understand any of this. And you thought I did. Though I was no longer a Christian, I had been raised Catholic. You knew this. I did not want the story of Christ's death to be your story and I had not found another story to tell you. How could I explain this to you?

"Who is that?" you asked, pointing to one of the women crying at the foot of the cross.

"That's his mother."

#3

We yearn. Stars burn, smolder, and remain molten, gushing at the core for eons. The universe is a reality engaged in acts of great passion. Galaxies wrap their giant arms around each other in consuming embraces. Black holes hungrily swallow everything that comes near them, their most brilliant obsession being light. Planets crave the sun. The moon desires the Earth. The Earth thickens and sways, and wobbles dizzily in the orbit of her attraction. Desire leads us. Heat sustains us. Passion transforms us.

You had an echocardiogram to assure your dentist that your heart murmur was nothing to worry about. That day I understood how it was possible to fall in love with technology. Before, people who fell in love with technology only angered me. But as I stood in

the exam room that day, seeing the valves of your small heart pulsing, hearing its voice, its rhythmic breath whispering, everything
changed. Your Sacred Heart was speaking into the room, filling the
space with its aching, hopeful presence, full of youth and optimism.

The voice within me whispered, Inside her is a heart that is
beating. *Inside her, a heart is beating and with each beat it moves her
blood, creating circulatory rivers that course through her being, managing
her life, sustaining her aliveness.*

In the exam room with a piece of equipment—a compilation of
metal and electronic circuits created by human imagination—I was
able to see, to listen, and be present to the inside of your healthy,
living body. Naturally, people fell in love with technology. No
wonder it had become a household god.

The technician tapped the keyboard methodically. In cool, cal-
culated movements, she moved the mouse to certain locations on
the image of the heart pumping on the screen before her. The best
science leads us back to the mystery. She took measurements and
gathered information. It was all very routine. It was all very scientific. But I was weeping.

#4

Imagine a universe devoid of passion. No one wanting anything. Nothing attracted to anything else. No sweet, painful longing. Imagine a universe involved with detachment, one that chose
to rise above its emotions.

Would a rose ever bloom if it didn't ache to do so?

#5

The human heart has a large, electromagnetic field, the largest
in the body. This field can be perceived across a room by the field
of another heart. The electromagnetic field of the heart changes
with the emotional state. DNA is affected by the electromagnetic

field of the heart, which is generated by emotions. The lives of our hearts can mutate our DNA. Feelings matter.

In fourth grade, you learned about the ancient Egyptians. They believed that after death, your heart is measured against Ma'at's feather of truth. You and your classmates acted out a scene about meeting the Goddess Ma'at after death in the place where she sat with her scales. I was in the play. I dressed up as the Goddess Ma'at and weighed each heart against my feather.

"Were you true to your heart?" I asked each small child, your friends, as they came to sit across the scales from me.

The Egyptians believed the heart has a soul. They called it the *Ab*—the heart-soul. *The soul of your heart is your longing.* If you were true to your heart, then it was as light as a feather and you were granted eternal life. If you had not been, and it was heavier than a feather, you were sent to the realm of the demons.

When the Egyptians mummified people, they put a scarab beetle in the place in the body where the heart once lived. Written on it were the words:

> *My heart, my mother*
> *My heart, my mother*
> *My heart of my becoming.*

You approached the scale. You were dressed as an Egyptian. You had a gold headband across your forehead. Underneath hung your long, light-brown curls. You wore a white dress tied with a gold sash at the waist. You had the blue eye makeup, *kohl*, on your eyelids, to protect your eyes from the bright Egyptian sun. You looked at me from under those blue lids, your brown eyes full of wonder as you placed your heart on the scales. The heart that had grown within me. *My heart, my mother.* The heart I had once felt beating in rhythm with mine. *My heart, my mother.* The heart that was now on its own, this most precious, sacred heart, the main compass we can use along this journey. *My heart of my becoming.* You placed your heart on the scale.

I, the Goddess Ma'at, looked at you. "Were you true to your heart?" I asked. "Were you true to your passion?"

#6

Always be true to the soul of your heart.

Epilogue

In my last visit to Domenica's cave, I was surprised to have her place a necklace over my head. When I looked down at it, I saw that it looked much like what I call a *Kali* necklace.

"Kali-Ma, the fierce Hindu goddess, means 'dark mother' and her associations with the womb are vast. She is the Creatrix, the nurturer, the triple Goddess. She is often portrayed as a demonic goddess but this is terribly inaccurate and one-sided. She is a loving mother, transformer, *'being-consciousness-bliss, illuminatrix.'* Kali is the mother of all living. She is *kundalini,* the female serpent, the spiral. She is *'the generative womb of all,'* the beginning and end of beings."[93]

Kali is often depicted wearing a necklace of human skulls. She created the sound of word, each skull engraved with a letter. "The letters were magic because they stood for primordial creative energy expressed in sound—Kali's *mantras* brought into being the very things whose names she spoke for the first time, in her holy language."[94]

After placing the necklace on me, Domenica said it was time to take my message out to the world—her message, the message of

---

[93] Barbara G. Walker. *The Women's Encyclopedia of Myths and Secrets*. 490-491.
[94] Ibid.,491.

Theresa C. Dintino

the *Womb with Wings* — and to wear this necklace of courage. I shuddered at first, thinking the skulls would bloody my shirt but then saw that they were skeletons of wombs with wings. Rather than human skulls, this was a necklace of *bucrania,* the skulls of bulls, images of the cosmic womb.

When she told me to take her message to the world, I was panicked that this meant she was leaving me. I realized how important this relationship in the otherworld had become to me. In her usual, detached way, Domenica said, *"Everything is always changing. I must transform. You must transform. You are helping me transform."*

Although I had considered that my interactions with the otherworld would change my world and me, I did not realize that my interactions with Domenica and her otherworld cave would help transform her. I now understand that it is reciprocal, this relationship, and so much more complex.

Also by Theresa C. Dintino

Ode To Minoa

When Aureillia, the young Snake Priestess in Bronze Age Crete, begins having visions of an unspeakable evil, her simple life is thrown into turmoil.

As a member of a Goddess-worshiping culture, her life is ruled by the cycles of the moon and a deep connection to Earth, but soon will be affected by a far greater force. Visions of the future lead Aureillia to a loss of innocence and the discovery of her extraordinary power and the power in every woman.

Stories They Told Me

In an underground temple on the island of Malta, Danelle and Aureillia witness a vision of the future that shocks and horrifies them. Danelle journeys to Africa. There, with the local shaman walking in and out of his own simultaneous lives, he explores the heartbreaking questions of his soul. Aureillia returns to her home in Bronze Age Crete, where shockwaves of a prophecy she told as a Snake Priestess years before resonate in ways unexpected. Can they find a way to change the future separation of men and women that appears to loom inevitable?

The Strega and The Dreamer

The Strega and the Dreamer is the tale of Italian immigrants coming to America from the Abruzzi region of Italy at the turn of the last century.

Eva is an Italian Strega, a midwife and healer, fully committed to her small hilltop village. Marcello is a man with a dream of

America—a dream that Eva does not share. Famine comes to the Abruzzi and Marcello goes to America, leaving his family behind as he searches for a more prosperous life.

Eva dedicates herself to her Strega duties and the people of the village. Though it is taboo for a woman to do so, with the help of a doctor from the city, she secretly learns of modern medicine. When Marcello finally calls for her, Eva has a decision to make. She must choose between staying in her beloved Abruzzi, where she has her family and her Strega calling, or moving to America, where midwifery is considered barbaric and is being systematically eliminated.

Welcoming Lilith: Awakening and Welcoming Pure Female Power

Lilith is a Goddess and mythological figure who is misunderstood. She is reputed to be Adam's first wife before Eve, and she represents the first powerful and liberated female in history. Then why was she banished?

Through commentary and reflection on the multifaceted aspects of Lilith, Theresa C. Dintino guides the reader on an exciting inner journey to reclaim her own repressed parts. By examining how these Lilith energies may show up in her own life, the reader is encouraged to do the work to bring them back to life.

Rituals included in the book offer the opportunity to explore these powerful but often feared aspects. Reclaiming the lost fragments—her power, her anger, her shadow, her sexuality, her creativity, and her deep inner truth—returns the female psyche to a state of wholeness and integration.

The Amazon Pattern: A Message from Ancient Women Diviners of Trees and Time

What is an Amazon Woman? Mythical or actual, what were these fierce women fighting for? Perhaps there is more to their story than we have been told.

In a forest in Northern California, Dintino encounters a Tree that tells her she does not like her pattern. Surprised and intrigued by this statement, Dintino asks the Tree what pattern it does like.

"What happened to the Amazon Pattern?" the Tree responds. "I want the Amazon Pattern."

This mysterious meeting propels Dintino onto the journey described in her book. With curiosity and wonder leading her, Dintino uncovers a thread of messages that ancient Amazon Women hid, discovers a lost tradition of priestess-diviners, and begins to understand and restore this mystical cosmology of Trees and Time called The Amazon Pattern.

Discover this ancient pattern that has been stored away in Time and find out what it has to offer today's world.

Notes from a Diviner in the Postmodern World: A Handbook for Spirit Workers

What does it mean to bring indigenous wisdom to the postmodern world? How do divination and ritual fit into modern society? How does one integrate ancient spiritual teachings into a Western mindset while remaining true to the original meaning?

Notes from a Diviner in the Postmodern World: A Handbook for Spirit Workers is a guidebook for both diviners and spirit workers of any tradition. In this book, Dintino describes what she calls the "landscape of the otherworld" revealed to her through spirits — ancestors, archangels, elemental and light beings — in her divinations.

Whatever your spiritual tradition, there's always a shared landscape of the otherworld. Understanding the landscape will help you navigate your own spiritual terrain.

Learning how to be an effective diviner and spirit worker also means that you must interact fully with the wisdom of the place where you live, which includes learning from all living things, including mountains and water.

This powerful handbook teaches you how to heal your world by exploring interdimensional realms and ultimately becoming a spiritual steward of the Earth.

Teachings from the Trees: Spiritual Mentoring from the Standing Ones

In Teachings from the Trees: Spiritual Mentoring from the Standing Ones, Theresa C. Dintino offers guidance and instruction about how to work energetically with the trees. She gives detailed accounts of what the trees have taught her and relates the story of her relationship to specific trees.

In this book you will learn how to:

* Locate and communicate with trees who will become your allies.
* Build healing space for your community.
* Release trapped or stuck spirits who were unable to properly cross into the ancestral realm.
* Clean-up locations on the land from infractions and trauma.
* Interact with guardians and groves.
* Steward the land and community you serve by becoming embedded in your local root system and developing a network of healing energy.

You will also meet some of Theresa's personal tree guides, including The Moon Tree, The Dragon Tree, and The Grandmother Oak.

The history and legacy of the human relationship to trees is a long one. It's time to reignite it for the benefit and care of Mother Earth.

Works Cited

Books

Ainsworth, Catherine Harris. *Italian-American Folktales.* Clyde Press, 1977.

Becker, Robert O., and Gary Selden. *The Body Electric.* Morrow, 1998.

Becker, Robert O. *Cross Currents: the Promise of Electromedicine, the Perils of Electropollution.* J.P. Tarcher/Penguin, 2004.

Buhner, Stephen Harrod. *The Lost Language of Plants: the Ecological Importance of Plant Medicines to Life on Earth.* Chelsea Green Publishing, 2002.

Canziani, Estella. *Through the Apennines and the Lands of the Abruzzi.* Heffer, 1928.

Castaneda, Carlos. *The Art of Dreaming.* Element, 2004.

Clow, Barbara Hand, and Gerry Clow. *Alchemy of Nine Dimensions: the 2011/2012 Prophecies and Nine Dimensions of Consciousness.* Hampton Roads Pub. Co., 2010.

Cummings, E. E. *100 Selected Poems.* Franklin Classics, 2018.

Dames, Michael. *The Silbury Treasure: the Great Goddess Rediscovered.* Thames and Hudson, 2004.

Dintino, Theresa C. *The Strega and the Dreamer.* CreateSpace, 2012.

Dintino, Theresa C. *Notes from a Diviner in the Postmodern World: A Handbook for Spirit Workers.* Wise Strega Books, 2016.

Dintino, Theresa C. *The Amazon Pattern: A Message of Ancient Women Diviners of Trees and Time.* Wise Strega Books, 2016.

Dintino, Theresa C. *Teachings from the Trees: Spiritual Mentoring from the Standing Ones.* Wise Strega Books, 2016.

Gimbutas, Marija. *The Civilization of the Goddess.* HarperSanFrancisco, 1991.

Gimbutas, Marija. *The Language of the Goddess: Unearthing the Hidden Symbols of Western Civilization.* Harper & Row. 1989.

Goody, Jack. *Death, Property and the Ancestors: a Study of the Mortuary Customs of the Lodagaa of West Africa.* Routledge, 2004.

Greene, Brian. *The Hidden Reality: Parallel Universes and the Deep Laws of the Cosmos.* Vintage Books, 2013.

Liebes, Sidney, et al. *A Walk Through Time: from Stardust to Us.* Wiley, 1998.

Lovelock, James. *The Ages of Gaia. A Biography of Our Living Earth.* Bantam Books, 1988.

Mellaart, James. *Çatal Hüyük: A Neolithic Town in Anatolia.* Thames & Hudson, 1967.

Moss, Robert. *The Dreamer's Book of the Dead: a Soul Travelers Guide to Death, Dying, and the Other Side.* Destiny Books, 2005.

O'Donohue, John. Anam Cara: *A Book of Celtic Wisdom.* Harper Perennial, 2004.

Streep, Peg. *Sanctuaries of the Goddess: the Sacred Landscapes and Objects.* Little, Brown, 1994.

Swimme, Brian, and Thomas Berry. *The Universe Story.* Arkana, 1994.

Thomas, Lewis. *The Lives of a Cell.* Penguin Books, 1978.

Walker, Barbara G. *The Women's Encyclopedia of Myths and Secrets.* 1986.

Walker, Matthew. *Why We Sleep, the New Science of Sleep and Dreams.* Penguin, 2018.

Wheatley, Margaret J. *Leadership and the New Science.* Berrett-Koehler, 2000.

Wheatley, Margaret J. *Who Do We Choose to Be?: Facing Reality, Claiming Leadership, Restoring Sanity.* Berrett-Koehler Publishers Inc., 2017.

Wohlleben, Peter. *The Hidden Life of Trees.* Greystone Books, 2018.

Woolf, Virginia. *A Room of One's Own.* Penguin Books, 1937. 2020.

Woolf, Virginia. *Moments of Being.* Pimlico, 1985. 2002.

Yeats, William Butler and M.L. Rosenthal ed. *Selected Poems and Two Plays by William Butler Yeats.* Collier Books, 1962.

Webpages

Discovering the Oscan Roots of My Strega Lineage | Strega-tree.com. https://stregatree.com/discovering-the-oscan-roots-of-my-strega-lineage/.

"Earth's Interior." National Geographic, 18 Jan. 2017, https://www.nationalgeographic.com/science/earth/surface-of-the-earth/earths-interior/.

"Home." Atmosphere - Biology Forums Dictionary, http://biology-forums.com/definitions/index.php/Atmosphere.

"John O'Donohue - The Inner Landscape of Beauty." The On Being Project, 31 Aug. 2017, https://onbeing.org/programs/john-odonohue-the-inner-landscape-of-beauty-aug2017/.

"Online Etymology Dictionary: Origin, History and Meaning of English Words." https://www.etymonline.com/.

SparkNotes, https://www.sparknotes.com/biology/cellstructure/cellmembranes/section1/.

Strega Tree Apothecary | A Center for Divination ... https://stregatree.com/.

"Structure of the Plasma Membrane." Khan Academy, Khan Academy, https://www.khanacademy.org/science/high-school-biology/hs-cells/hs-the-cell-membrane/a/structure-of-the-plasma-membrane.

"The Carbon Cycle." Petroleum, http://www.petro-leum.co.uk/carbon-cycle.

The Editors of Encyclopaedia Britannica. "Membrane." Ency-clopædia Britannica, Encyclopædia Britannica, Inc., 25 Sept. 2019, https://www.britannica.com/science/membrane-biol-ogy.

"Welcome! " Home of the Labyrinth Movement, http://veridi-tas.org/

"Wendell E. Berry." National Endowment for the Humanities (NEH), https://www.neh.gov/about/awards/jefferson-lec-ture/wendell-e-berry-biography.

strega tree apothecary

Ritual based remedies for reconnection to yourself, ancestors, and the natural world

Visit our online apothecary at stregatree.com for your spiritual care needs
Each product comes with or is a ritual.

Protective Balms
for the mothers
evil eye remedy
remedy to heal violation
the big offering

Inner Earth Blends
auric shield spray
aberewa's below tonic

Wedeme Heart Blends
the heart healing for when the heart is broken
heart opening
rapid heart movement: return to origin reclaiming our passion
and purpose
heart speak: universal oneness remedy

Medicine Jewelry
Guided Meditation Journeys
Books
Divinations
Consultation Calls For Keepers of the Membranes
Classes

And sign up to follow our blog to continue learning.

stregatree.com

293

www.ingramcontent.com/pod-product-compliance
Lightning Source LLC
Chambersburg PA
CBHW070018100426
42740CB00013B/2547